EMPTY CAGES

EMPTY CAGES

FACING THE CHALLENGE OF ANIMAL RIGHTS

Tom Regan

ROWMAN & LITTLEFIELD PUBLISHERS, INC.
Lanham • Boulder • New York • Toronto • Oxford

ROWMAN & LITTLEFIELD PUBLISHERS, INC.

Published in the United States of America
by Rowman & Littlefield Publishers, Inc.
A wholly owned subsidiary of The Rowman & Littlefield Publishing Group, Inc.
4501 Forbes Boulevard, Suite 200, Lanham, Maryland 20706
www.rowmanlittlefield.com

PO Box 317
Oxford
OX2 9RU, UK

British Library Cataloguing in Publication Information Available

Library of Congress Cataloging-in-Publication Data

Regan, Tom.
  Empty cages: facing the challenge of animal rights /
Tom Regan.
     p. cm.
Includes bibliographical references and index.
  1. Animal rights—United States. 2. Animal welfare—United
States. I. Title.
  HV4764.R44 2003
  179'.3—dc21   2003010534

  ISBN 0-7425-3352-2 (cloth : alk. paper) — ISBN 0-7425-4993-3 (pbk. : alk. paper)

Printed in the United States of America

♾™ The paper used in this publication meets the minimum requirements of
American National Standard for Information Sciences—Permanence of Paper
for Printed Library Materials, ANSI/NISO Z39.48-1992.

To Muddlers, everywhere.

How we treat our fellow creatures is only one more way in which each of us, every day, writes our own epitaph—bearing into the world a message of light and life or just more darkness and death, adding to its joy or its despair.

—Matthew Scully

Take sides. Neutrality helps the oppressor, never the victim. Silence encourages the tormentor, never the tormented.

—Elie Wiesel

No one has a right to sit down and feel hopeless. There is too much work to do.

—Dorothy Day

CONTENTS

FOREWORD *Jeffrey Moussaieff Masson*   ix

PROLOGUE The Cat   1

    PART I Norman Rockwell Americans

1 **WHO ARE YOU ANIMAL RIGHTS
   ADVOCATES ANYWAY?**   9

2 **HOW DID YOU GET THAT WAY?**   21

    PART II Moral Rights: What They Are and Why They Matter

3 **HUMAN RIGHTS**   37

4 **ANIMAL RIGHTS**   53

    PART III Saying and Doing

5 **WHAT WE LEARN FROM ALICE**   77

    PART IV The Metamorphoses

6 **TURNING ANIMALS INTO FOOD**   87

7 **TURNING ANIMALS INTO CLOTHES**   107

8 **TURNING ANIMALS INTO PERFORMERS**   125

9 **TURNING ANIMALS INTO COMPETITORS**   141

CONTENTS

10   **TURNING ANIMALS INTO TOOLS**   159

     PART V   Many Hands on Many Oars

11   **"YES . . . , BUT . . ."**   181

EPILOGUE   The Cat   199

ACKNOWLEDGMENTS   201

NOTES   203

INDEX   221

ABOUT THE AUTHOR   229

FOREWORD

Jeffrey Moussaieff Masson

The book you are holding in your hands is, in my estimation, the single best introduction to the topic of animal rights ever written. Nobody has done more to articulate what "animal rights" means and should mean than Tom Regan. Universally recognized for decades as the leading philosophical spokesperson of the animal rights movement, Tom Regan's views have always been radical, in the original sense of that word: going to the root. This is what enables him to condemn, on purely moral grounds, *any* animal experimentation, whatever the perceived benefit to humans, a position I wholeheartedly endorse, and which I first heard expressed most eloquently by Tom Regan.

Tom Regan's philosophy about animals is original to its core. It is not dependent on any prior system. It is not tied to the doctrines of utilitarianism or any other traditional point of view. It is the product of a unique combination of head and heart. This is what makes Tom so beloved by people who care about animals and what makes this particular book so refreshing. Its pages overflow with profound ideas, clearly and simply stated. Though written by a philosopher, you do not need a degree in philosophy to understand and appreciate this powerful book.

Tom updates what is perhaps the most famous (and justly so) saying of the animal rights movement, proposed long ago by Jeremy Bentham: "The question is not 'Can they reason?' nor, 'Can they talk?' but, 'Can they suffer?' " Tom adds something equally important but not recognized until he formulated it. The question is not only can animals suffer but are they the subjects-of-a-life? This is one of those phrases that resonates long after you read it. It begins to sink in, and you realize that you have been exposed to a whole new idea, one of those potentially life-altering insights. Animals have a past, a story, a biography. They have histories. Mink and bears, elephants and dolphins, pigs and chickens, cats and dogs: each is a unique somebody, not a disposable something.

Think of the many implications: animals have mothers and fathers, often siblings, friendships, a childhood, youth, maturity. They go through life cycles much the way humans do (the psychoanalyst Erik Erikson earned his reputation by describing these phases in the lives of humans, but they are just as important in the lives of animals). Moreover, as Tom has said, and this is another of those illuminating phrases that will not leave you alone (gnawing, for example, at your conscience), their lives can go better or worse for them, whether or not anyone else cares about this.

Opponents of Tom often say we cannot possibly know what makes an animal happy. Nonsense. Nothing could be easier. A cow wants to live, to feed her young, to be outdoors in a natural world full of wind and sunshine and other natural things. A cow is happy when a cow does what cows have evolved to do: have friends and family and a life. Not a death. *This* is what a cow wants to do; *this* is what makes a cow happy. When you think of what is the worst thing that can happen in the life of any animal, you understand that it is an untimely death, and so Tom's philosophy tells us that we must do everything in our power to see to it that no animal dies when death is not natural, necessary, or required on grounds of mercy.

Untangle all the complex strands of Tom's simple statement, and you realize that you are taking an intellectual voyage that will bring you to places you may never have thought of visiting. You will be faced with implications you may never have considered, as happened to me just after reading Tom's book. After much research, my family found the Volvo Cross-Country station wagon to be the best car built in terms of child safety (and we have two small children). It only came in leather where I live (New Zealand). How seriously could I be taking Tom Regan's insights if I could support the killing of a dozen cows for my car? No way. That was out of the question for me.

Or think about eggs: how are the chickens who produce eggs treated? How much credence could I give to the statements of those who profited from selling the eggs? And whose eggs were they anyway? If I took Tom's ideas seriously and I purchased eggs, was I not supporting practices that routinely killed animals because they were not laying eggs fast enough? Eggs I didn't need in the first place? How can one justify terrorizing and killing innocent animals? If hens are subjects-of-a-life, was my decision showing respect for them? If their lives go well or poorly, was my decision helping or hindering their well being? So much for eggs.

I am not sure, but I believe it was Tom who first made me aware that taking the life of an animal, any animal, was an important matter, a momentous moment, not to be taken lightly. We could not hide behind words or try to conceal what we were doing by talking about it in imprecise or obscure terms. Today, even as I write these words, Americans are engaged in doing precisely that, killing people while they talk about shock and awe and ordinances. In this book, Tom explains that we must use words that everybody understands in ways that they have always been used and understood. He will not allow the kind of obfuscation I have just indicated, especially when practiced by animal abusers who hide behind the rhetoric of "humane treatment" and "responsible care." Tom is constantly recalling us to our own best instincts.

I am convinced that animals, all animals, feel love, much the same way that humans do. Tom, I know, agrees with me. And here is his book, written with love, asking us to do only one thing, but it is radical: to live in ways that show respect for animals even as we strive to live in ways that show respect for one another. Read this book and see if you don't come away convinced that this is the single best hope for our planet at this dangerous time in its existence.

PROLOGUE: THE CAT

A few years ago, the Home Box Office network aired a program entitled "To Love or Kill: Man vs. Animals." It told a fascinating and, at the same time, a disturbing story about how different cultures treat the same animals differently. One especially chilling segment took viewers out to dinner in a small Chinese village. You know how, in some American restaurants, patrons get to choose from among live lobsters or live fish? And how, after they make their selection, the animal is killed, and the chef cooks a meal of their choice? At this Chinese restaurant, things are the same except the menu is different. At this restaurant, patrons get to select from among live cats and dogs.

The video takes its time. First we see the hungry patrons inspect the cats and dogs, jammed cheek by jowl into wooden cages; next we see them talk it over; then we see them make their selection; finally we see a man (the cook, I assume), using long metal tongs, yank a fluffy white cat from her cage and hurry into the kitchen. What follows does not make for pleasant reading, so feel free to skip the next paragraph.

While the cat claws and screeches, the cook hits her several times with an iron bar. Clawing and screeching more now, she is abruptly submerged in a tub of scalding water for about ten seconds. Once removed, and while still alive, the cook skins her, from head to tail, in one swift pull. He then throws the traumatized animal into a large stone vat where (as the camera zooms in) we watch her gulp slowly, with increasing difficulty, her eyes glazed, until—her last breath taken—she drowns. The whole episode, from selection to final breath, takes several minutes. When the meal is served, the diners eat heartily, offering thanks and praise to the cook.

I have never been more stunned in my life. I was literally speechless. Like many Americans, I already knew that some people in China, Korea, and other countries eat cat and eat dog. The video didn't teach me any new fact about dietary customs. What was new for me, what pushed me back in my chair, was *seeing* how this is done, *seeing* the process. Watching the awful shock and suffering of the cat was devastating. I felt a mix of disbelief and anger welling up in my chest. I wanted to shout, "Stop it! What are you doing! Stop it!"

But what made matters worse, at least for me, was how the people behaved. For them, everything was just so ordinary, just so ho-hum, just so matter-of-fact. The diners said, "We'll have this cat for our dinner" the way we say, "We'll have this roll with our coffee." And the cook? The cook could not have cared less about the cat's ordeal. The poor animal might just as well have been a block of wood as far as he was concerned. I have never seen people behave so nonchalantly, so comfortably, so indifferently in the face of an animal's suffering and death. I don't think many Americans could watch this episode and not ask themselves, as I asked myself, "What is this world coming to?"

VARIATIONS

In the years since I first saw "To Love or Kill," I have imagined different variations of the episode I have just described. First variation: Everything is the same as in the original video except the dogs and cats are housed in large cages rather than jammed together. I ask myself, "Would making their cages larger make a difference in my thinking? Would I say, 'Well, since the cat lived in a larger cage, I no longer object to what happened to her'?" My answer is always the same. I would still object to what happened to her.

Second variation: In addition to living in a larger cage, the cook handles the cat gently and ends her life by giving her a shot of sodium pentobarbital, from which, to all appearances, she dies peacefully. Aside from these changes, everything else in the video remains the same. I ask myself the same kinds of question. "Would these changes make a difference in my thinking? Would I say, 'Well, since the cat lived in a larger cage, was treated gently, and died peacefully, I no longer object to what happened to her'?" My answer is always the same. I would still object to what happened to her.

Does this mean that I think these imaginary variations are just as bad as the original? No. Larger cages are better than smaller cages. Gentle treatment is better than violent treatment. Nevertheless, when that fluffy white cat is killed and skinned for dinner, even if she had lived in a larger cage and was killed without undue suffering, I would still want to shout (or at least plead), "Stop it! What are you doing? Stop it!" I cannot help thinking that the vast majority of people throughout the world, including many Chinese and Koreans, would agree with me.

ANIMAL RIGHTS ADVOCATES

For reasons I explain in part I, people like me, people who believe in animal rights, feel the same way about eagles and elephants, pigs and porpoises, as most people feel about cats and dogs. Don't get me wrong. Animal Rights Advocates (ARAs) don't want pigs sleeping in our beds or elephants riding in our cars. We don't want to make "pets" of these animals. What we want is something simpler: we just want people to stop doing terrible things to them.

Why do ARAs think this way? What explains our beliefs and values? There is no one-size-fits-all answer. ARAs take different paths to reach the same destination. It is important for people who are not ARAs to know something about those of us who are; it increases the chance of polite discussion. Which is why I will be saying something about my journey, along with the journeys of others.

My path has this odd twist to it. Part of the reason I became an ARA is because I studied philosophy. My teachers taught me to prize clear, rigorous, logical, fair thinking when I found it in others and challenged me (my, how they challenged me!) to bring my own thinking up to these lofty standards. In quiet homage to them, this is what I have tried to do in my philosophical writing for the past thirty years and more.

I know there is a stereotype of ARAs out there that pictures all of us as emotionally unbalanced bunny-huggers who wouldn't recognize a logical argument if one fell on us. I will address the origin of this and other ARA myths in chapter 1. Here, it is enough to express my hope that reading about my journey will go some way toward taking the air out of this particular stereotype. There is a rigorous, logical philosophy that supports what ARAs believe, one that treats fairly those with whom we disagree. In part II, I do my best to explain this philosophy, as clearly and as simply as I can. For those looking for more by way of abstract philosophy, one place to begin is with the companion volume to the present work, *Animal Rights, Human Wrongs: An Introduction to Moral Philosophy,* in which I defend animal rights by critically examining competing moral theories.

Explaining this philosophy also provides an opportunity to address another myth about ARAs: that we are misanthropic. We may love animals, but by golly we hate human beings. My journey toward animal rights illustrates how far this is from the truth. I would never have become an animal rights advocate if I had not first been a human rights advocate, especially for those humans (the very young and the very old, for example) who lack the understanding or power to assert their rights for themselves. ARAs do not hate humanity. How could we? Any success we might achieve in the days and years ahead requires the cooperation of the other human beings with whom we share this fragile planet. In the struggle for animal rights, all humans are potential allies whose dignity and rights ARAs unreservedly affirm.

MORE VARIATIONS

Earlier I described two variations on the cat episode. Here is another one. Variation three: What happens is exactly as shown in the original video except in this one I confront the cook and charge him with cruelty. He is shocked that I think so ill of him. He treats his cats and dogs "humanely," he insists, with "due regard for their welfare." I say, "You can't be serious!" He replies, "I am!"

What are we to make of a disagreement like this one? Should we say that the cook treats the fluffy white cat humanely because he says he does? That he acts with due regard for the cat's welfare because this is what he says? I don't think so. Humaneness is not in the eye of the beholder. The cook acts inhumanely. This is an objective fact in the world, not a subjective projection onto it.

To make my point clearer, consider this scenario. Variation four: Everything is the same as in the original video except it is *your* cat that the cook takes to the kitchen. Not for a moment would you say, "Yes, the cook certainly treated my cat humanely; after all, this is what he said he did." Not for a moment would you even *dream* of saying such a thing. Well, inhumane treatment does not become humane treatment just because some *other* cat is on the receiving end. If the cook says he treats cats humanely, we are certainly right to say, "No, you do not."

The reason I have included this fourth variation has little to do with what a cook in China might say and much to do with the actual words spoken by representatives of the major animal user industries. (I examine their rhetoric in part III). Like the Chinese cook in the third variation, representatives of the meat industry and greyhound racing, for example, *say* their industries treat animals humanely; like him, they *say* they always show due regard for their welfare. However, after we confirm (in part IV) that these industries treat animals just as badly if not worse than the cat was treated by the Chinese cook, it will be hard to believe their spokespersons anymore.

Some people, I am sure, will doubt the truth of what I have just said. Surely these industries do not treat animals just as badly (let alone worse) than the Chinese cook. Surely I must be exaggerating. Would that this were true. As we will see, compared to how animals are treated by the major animal user industries, and despite industry and government assurances to the contrary, that fluffy white cat was one of the lucky ones.

LIMITATIONS

My discussion in part IV is limited for the most part to the American scene. Much as I would have liked to have been able to include discussions of how the major animal user industries operate throughout the world, both the constraints of space and the limits of my knowledge worked against my doing so. In general, however, I do not think that how these industries do business in other countries differs greatly from how they do business in America. Granted, sometimes some animals in some places might be treated better, just as sometimes some animals in some places might be treated worse. Still, as a general rule, I do not think there are vast, systemic differences from one nation to the next. Whether this is true or not, readers can decide by consulting the relevant international resources that will be found at www.tomregan-animalrights.com, a website that offers a wide variety of resources relevant to the topics discussed in this book in particular, and to animal rights in general.

A second limitation should be noted. Humans exploit so many different kinds of animals, in so many different kinds of ways, that it is not possible to cover every form of abuse. Organized dog fighting. The whaling industry. The plight of America's wild horses. Manatee preservation. The anachronism of "modern" zoos. The barbarities of roadside animal displays. The poaching of African wildlife. Bullfighting. The many torments animals endure in the name of religious practices and festivals. It is not hard to make a long list of omissions.

In lieu of trying to cover many practices superficially, I will be describing a few in some depth. Readers looking for more information, both about the issues covered in these pages as well as those that are not, will find this on the website mentioned earlier. Other resources on the site include photographs and videos that depict the beauty and dignity, the grace and mystery of other animals. In addition, some of these resources (the hard ones) realistically depict the treatment animals receive at the hands of the major animal user industries. Be forewarned (and you will always have the choice to view them or not): these visuals do not try to conceal or minimize the tragic truth. Billions of animals live lives of abject misery and go to their death in the unfeeling clutches of human cruelty. These are painful truths, but truths they are. One challenge ARAs face is to make the invisible visible; otherwise, people will never fully understand the history of the meat on their plate or the wool on their back, for example. In this regard, the "hard" photographs and videos play an essential educational purpose.

A FINAL VARIATION

We return to the cat one last time, in the epilogue, where I describe a fifth and final variation. Prior to this, in part V, I explore a variety of ways in which people are turned off by ARAs and try to put these turn-offs in perspective. The future for animals is bleak if too few people want to make the goals of animal rights a reality. Like other social justice advocates, ARAs make our full share of mistakes. My hope is that people will not let the self-righteousness, tastelessness, or violence of a small handful of ARAs prevent them from becoming ARAs themselves.

NORMAN ROCKWELL
AMERICANS

WHO ARE YOU ANIMAL RIGHTS ADVOCATES ANYWAY?

Do animals have rights? Different people give different answers. Sometimes people give different answers because of a disagreement about the facts. For example, some people believe cats and dogs, chickens and hogs do not feel anything; others believe they do. Sometimes different answers are given because of a disagreement over values. For example, some people believe animals have no value apart from human interests; others believe the opposite. Disagreements of both kinds are important certainly, and both will be explored along the way. As important as these kinds of disagreements are, neither touches a more basic source of division, this one concerning the idea of animal rights itself.

Some people think this idea is synonymous with being kind to animals. Since we should be kind to animals, the inference is obvious: animals have rights. Or they think animal rights means avoiding cruelty. Since we should not be cruel to animals, the same conclusion follows: animals have rights. Given either of these two ways of understanding animal rights, it is hard to explain why the idea is so controversial, with animal rights advocates on one side and animal rights opponents on the other.

The heated, often acrimonious controversy that pits advocates against opponents tells us that these familiar ways of thinking (we should be kind to animals; we should not be cruel to them) fail to capture the real meaning of animal rights. Its real meaning, as it turns out, is both simple and profound.

Animal rights is a simple idea because, at the most basic level, it means only that animals have a right to be treated with respect. It is a profound idea because its implications are far-reaching. How far-reaching? Here are a few examples of how the world will have to change once we learn to treat animals with respect.

We will have to stop raising them for their flesh.
We will have to stop killing them for their fur.
We will have to stop training them to entertain us.
We will have to stop using them in scientific research.

Each example illustrates the same moral logic. When it comes to how humans exploit animals, recognition of their rights requires abolition, not reform. Being kind to animals is not enough. Avoiding cruelty is not enough. Whether we exploit animals to eat, to wear, to entertain us, or to learn, the truth of animal rights requires empty cages, not larger cages.

UNTRUTH IN LABELING

Opponents think animal rights is an extreme idea, and it is not unusual for them to pin the label "extremists" on animal rights advocates. It is important to understand how this label is used as a rhetorical tool to prevent informed, fair discussion; otherwise, chances are we won't have an informed, fair discussion.

"Extremists" and "extremism" are ambiguous words. In one sense, extremists are people who will do anything to further their objectives. The terrorists who destroyed the twin towers of the World Trade Center were extremists in this sense; they were willing to go to any lengths, even if it meant killing thousands of innocent human beings, to further their ends.

Animal rights advocates (ARAs) are not extremists in this sense. Let me repeat this: ARAs are not extremists in this sense. Even the most militant advocates of animal rights (the members of the Animal Liberation Front, say) believe there are absolute moral limits to what can be done in the name of animal liberation, acts that should never be performed, they are so bad. For example, the ALF opposes hurting let alone killing human beings.

In another sense, the word *extremist* refers to the unqualified nature of what people believe. In this sense, ARAs are extremists. Again, let me repeat this: ARAs really are extremists, in this sense. ARAs really do believe that it is always wrong to train wild animals to perform tricks for human amusement, for example. But in *this* sense, *everyone* is an extremist. Why? Because there are some things all of us (one hopes) oppose unqualifiedly.

For example, everyone reading these words is an extremist when it comes to rape; we are against rape all the time. Each of us is an extremist when it comes to child abuse; we are against child abuse all the time. Indeed, all of us are extremists when it comes to cruelty to animals; we never favor that.

The plain fact is, extreme views sometimes are correct views. That being so, the fact that ARAs are extremists, in the sense that we have unqualified beliefs about right and wrong, by itself provides no reason for thinking that we must be mistaken. So the question to be examined is not, "Are ARAs extremists?" It is, "Are we right?" As we shall see, this question is hardly ever fairly asked, let alone fairly answered. Collusion between the media and powerful special interests sees to that.

THE MEDIA

One barrier to fair discussion of animal rights is the media. As so often happens today, our perception of the "real world" is based on what we see on television or read in the newspaper. This should raise a red flag immediately. Perhaps Paul Watson exaggerates when he states that "[T]he media is only concerned with four elements: sex, scandal, violence and celebrities, and if you don't have one of those elements in your story then you don't have a story." Still, there's a lot of truth in what Watson says. Safe landings? Hard to get those covered. The media loves a plane crash. Add some sex, scandal, and a few celebrities, mix and stir and you're vying for front page coverage. Any doubts about this, just watch the news tonight or read the paper tomorrow.

Because the media looks for what is sensational, they can be counted on to cover animal rights when something unlawful or outlandish occurs. Members of the Animal Liberation Front firebomb a lab. An antifur activist throws a pie in Calvin Klein's face. These are the sorts of stories we get to watch or read. As for the peaceful protest that took place outside a fur store yesterday, or the lecture on animal rights given at the law school last night? Hardly ever covered. Non-sensational animal rights news doesn't "bleed" enough for the media's tastes. No wonder the general public views ARAs as a band of merry pranksters and social misfits. All too often, this is the only message that works its way through the media's filters.

SPECIAL INTEREST POLITICS

That the general public tends to have a negative picture of ARAs is not the result only of the media's appetite for the sensational; it is also due to what the media is fed by the public relations arms of major animal user industries. By "major animal user industries" I mean the meat industry, the fur industry, the animal entertainment industry, and the biomedical research industry, for example. The people who work in these industries speak with one voice, tell the same story, even use the same words to denigrate their common enemy: animal rights extremists.

The origin of the most recent chapter in this story here in the United States is not hard to find. It begins in 1989 with the publication of the American Medical Association's white paper "Use of Animals in Biomedical Research: The Challenge and the Response." Among the AMA's recommendations: People who believe in animal rights "must be shown to be not only anti-science but also (a) responsible for violent and illegal acts that endanger life and property, and (b) a threat to the public's freedom of choice." ARAs must be seen as people who are "radicals," "militants," and "terrorists," who are "opposed to human well being." By contrast, sane, sensible, decent people must be shown to favor animal welfare, understood as humane, responsible use of animals, by humans, for humans.

The AMA's strategy was both simple and inspired. If the public's perception of using animals in research could be structured as a contest between know-nothing animal rights extremists who hate humans and have an insatiable appetite for violence, on the one hand, and wise scientific animal welfare moderates, true friends of humanity, on the other, ARAs would be repudiated and the ideology of humane, responsible use would prevail.

Since 1989, a steady stream of press releases, memos, e-mail messages, press conferences, and website miscellany, denouncing ARA extremists and lauding reasonable animal welfarists, has flowed from the AMA's and other biomedical research industry's public relations offices straight into the hands of reporters, news directors, and editors. How does this work? Here is one example.

The Foundation for Biomedical Research describes itself as "the nation's oldest and largest organization dedicated to improving human and animal health by promoting public understanding and support for the humane and responsible use of animals in medical and scientific research." FBR's website includes a page entitled "Journalist Resources," featuring three links. One is "Expert Opinion," which is described in this way: "FBR works to bring scientists and journalists together to inspire exceptional, outstanding and ongoing news coverage that contributes to public understanding and appreciation for the humane and responsible use of animals in medical and scientific research. When you need to quote an expert from the American research community, contact us first."

"To inspire exceptional, outstanding . . . coverage." That's positive and appealing. Who could be against that?

A second link is "FBR News Tips," described as "a monthly tip sheet for journalists that promotes story ideas that will strengthen public understanding and respect for the humane and responsible use of animals in medical research. It provides a summary of the latest medical discoveries, as well as reliable contact information. In every case, the research described demonstrates the essential need for lab animals in medical research."

"Humane and responsible use of animals in medical research" that is "essential." Hard to be against this, either.

And the third link? This one is "Animal activism," where FBR presents "a record of all known criminal activities committed in the name of 'animal rights' since 1981."

Let's see, now. "Animal activism" equals "criminal activities committed in the name of 'animal rights'," which equals "illegal and violent acts." If *that's* what "animal rights" involves, who (except those who support criminal, illegal, and violent acts) could possibly be for it?

There we have the basic story: Animal welfare moderates versus animal rights extremists. Wise scientists who treat animals humanely versus know-nothing, emotionally overloaded ARAs bent on destruction. This is the message special interest groups like FBR spoon-feed the media. Does it work? Does the media slant its coverage because of efforts like FBR's? Before we answer, let's do some imagining. Here we have an earnest forty-something reporter, lucky to have a permanent job; his salary, together with his wife's, falls far short of being enough to cover all the bills, now that both their children are attending prestigious colleges. His beat includes biomedical research. On a monthly basis, he receives FBR's tip sheets. On a daily basis, he receives the latest installment of authoritative quotes from "experts" who support research using animals. And on a timely basis, he receives an up-to-date inventory of "criminal activities committed in the name of 'animal rights.'"

So let us ask ourselves: what are the odds of this reporter's giving an impartial, fair story about the "latest medical break-through using animals"? Might the odds be just a tiny bit skewed in one direction rather than another? Should we mention that among the newspaper's biggest advertisers are major animal user industries, including economically powerful interests (major pharmaceutical companies, for example) represented by FBR? Or that the reporter's 401(k) is heavily invested in these same industries, as are those of the newspaper's publisher and editorial staff? Can we really think, when we think about it objectively, that the odds of an impartial, fair story about the "latest medical breakthrough using animals" are even-steven?

There may be some people who will answer yes, but my experience tells me they would be in the minority. Most people, once they understand how the cards are stacked, understand why the news is dealt the way it is. Remember the old adage He who pays the piper calls the tune? Its truth did not pass away when paid pipers became an extinct species. The plain fact is, many people have a negative image of animal rights because much of the media presents ARAs in a negative light. And much of the media presents ARAs in a negative light because the media is relentlessly fed a negative image by the spokespersons for the financially powerful and influential major animal user industries. It's not all that surprising, once we stop to think about it.

ALL ABOARD!

With so prestigious a group as the AMA having raised the sails, it did not take long for other major animal user industries to come on board. The meat industry. The animal entertainment industry. Sport hunters and rodeo enthusiasts. The story is everywhere the same. Animal welfare moderates versus animal rights extremists. Law-abiding citizens versus law-breaking terrorists. By way of example, consider the following discussion of animal welfare and animal rights from the Fur Information Council of America. First, we have a description of the sane, sensible position of those who favor animal welfare:

> Animals enrich our lives in many ways. They provide food, clothing and companionship. Animals used for medical research have given us important advances in medicine that have saved millions of lives. Most people today recognize that the use of animals under humane circumstances is important.
> Animal welfare organizations also support the wise use of animals under humane conditions. The animal welfare ethic has been promoted over the past century by many groups, including the fur industry. Working with the government and the veterinary community, industries that involve animal use have adopted high standards for the treatment of animals. For instance, today there are strict regulations governing livestock; guidelines have been implemented for the care of animals used in medical research; and humane care standards have been implemented by the fur industry.

Next, we have a description of the "out-of-touch-with-reality" extremists who favor animal rights:

> In the past few years, however, an extreme movement called "animal rights" has emerged. The basic philosophy of these groups dictates that humans have no right to use animals for any purpose whatsoever. These groups oppose the use of animals for food, clothing, medical research, and in zoos and circuses. . . .

The majority of Americans support animal welfare groups, but do NOT support [any] out-of-touch-with-reality, publicity-hungry animal rights groups. . . . Animal welfare groups support humane treatment and responsible care of animals while the animal rights philosophy not only condemns the use of all animals for any purpose but it also is known for its increasingly terroristic tactics. The current mindset of the animal rights movement is, "Believe what I believe . . . or else."

True to the spirit of the AMA's white paper, the debate over fur is framed here as a contest between animal welfare moderates, who favor "humane treatment and responsible care of animals," and animal rights extremists who, like the criminals who blew up the twin towers of the World Trade Center, resort to "terroristic tactics."

But (you might well ask) is this true of all ARAs? Do we all favor terrorism and intimidation? This is what the Fur Information Council is saying. They presume to tell us what "[t]he current mindset of the animal rights movement" is, not what a small handful of ARAs think. *The mindset of the movement* is, "Believe what I believe . . . or else," where the "or else" carries with it the threat of one "terroristic tactic" or another. ARAs must really be terrible people.

"THEY WOULD NEVER DO THAT, WOULD THEY?"

Having adopted a proactive strategy, one pillar of which is the depiction of ARAs as lawless terrorists, the major animal user industries face a daunting challenge. For their strategy to work, there *has to be* illegal, terroristic activity attributed to ARAs. And not just a little. What is needed is a lot. It did not take long before anti-ARA forces decided that they would need to do a little freelance terrorist work of their own.

Consider this possible scenario. Why not hire someone to infiltrate the animal rights movement, as an agent provocateur, with one main purpose: to find a malleable person in the movement who could be "encouraged" (shall we say) to try to do something that would really discredit ARAs. Like, maybe this person could be "encouraged" to try to murder someone. And not just anyone. No, the "someone" should be a pillar of the community, someone who (what an odd coincidence) just happened to be a leader in a major animal user industry, someone who just happened to have been famously outspoken in his criticisms of ARAs. An attempt on his life would be perfect. It would show the public that ARAs really are extremists who will stop at nothing to further their ends. It is not hard to visualize the headline: "Animal Rights Terrorist Attempts to Murder Pillar of Community."

A few problems would have to be solved. It takes time to find the right person for the job. It takes money to pay all the players. Who is going to come up with the necessary cash? Well, suppose the pillar himself could pay for the attempt on his life. Suppose the pillar himself (such is his influence) could arrange to have the local police on hand to arrest the would-be murderer. "Nah," you might say, "This is too fanciful, too conspiratorial. I don't think anyone in a major animal user industry would ever do anything like this." Think again.

Leon Hirsch, past president of the Norwalk, Connecticut-based U. S. Surgical Corporation, played the role of the pillar of the community. Hirsch's former company manufactures staples used in place of ordinary sutures in many operations. During Hirsch's tenure, physicians received training by practicing on live dogs, who were vivisected, then killed. ARAs (led by Friends of Animals, also located in Norwalk) mounted an in-your-face campaign against Hirsch and his company back in the late 1980s. His ingenious way of getting even was to put up the necessary money to arrange for an ARA to try to murder him.

On November 11, 1989, a man on the payroll of a firm Hirsch had hired drove a young woman named Fran Trutt, a self-professed ARA, along with her two recently purchased pipe bombs, from New York City to Norwalk. When she placed the bombs adjacent to Hirsch's parking space, Hirsch's friends in the Norwalk police department just happened to be on hand to arrest her.

The resulting story (not the bombs, which never exploded) was the real bombshell. There it was: "Animal Rights Terrorist Attempts to Murder Pillar of Community." As John C. Stauber and Sheldon Rampton observe, "Normally, of course, company presidents do not arrange their own murder, but Hirsch was neither crazy nor suicidal. He was trying to engineer an embarrassing scandal that would discredit the animal rights movement."

Hirsch would have succeeded, too, except for one thing: the ensuing trial brought to light extensive tape transcripts that implicated everyone, from Hirsch on down, who had hatched the plot to discredit ARAs. Friends of Animals sued Hirsch, who sold U. S. Surgical in 1998, but their suit was unsuccessful, and he never faced any criminal charges. Perhaps not surprisingly, Fran Trutt was the only person to serve time (a year in prison, followed by a year on probation). She seems to have left the movement.

IT ONLY GETS WORSE

This is not the only case where people in major animal user industries have taken on the job of trying to make sure there is enough "ARA terrorism" to go around. Books, not just people, can be deceiving. The infamous Ku Klux Klan leader, David Duke, knows this. One of his books, *African Atto*, is a manual written for violent black street gangs, supposedly authored by an "insider" (that is, a gang member). Another of his books (like the first, this one was not published under Duke's name, for obvious reasons), is a sex manual written by and for the "liberated" woman. You know the type: mindless of "family values," lusting after sexual adventures with the next guy to turn the corner.

In both cases, Duke's books were written to reinforce prejudicial stereotypes of the sort Duke wants his constituency to fear: the predatory black male, in the one case, the liberated woman (whatever her race), in the other. Given the familiar stereotype of ARAs as misanthropic violent lawbreakers who are antiscience, antireason, anti-American, anti-everything any decent human being values, one might expect to find a fraudulent animal rights exposé written by someone posing as an ARA insider.

This expectation was fulfilled with the publication of *A Declaration of War: Killing People to Save Animals and the Environment*, written anonymously by an author identified only as "Screaming Wolf." A real charmer, Screaming Wolf makes it clear that there is no limit to the violence real ARAs ("liberators") are prepared to carry out. It is not just the university researcher who uses animals in harmful studies, not just the furrier, not just the hunter, whose lives are at risk; it is the researcher's children, the furrier's rabbi or minister, the hunter's friends or business associates. In short, *anyone* can be chosen as a legitimate, justifiable victim by the army of "liberators" who have decided the time has come to kill people in order to save animals and the environment.

Haven't the major animal user industries been saying as much? Screaming Wolf (a liberator "insider") is only confirming what these industries have been saying about ARAs all along. The industries could not have done a better job of discrediting ARAs if they had hired some fictitious Screaming Wolf to write this book for them.

And that is precisely what happened. At least this is the judgment I reached when I reviewed the book, more than a decade ago, a judgment that, to date, no one has successfully refuted. *A Declaration of War* is nothing more than a work of fraudulent provocation, a work of fiction disguised as fact. And a clever work of fiction it is. For liberators, you see, will rarely take credit for their actions. In general, they prefer to remain anonymous.

Consider the illogic of this logic. Suppose a researcher's car is blown up. Or she dies or disappears mysteriously. Or strangers rape her daughter. Then liberators will either take credit for this or they will not. If they do, then they did it. If they don't, then they probably did it anyhow. Here, most assuredly, is a strategy that *cannot fail* to create the appearance that animal rights terrorism is on the rise.

And the moral of the story is? The moral of the story is simple. The next time the media shows or tells a story about "animal rights terrorism," we should all think twice before buying into its veracity. We do not know how often the violent, unlawful acts the media attributes to ARAs actually were paid for by someone trying to do what Leon Hirsch tried to do: discredit the animal rights movement by encouraging impressionable ARAs to break the law. And we do not know how often the violent acts the media attributes to ARAs actually are carried out by people who, paid or unpaid, have nothing to do with the movement. What we do know is, all this happens some of the time, which should be reason enough to make us raise a skeptical eyebrow when we open tomorrow morning's paper and read "Animal Rights Terrorists" do one bad thing or another.

NORMAN ROCKWELL AMERICANS

Let me be perfectly honest. My wife Nancy and I have been involved in animal advocacy for more than thirty years. During this time, we have met some people we would not want to do any baby-sitting. Misanthropic people, mean-spirited to the core. People who hate hunters, hate trappers, hate butchers, hate every living, breathing human being, even themselves. We have also met ARAs who could be described (to speak charitably) as weird, kooky, or strange, and others who have no respect for reason or science. Moreover, we have known ARAs who believe violent, criminal acts, as well as personal threats made against animal users or their family members, when done in the name of animal liberation, are morally justified. Yes, some ARAs are prepared to go this far.

For a variety of reasons, the attitudes and values of the ARAs I have just described are regrettable. One reason concerns the public's perception of animal rights. The violent, lawless behavior of a few, the hateful attitudes of a handful, is grist for the opponents of animal rights' mill. Representatives of the meat and fur industries, for example, want nothing more than to have the general public accept the accuracy of the stereotype of ARAs as misanthropic violent lawbreakers. Fortunately for industry spokespersons, some ARAs cooperate by actually being this way. They don't have to be invented.

If I have learned anything from my years of involvement in animal rights, it is that the ARAs who fit the stereotype are the rare exception, not the rule. The great majority of ARAs are just ordinary folks: neighbors and business associates; the family that runs the print shop or cleaners down the street; the guy next to you on the exercise bike at the gym; students and teachers in the local schools; the woman who sings solos in the church choir; teenagers who belong to Luther League or Wesley Fellowship; the couple that volunteers for Meals on Wheels; homemakers, nurses, and physicians; counselors and social workers; whites, blacks, browns, reds, yellows, of every shade and hue; rich, poor, middle class; the old and the young; Protestants, Catholics, Jews, Muslims, Hindus, and every other faith, including those with no faith; political liberals and conservatives; people who love family and country, who work hard, mow their lawn, and pay their taxes.

Moreover, while the ARA message the public receives is one of negativity (ARAs are against greyhound racing, against sport hunting, against rodeo, for example), the other, positive side of the story hardly ever gets told. With rare exceptions, ARAs are for love of family and country, for human rights and justice, for human freedom and equality, for compassion and mercy, for peace and tolerance, for special concern for those with special needs (children, the enfeebled, the elderly, among others), for a clean, sustainable environment, for the rights of our children's children's children—our future generations.

In a word, the vast majority of ARAs are Norman Rockwell Americans, straight off his famous Thanksgiving cover for the old *Saturday Evening Post,* only with this noteworthy difference. We'll pass on the turkey, thank you. We don't eat our friends.

So let us put an end to the untruths that the major animal user industries spread about "animal rights extremists." Not all ARAs are violent lawbreakers, and "[t]he current mindset of the animal rights movement" is not "'Believe what I believe . . . or else.'" This is just special interest propaganda meant to forestall fair, informed discussion. That said, it has to be acknowledged that ARAs are, well . . . we are . . . different from most people. Especially if you're a Muddler, you have to wonder how we got that way. Answering this question is a good place to begin our discussion.

HOW DID YOU
GET THAT WAY?

In today's world, animal rights advocates stick out like a sore thumb. We don't eat meat. We don't drink milk, or eat cheese or eggs. Wear fur? Forget it. We don't even wear leather or wool. ARAs are so obviously out of step with the dominant cultural drumbeat that one has to wonder what quirk of nature or stroke of fate made us the way we are. This is a question I have asked myself many times. I do not pretend to know all the answers. I may know some. Here is what my experience has taught me.

ANIMAL CONSCIOUSNESS: THE DAVINCIANS

Some children seem to be born with what I call animal consciousness. From an early age, they have the ability to enter into the mystery of the interior lives of animals, the life that goes on "behind their eyes," so to speak. It is not something they are taught, not something they have to "figure out," not a conclusion they reach after going through a complicated chain of scientific or moral reasoning. I don't mean to suggest that these children are omniscient. Like the rest of us, they do not know everything: all the odors dogs smell when romping through the woods or what dolphins "see" through their sense of sound, for example. Some things remain forever mysterious to all of us.

What I mean is this. At a young age, some children are able to empathize with animals, to make the life of the "other" part of their own, so much so that they feel a real kinship with them. They know when animals are enjoying themselves, when they are distressed, what they find interesting and challenging, the things that bore them, and the others that scare them. Dogs and cats, bears and lions, whales and seals: these children have a rapport with other animals that goes beyond their ability with words. They know more than they can say.

The bonds that unite these children and animals are the bonds of a special kind of friendship, a friendship that expresses itself in respect and loyalty. The relationship between the child and the animal (to use the helpful language of Martin Buber) is that of "I–Thou," not "I–It." Animals known, as well as animals imagined, are unique somebodies, not generic somethings.

How do these precocious children know what they know? Here is the best analogy I can offer. Think of the most loyal friends you have ever had. Ask yourself how you know they are loyal. It is not by observing their loyal behavior on one day, then the next, and so on, through all the years of the relationship, until one day you devise the hypothesis, "Maybe my friends are loyal?" Instead, it is by *knowing the persons* who are your friends, knowing *who they are*. The same, I think, is true of these children. They know that what happens to other animals matters to them because they know them.

This knowledge makes a difference to how these children want to behave. Once they understand what meat is, where it comes from, for example, they want nothing to do with it. To kill animals for sport or to keep them in tiny cages? Absolutely unthinkable. Friends take care of friends. Friends are loyal to friends. Friends speak out for and try to protect friends. For these children, animals are their friends. To eat a dead friend is something they would never want to do (which is not to say that their parents might not make them do it anyway).

I call these children DaVincians, after Leonardo da Vinci (1452–1519), the greatest mind of the Italian Renaissance, famous for some of the world's most magnificent paintings, including *The Last Supper* and the *Mona Lisa,* and renowned for the great sweep of his intellect, which took in all that was known while he was alive, extending to anatomy, astronomy, mathematics, and natural history. Less well known but highly relevant in the present context is Leonardo's untutored love of animals. The historian Edward MacCurdy writes that "[t]he mere idea of permitting the existence of unnecessary suffering, still more that of taking life, was abhorrent to him."

Early in life, by all accounts, he adopted a vegetarian diet, for ethical reasons. Sparing no sarcasm, Leonardo assails human vanity in these words: "King of the animals—as [humans] have described [themselves]—I should rather say king of the beasts, thou being the greatest—because thou dost help them, in order that they give thee their children for the benefit of the gullet, of which thou has made a tomb for all animals." Our stomach "a tomb"? An arresting image, to say the least. Even milk and cheese were suspect because they involve theft. "Of the beasts from whom cheese is made," he writes, "the milk will be taken from the tiny children."

The most famous quotation attributed to Leonardo also happens to be the one that has occasioned the most controversy. Jon Wynne-Tyson makes the attribution in his book *The Extended Circle: A Commonplace Book of Animal Rights.* According to Wynne-Tyson, Leonardo writes the following: "I have from an early age abjured the use of meat, and the time will come when men such as I will look upon the murder of animals as they now look upon the murder of men." Since the publication of *The Extended Circle,* it has become a commonplace to find these words attributed to Leonardo in the vegetarian community.

As it turns out, however, these words cannot be found among Leonardo's collected works; they are only to be found in a work of fiction, *The Romance of Leonardo da Vinci,* by Dimitri Merejkowski. It may very well be true, therefore, that Leonardo himself never said what Wynne-Tyson attributes to him. Even so, knowing what we do about the man, it is not unreasonable to believe that they cannot be far from expressing his personal convictions.

Leonardo's animal consciousness extended beyond his abhorrence for meat. He was keenly interested in understanding flight (his notebooks contain pictures of rudimentary helicopters, for example) and could not bear the sight of birds in captivity. The story is told of how, on many occasions, he would purchase birds, lift them from their prisons, and then (we must imagine he held them ever so gently) he set them free.

Not many ARAs are DaVincians. At least this is what other ARAs have told me. Most of us lack the natural empathy and sympathy of DaVincians, lack their (it seems) innate desire to help and protect. For most ARAs, our initial understanding of animals is a hand-me-down understanding. Successfully acculturated, we uncritically internalize the cultural paradigm. We see animals as our culture sees them. Because the paradigm in American culture in particular, and Western culture in general, sees other animals as existing for us, having no other purpose for being in the world than to serve human needs or satisfy human desires, we see them that way too. Thus it is that pigs, for example, fulfill their purpose when they end up as lunchmeat between two slices of bread.

A CHANGE IN PERCEPTION

In 2000 two independent filmmakers, James LaVeck and Jenny Stein, released *The Witness.* The film tells the inspiring story of Eddie Lama, a tough-talking New Yorker who accepted the cultural paradigm for most of his life. Eddie's

Figure 2.1.

journey toward animal consciousness began when he was asked to take care of a cat. No one can improve on the story as he tells it in *The Witness*, and I won't try to do that here. However, one thing Eddie says has always stuck with me. Because of the time he spent with the cat, and what he began to learn, Eddie experienced what he describes as "a change in perception."

I liken his idea to the experience we have when we look at optical illusions, the one reproduced in this chapter, for example. When we first look, we see the image one way; then (how long this takes varies from person to person) a second image reveals itself. First we see the vase; then we see the faces. Or vice versa.

Eddie's change in perception did not concern an optical illusion; it concerned a living, breathing animal being. Whereas before he had seen animals as pieces of potential human utility, as something to eat or wear or experiment on, he now began to see them the way DaVincians do: as unique somebodies, with lives of their own, in need of protection.

ANIMAL CONSCIOUSNESS: THE DAMASCANS

Different people undergo this "change in perception" in different ways, for different reasons, and at different times. Some people experience this change in the blink of an eye. To continue with the analogy: one minute they see the vase, the next minute they see the faces. I call these people Damascans, after the Biblical story of Saul on the road to Damascus.

Saul (you may recall) had been called to Damascus to help silence all the favorable talk about a man named Jesus, toward whom Saul and his friends felt great enmity. As he walked along the road to Damascus, so the story goes, Jesus miraculously appeared and spoke to Saul directly. That was enough to change Saul's life forever. Saul, the Detractor, became Paul, the Apostle, the author of such New Testament books as Romans, and First and Second Corinthians.

Damascans enter animal consciousness in a similar way. One minute they accept the cultural paradigm; the next minute they do not. I remember listening to an older German activist tell how one day, during the Second World War, he emerged from a bomb shelter to encounter a horse running wildly down the street, ablaze from nose to tail because the gasoline covering her body had caught fire. As the mare passed, she looked directly at the then young boy, her eyes full of terror and accusation. It was (the man said) as if she were asking him, "What have I done to deserve this? Why aren't you helping me?"

From that moment on, the man was infused with animal consciousness. Once his mind and heart were opened, he was able to enter the interior lives of animals through empathy and compassion, something he was never able to do before. What happened to animals mattered to him. Because they had no voice, he would speak for them, asking of others the same questions the horse had asked of him: "What have animals done to deserve the treatment they receive? Why aren't you helping them?"

On another occasion, Nancy and I were eating dinner next to a young woman who was dining alone. We exchanged a few words, one thing led to another, and without knowing our own views she began to tell us about how she had grown up on a small farm where she raised a lamb. Every morning, before she went to school, she would visit the lamb, brushing her, cleaning her, feeding her. And every afternoon, after school, she would do the same things. Until one day, when she went to the barn after school, the lamb was gone, and the evening meal was lamb chops.

This young woman (she was in her midtwenties) was almost in tears as she told her story. "To this day," she said, "I've never forgiven my parents." But from that day forward, her life was infused with animal consciousness. Not the plight of one lamb, but the plight of all animals became a doorway through which she entered the world.

ANIMAL CONSCIOUSNESS: THE MUDDLERS

More animal rights advocates are Damascans than DaVincians. This reflects my experience, in any event. When it comes to how we see other animals, more people are changed because of a single, transforming experience than are born with and never lose their natural empathy. However, if my experience is reliable, the majority of ARAs are not DaVincians, and not Damascans either. Nothing in the genes. Nothing so dramatic. Rather, most people who become ARAs just muddle along in life, first learning one thing, then another; experiencing this, then that; asking some questions, finding some answers; making one decision, then a second, then a third. Men, it seems to me, have a special talent for taking their time about it. We tend to want more by way of rational proof, more by way of logical demonstration; there are *so* many things we think we have to "figure out" before we can permit ourselves to come down on the side of animal rights. At least this was true in my case, as I will explain shortly.

Whatever the path taken, and however long it takes, Muddlers (as I call them) grow into animal consciousness step by step, little by little. To speak metaphorically, it just takes us awhile to see the vase rather than the faces, or vice versa. Even so, the transformation is noteworthy and, once it occurs, permanent. For Muddlers, a day finally dawns when we look in the mirror and, to our surprise, we see an Animal Rights Advocate looking back at us.

The archetypes I have described (DaVincians, Damascans, Muddlers) are not restricted to animal consciousness. I have known some children who have been born without a mean bone in their bodies. Their sensitivity and kindness, their empathy and compassion for everyone around them, are apparent from the moment they are able to interact with others. The good they exude is boundless and nondiscriminatory. It is as if these children do not see the color of another person's skin or how different some people are from them when it comes to their dress, language, and customs, for example. These children are to other humans what some children are to other animals. And, of course, sometimes an exceptional child will combine both capacities.

In addition, some people, like the Damascans I have described, recognize and overcome various prejudices against humans because of a single transforming experience. And still others just muddle along, growing slowly but surely toward the sensitivity and respect for other humans that some children bring with them when they enter the world, qualities that, once acquired, are retained undiminished throughout their lives.

I should note as well that the three archetypes I have described do not exhaust all the possibilities even in the case of animal consciousness. For example, Kim Bartlett who, together with Merritt Clifton and their son, Wolf, publish *Animal People*, writes about her experience as follows:

> I believe that the normal acculturation of children (into religion; the educational system; the acceptance of meat-eating or at least the prevalence of cruelty) . . . has the effect of stifling and stunting whatever awareness the child may have been born with. You might have a child who was born in an enlightened state only to have the enlightenment turned completely off by the acculturation process.

In other words, children can be born DaVincians only to have their animal consciousness stunted or drained from them. Kim knows whereof she speaks. It happened to her:

> I know that I went into a deep state of denial after learning that I was eating animals at about age 5 or 6, so I know what can happen to a child—even one who is emotionally sensitive to an extreme that is personally and socially maladaptive.

In time Kim was able to reclaim her DaVincian ways, something her son Wolf has never lost:

> Wolf was never "turned off." He was never told that animals were anything but his kin, and he was never indoctrinated into any religion. When he would ask about spiritual or moral matters, I would tell him what I think and what things other people think or what various religions teach, but always encouraging him to decide what he believes. When Wolf found out that other people eat animals, discussions went on for a very long time about it (and still go on sometimes), with Wolf concluding that it is wrong to eat animals "because animals don't want to be eaten."

I hope I will not be misunderstood, therefore, when I use the ideas I have been explaining in the pages that lie ahead. When it comes to how different people perceive animals, not everyone is either a DaVincian, or a Damascan, or a Muddler. The world is more complicated than that.

As a Muddler myself, I think I know something about this way of reaching animal consciousness. In fact, this book (as the dedication states) is for Muddlers, everywhere. Resolute DaVincians don't need to read it. Born with an animal consciousness they never lose, they already have what Muddlers are in the process of possibly acquiring. And while all writers hope their words have some power for the good, I would be fooling myself if I believed that my words alone might have the power to change how people see animals, in the blink of an eye, the way the world changes for Damascans.

No, if my words can be of any possible use to anybody, it will be to people who are growing slowly into animal consciousness, maybe even those who are starting from a place at or near ground zero. Beginning in this chapter, I share some of the noteworthy features of my journey, not because it is so exceptional but because it is, well—because it is so ordinary.

A MUDDLER'S LIFE

For almost half my life, I had only the faintest glimmer of animal consciousness. We had cats and dogs at home while I was growing up, and Nancy and I had a dog (we called him Gleco) early in our marriage, before our children were born. So, yes, I had a fondness for companion animals, but nothing more.

Like many boys of my generation, I loved to go fishing, and though I never hunted, I envied the older boys in my neighborhood who did. I remember pleading with my parents to buy me a rifle and to let me join my friends on the first day of deer season, but they would have none of it. In high school and college, I willingly dissected animals in biology labs. And not only did I enthusiastically eat meat of every type and cut, I worked as a butcher during my college years. On a daily basis, I entered the dead bodies of cows, calves, and pigs, up to my elbows. I sliced. I diced. I cubed. I ground. I trimmed. I hacked. I sawed. Their cold flesh conformed to my cold will. Back then, I did not find butchering bloody, only bloody hard. So successfully did I internalize the cultural paradigm that I bought Nancy a stylish mink hat for her birthday. My only regret was that I couldn't afford to buy her a full-length fur coat.

Although I wrote a great deal during my high school and college years, and even more after I went on to study philosophy in graduate school, I cannot recall ever writing a paper about animals. There was a letter I sent to Nancy, however, two years before we were married, in which I included my views about animals, using elephants as an example. Ever the steamy romantic (I was twenty at the time), I wrote the following:

> I think we must be careful to distinguish between our love for elephants and our love for persons. Martin Buber discusses the radical distinction between the I–elephant and the I–person relationships. My relationship to an elephant is an I–It relationship, an I–Thing. It does not demand of me personal kindness or affection . . . nor does it demand any claim to equality, freedom, and etc. An elephant is a thing, an it, and my relationship to it will always be tempered by this. . . . The relationship between one person and another, however, is an I–Thou relationship; it is an I, Tom Regan, facing a Thou, you, Nancy Tirk [Nancy's maiden name]. The relationship *is* tempered by equality, freedom, and etc. . . . To treat people as "things" is to treat them as elephants, cucumbers or sack dresses. To love them as 'things' is, in fact, not to love *them* at all.

Elephants are things, like cucumbers and sack dresses. Our relationship to other animals does not require "personal kindness or affection . . . nor . . . any claim to equality, freedom, and etc." Talk about successful acculturation! I had internalized the cultural paradigm so completely, so blindly, that I thought I was being an original thinker because I thought this way. If we picture lack of concern for animals as a large, unilluminated cave, you could say that, at this point in my life, my back was up against the rear wall. I was living on the same planet as DaVincians, but we certainly inhabited two totally different moral universes.

After our children were born, Nancy and I were your typical American parents. We put meat on the table, day in and day out (otherwise, how could our children get their protein?). I grilled hot dogs and hamburgers on the Fourth of July. Nancy roasted a big-breasted turkey every Thanksgiving. And the whole family went to McDonalds and Burger King, to zoos and circuses, where a good time was had by all.

In large measure, then, my beliefs about and attitudes toward animals were quite unremarkable throughout my youth and into young adulthood. In fact, I might never have grown any further in animal consciousness if America had not gone to war.

FIRST STEPS

When I began teaching philosophy, America was fighting in Vietnam. The government's rationale for the war appealed to the domino theory: if we did not defeat the communists in Vietnam today, they would be sleeping in our bedrooms tomorrow.

Many people of my generation, not to mention many more of college age, actively opposed America's role in the war. Nancy and I were no exceptions. We thought the war was wrong, that the violence could not be justified. Tens of thousands of innocent civilians, many of them children, were being killed or maimed, their homes destroyed. Young men, the age of students in my classes, were being drafted, trained, and shipped overseas, often to return wrapped in black body bags. These young men, we believed, had every right to refuse to serve in *this* war without having to believe, like Quaker pacifists, that *all* wars are wrong. People needed to speak out. The tragic loss of human life had to stop.

To that end, Nancy and I, along with a handful of others, organized North Carolinians against the War, a statewide grassroots group that sought to end American involvement. Nancy baked a ham and served a large bowl of potato salad, brimming with eggs and mayo, at NCAW's first meeting, which we hosted in our home. When hundreds of thousands marched on Washington to voice their opposition to the war, the Regan family was represented.

It occurred to me at the time that I might be able to contribute something to the antiwar movement as a philosopher, not just as an organizer and protester. After all, philosophers are trained to think critically and to argue rigorously. This is how we find important truths. If the war was wrong, as I believed it was, and if young men of draft age had a right to refuse to serve, as I believed they did, this should be something I could prove.

Armed with my faith in reason, I plunged into the voluminous philosophical literature on war and human rights. One day found me in the stacks of the university library. I took a book off a shelf entitled *An Autobiography: The Story of My Experiments with Truth*. The author was someone whose name I recognized and whose views I knew something about, but only indirectly; I had never actually read anything he had written. His name was Mahatma Gandhi.

What a fateful choice! The book helped change the future direction of my life. I did not agree with Gandhi's pacifism. *Sometimes*, I believed (and still do), the use of violence is not wrong. *Some* wars, I believed (and still do), can be morally justified. But not when a war involves unnecessary violence, which is what I believed was true of the Vietnam War. Not when the conduct of the war violated human rights, including the rights of young men of draft age.

Beyond his pacifism, Gandhi had a novel challenge for me that went directly to the habits of my life. Though written for any and every reader, he seemed to be addressing me personally. It was as if he wanted to know how I, Tom Regan, could oppose unnecessary violence, such as the war in Vietnam, when *humans* are the victims, and support this same kind of violence (unnecessary violence) when the victims are *animals*. "Please do explain to me, Professor Regan," Gandhi's voice asked from the page, "what those dead body parts (AKA 'pieces of meat') are doing in your freezer? Please do explain, Professor, how you can bring antiwar activists together in your home and serve them a victim of another kind of war, the undeclared war humans are waging against animals?" I'm not sure, but I thought I detected a sly, sarcastic smile on the Mahatma's face.

Gandhi clearly was right about some things. Eating animals, eating their flesh, as I did, certainly supported their slaughter, a truly horrible, violent way to die, something I would later come to know first-hand when, despite having a strong aversion to doing so, I watched hogs, chickens, and cows meet their bloody end.

Moreover, from what I had begun to learn about nutrition, I knew my good health did not require animal flesh in my diet. So the logic was fairly obvious: the violent slaughter of animals for food was unnecessary. Was my fork, like napalm, a weapon of violence? Should I become a vegetarian, for ethical reasons?

This was not an idea I wanted to embrace. Change, especially when it means altering the habits of a lifetime, is never a welcome prospect. So I did what any red-blooded, rational human being would do: I tried to avoid coming to terms with the question that was really troubling me. Instead, I threw myself into asking bigger, impersonal questions—about the justice of capitalism, the future of civilization, the threat of nuclear annihilation. But even as I tried to find a comfortable place for my gnawing sense of moral inconsistency, bedded down in the dark recesses of my unconscious, Gandhi's ghost would not go away. We never resolve conflicts of conscience by pretending they do not exist.

As it happened, it was during this same time that Nancy and I had to deal with Gleco's sudden death. For thirteen years he had been our all but constant companion. Then, one day, he was dead. Such grief Nancy and I shared! So many tears! Emotionally, we were a mess, our sense of loss so great.

From my reading of Gandhi I had learned how some people in India regard *eating cow* as unspeakably repulsive. I realized I felt the same way about cats and dogs: I could never *eat them*. Were cows so different from cats and dogs that there were two moral standards, one that applies to cows, another that applies to cats and dogs? Were pigs so different? Were any of the animals I ate so different? These were the questions that would not go away. Before I was ready to accept them, I already knew my answers.

The more I thought about it, the more convinced I became that something had to give: *either* I had to change my beliefs and feelings about how companion animals should be treated, *or* I had to change my beliefs and feelings about the treatment of farmed animals. In time, unable to find an honest way around the dilemma—and, given the power of old habits and the gustatory temptations associated with lamb chops, fried chicken, and hamburgers grilled on the barbie, I have to confess that I fairly desperately wanted to find one—I chose the latter alternative.

In my case, then, it was a combination of the life and thought of Gandhi, on the one hand, and the life and death of a four-legged canine friend, on the other—a classic combination of the head and the heart—that motivated me to begin my journey toward an expanded animal consciousness. My first steps (and Nancy was alongside or ahead of me, every step of the way) involved asking ethical questions about the food I ate. The answers I reached in the early 1970s resulted in my decision to become an ovo-lacto vegetarian. Somehow, back then, I was able to convince myself that while it was wrong to eat animals, it was all right to eat eggs and dairy products as part of my everyday diet.

"THERE'S A MOVEMENT OUT THERE . . . SORT OF."

The decision to become a vegetarian was something done in private, so to speak. At the time, I had no idea that vegetarianism had a long history populated with famous people (Ovid, Plutarch, Charlotte Bronte, Susan B. Anthony, Weird Al Yankovic, to name a few). Moreover, I was largely unaware that there were organizations and publications that promoted a vegetarian lifestyle, some for reasons of health (a vegetarian diet is good for you), others for ethical reasons (a vegetarian diet shows respect for animals). Much to my surprise, I discovered that there were national and international conferences organized around vegetarianism in particular, animal protection issues in general. There was something that looked like a "movement" out there, or at least something that was trying to become one. It was an exciting time to be alive. The first international animal protection conference Nancy and I attended will be forever etched in the aging folds of our graying memory.

The conference took place at Cambridge University in the summer of 1978. Hosted by one of England's venerable animal societies, it focused on the ethical ties that bind humans to other animals and featured leading thinkers from throughout the world. It was an honor just to be in their presence.

You can imagine our surprise, therefore, when Nancy and I went to the first evening's dinner and found that beef Wellington was the main course. Things went steadily down hill from there. Breakfasts included ham, bacon, kippers, and sausage. Lunches were redolent with all manner of cuts of meat, some of which (various sweetbreads and slabs of bloody tongue, for example) no American had seen before or has seen since. Venison was served the second evening. Roast leg of lamb the third. And for the gala final evening's banquet? Veal cordon bleu.

Among those in attendance were a handful of like-minded vegetarians. Banding together, we asked, in the most polite manner, for some accommodation. If we were going to spend the day talking about our duties to animals, we said, we preferred not to spend our meals eating them.

The request was received as heretical. How dare we ask for special treatment! If the organizers had had a branding iron at their disposal, I do not doubt for a moment that some of them would have burned the letter *V* into our foreheads, the better to shame us for our vegetarian insolence. Consigned to a table in a far dark corner of the dining hall, away from the other diners (lest they be contaminated by our presence), the rebellious vegetarians were treated as moral untouchables. And this by people who said they cared about animals. It was the first (but not the last) time Nancy and I learned that different people sometimes understand animal protection differently.

It was an important lesson. When we returned home from Cambridge, we were emboldened. We had a clearer understanding of who we were and what we believed. We were not about to change. The people operating the venerable English animal society would have to change. And (over time) they did. Eight years later, when they hosted another international conference on animal protection, no meat was served. Only by then the vegetarians had evolved into vegans and again wanted a different accommodation. But that's another story.

AN EXPANDING ANIMAL CONSCIOUSNESS

Our first step toward a more expansive animal consciousness was soon followed by others. Nancy and I learned about cruelty-free products, including cosmetics, toiletries, and household cleaners that are not tested on animals. We stopped going to zoos and circuses, and all my fishing equipment was relegated to the attic. Fur became a thing of the past even as we continued to find no inconsistency in wearing leather belts, gloves, and shoes, or in buying wool pants, sweaters, and jackets.

As for the use of animals in science, I approached this topic cautiously, and my first thoughts stopped well short of the abolitionist ones I hold today. Even while I called for "a vast reduction in research involving animals," I left open the possibility that some of this research could be justified. What sort of research would this be? Where did I draw the line? Suffice it to say that, during this period of my life, hard as it is to understand today, I defended major auto manufacturers, like General Motors, when they killed baboons in crash tests designed to make seat belts safer. Unlike DaVincians and Damascans, there were limits to the protection I was willing to give.

Terminology

One thing I began to understand is how hard it is to talk about everything I wanted to talk about, without coming up for air, so to speak. It took awhile, but eventually I understood that you don't have to believe in animal rights, as a philosophical concept, to believe that animals should not be turned into food or made into clothes. DaVincians believe the same things. So do those Damascans who have achieved full animal consciousness because of a transforming experience. When it comes to what is really important, *how* different people form their convictions is less important than *what* convictions they form. In the present case, the unifying convictions can be summarized using this simple image: Animals are in cages, and they should not be there. Or (alternatively): Not larger cages, empty cages. DaVincians, Damascans, and (if they complete the journey) Muddlers all arrive at the same place using different routes.

These differences are both real and important. For reasons of linguistic economy, however, it is helpful to use a single expression to refer to the beliefs that unite DaVincians, Damascans, and Muddlers. Given where our culture is in its evolution, and in view of the terminology framing the current debate, I will continue to use (as I have been using) "Animal Rights Advocates" (ARAs) to denote the abolitionist convictions shared by anyone with full animal consciousness, whatever path they took to get there.

GOING BACKWARD BEFORE MOVING FORWARD

So here, roughly, is where I had arrived: Being both male and a Muddler, there was *so* much I thought I needed to "figure out." Because of my evolving animal consciousness, I began to wonder about an idea that would have seemed impossible just a few years before: the idea of animal rights. Is such an idea even intelligible? What does it mean? Why would anyone think in these terms? What would be the implications? I realized I did not know how to answer these questions. Worse, I realized I did not know how to answer the most basic questions about *human* rights. How, then, could I possibly answer my questions about animal rights? It did not take great philosophical wisdom on my part to know the answer to that question.

Having come this far in my life, to the point where the possibility of animal rights was an idea I wanted to explore, I reluctantly decided I would have to go backward before I could move forward. I would have to return to my questions about human rights. In the next chapter I describe the most important things I learned when I did so.

MORAL RIGHTS:
WHAT THEY ARE AND
WHY THEY MATTER

HUMAN RIGHTS

Human rights have shaped our history. Legions of ordinary people have died and royal heads have rolled in their defense. The framers of America's Declaration of Independence certainly believed in them. They maintained that the sole reason for having a government in the first place is to protect citizens in the possession of rights no government can give to them, what today we call our human, our moral rights.

What has been true in the past remains true today. Belief in human rights is pervasive throughout representative democracies. As an advocate of human rights, I take my stand with America's founders. The young men who were sent to fight in Vietnam had moral rights, including the rights to life, liberty, and bodily integrity. So did the Vietnamese children who were killed and maimed in the conflict. And each had these rights whether the U.S. government, or any other government for that matter, recognized them.

Clearly, when people are willing to give their own lives or take someone else's, something of great value must be at stake. What precisely (or even vaguely) is it? The more I learned about what other philosophers thought, the more confused I became. I decided to back into an answer. Instead of asking, "What are human rights and why do they matter?" I went to the haystack of worst-case scenarios to find what I was looking for. Let me explain.

America's cup runneth over with periods during which some of us have done horrible things to others of us. These worst case scenarios include the genocidal programs carried out against Native Americans, the enslavement of African Americans, and the forced internment of Japanese Americans. These are the places to look to find violations of human rights on a large scale. However, American history teaches that the same evil sometimes occurs in a smaller theater, so to speak. The infamous Tuskegee syphilis study is a case in point.

THE TUSKEGEE SYPHILIS STUDY

The time: 1932. The place: Tuskegee Institute (now Tuskegee University), in Tuskegee, Alabama, among the nation's oldest, most respected African American institutions of higher learning. The study's sponsor: the U. S. Public Health Service. The participants: 399 impoverished African American men who volunteered to receive, without charge, what they were told was "special treatment" for their "bad blood," not knowing that in fact they suffered from syphilis and that the "medicine" they were given was not medicine at all and would have no therapeutic effect.

Also unknown to the participants was the reason for the study. It was not to help them recover from their illness; it was not even to find a cure for syphilis; instead, the study was conducted to determine what would happen to the men if their condition went untreated. To learn this, the researchers thought, would help physicians understand the long-term effects of syphilis. Armed with this knowledge, syphilis sufferers in the future could receive better treatment.

Remarkably, in a country founded on "the rights of man," the study was carried out on these uninformed, trusting men, from 1932 to 1972—for *forty* years—with funds from, and with the knowing support of, the United States government.

All this is bad enough. What makes matters worse is that even after it became known, in 1957, that syphilis can be treated successfully using penicillin, the researchers withheld the cure. The results? By the time the true purpose of the study was exposed, twenty-eight men had died from the disease, another one hundred had died from related complications, forty wives had been infected, and nineteen children had been born with syphilis. This is the tragic legacy of the Tuskegee study.

Advocates of human rights universally condemn what happened at Tuskegee. If I could understand why the rights of the human "guinea pigs" were violated in this particular case, I could understand human rights in general. That was my strategy. I think it worked. Here's what I learned.

MORAL PROTECTION: NO TRESPASSING

To possess moral rights is to have a kind of protection we might picture as an invisible No Trespassing sign. What does this sign prohibit? Two things. First, others are not morally free to harm us; to say this is to say that others are not free to take our lives or injure our bodies as they please. Second, others are not morally free to interfere with our free choice; to say this is to say that others are not free to limit our free choice as they please. In both cases, the No Trespassing sign is meant to protect our most important goods (our lives, our bodies, our liberty) by morally limiting the freedom of others.

Things are different when people exceed their rights by violating ours. When this happens, we act within our rights if we fight back, even if this does some serious harm to the aggressor. However, what we may do in self-defense does not translate into a general permission to hurt those who have not done anything wrong. The men used in the Tuskegee study, for example. All were innocent of any wrongdoing. None was threatening anyone. In their case, any injury suffered, any death caused, and any freedom lost was both unprovoked and unjustified. The researchers who conducted the study trespassed on the most important goods of their victims.

MORAL STATUS: EQUALITY

Moral rights breathe equality. They are the same for all who have them, differ though we do in many ways. This explains why no human being can justifiably be denied rights for arbitrary, prejudicial, or morally irrelevant reasons. Race is such a reason. To attempt to determine which humans have rights on the basis of race is like trying to sweeten tea by adding salt. What race we are tells us nothing about what rights we have.

The same is no less true of other differences between us. Nancy and I trace our family lineage to different countries—she to Lithuania, I to Ireland. Some of our friends are Christians, some Jews, some Moslems. Others are agnostics or atheists. In the world at large, a few people are very wealthy, many more, very poor. And so it goes. Humans differ in many ways. There is no denying that.

Still, no one who believes in human rights thinks these differences mark fundamental moral divisions. If we mean anything by the idea of human rights, we mean that we *have them equally*. And we have them equally regardless of our race, gender, religious belief, comparative wealth, intelligence, or date or place of birth, for example. The researchers who conducted the Tuskegee study had moral rights. So did the men in their care. And all had them equally. That some researchers thought otherwise only shows how mistaken they were.

MORAL WEIGHT: TRUMP

Every serious advocate of human rights believes that our rights have greater moral weight than other important human values. To use an analogy from the card game bridge, our moral rights are trump. Here is what this analogy means.

A hand is dealt. Hearts are trump. The first three cards played are the queen of spades, the king of spades, and the ace of spades. You (the last player) have no spades. However, you do have the two of hearts. Because hearts are trump, your lowly two of hearts beats the queen of spades, beats the king of spades, even beats the ace of spades. This is how powerful the trump suit is in the game of bridge.

The analogy between trump in bridge and individual rights in morality should be reasonably clear. There are many important values to consider when we make a moral decision. For example: How will we be affected personally as a result of deciding one way or another? What about our family, friends, neighbors, fellow Americans? It is not hard to write a long list. When we say, "rights are trump," we mean that respect for the rights of individuals is the most important consideration in "the game of morality," so to speak. In particular, we mean that the benefits others derive from violating someone's rights never justifies violating them.

The researchers who conducted the Tuskegee study thought they were doing something good for humanity. Future syphilis sufferers, they believed, would benefit from what the study revealed. There is no reason to doubt or deny their good intentions. Nevertheless, respect for the rights of the individual trumps such considerations. The Tuskegee study illustrates why good ends do not justify evil means. What the researchers did was wrong, and it was wrong because they placed the good of the many above respect for the rights of the few.

MORAL CLAIMS: JUSTICE

For forty years the participants in the Tuskegee study trusted their caregivers. Once the truth was revealed, they invoked their rights. What does this mean? The contrast between claims of rights and requests for generosity highlights the answer.

I happen to want a fancy sports car. Said sports car also happens to cost more than Nancy and I paid for our house. Bill Gates (as everyone knows) has more money than he knows what to do with. I write to him:

Dear Bill:

I want an Audi TT 3.2-litre six-cylinder sports coupe with a direct shift gearbox. I can't afford the asking price. I know you can. So I would appreciate it if you would send me a money order (by Express Mail, if you don't mind) to cover the cost.

Your friend,

Tom

One thing is abundantly clear. I am not in a position to demand that Bill Gates buy me an Audi TT. Receiving a car from him—any car—is not something to which I am entitled, not something I am owed or due. If my good friend Bill bought me the car of my dreams, his gift would distinguish him as uncommonly generous (or uncommonly foolish), not uncommonly fair.

When we invoke our rights, by contrast, we are not asking for anyone's generosity. We are not saying, "Please, will you kindly give me something I do not deserve?" On the contrary, when we invoke our rights, we are demanding fair treatment, demanding that we receive what is our due.

Part of the special tragedy of the Tuskegee study arises because of the trust the impoverished men placed in the researchers. In their time, in that place, and in those circumstances, it never occurred to the men with the "bad blood" to invoke their rights. Why would they? They thought they were receiving state of the art medical treatment, treatment they could no more afford than I can afford an Audi TT. How we wish they had known the truth earlier! How we wish they had understood the injustice being done to them from the start! In time, after scores of deaths and generations of suffering, the day came when the survivors finally understood. When they invoked their rights, they were not asking for any favors.

MORAL WRONGS: ASSISTANCE

The Tuskegee study illustrates how the victims of injustice sometimes do not understand when or why their rights are being violated. Members of vulnerable populations (children and the poor, for example) are frequent victims. Because of their vulnerability, children and those living in poverty are easy prey to those seeking some benefit, whether personal or public. When the vulnerable are used as means to such ends, people who understand the wrong done have a duty to intervene, to stand up and speak out in defense of the victim. Moreover, the duty here is itself a demand for justice, not a plea for generosity. These victims are owed assistance from us; help is something they are due, not something it would be "awfully nice" of us to render. The less able humans are to defend their rights, the greater is our duty to do this for them.

Limited in our power and influence, we cannot do everything to defend every victim of injustice. For all of us, however, what we can do is more than nothing. That we cannot do everything for all the victims of injustice does not mean that we should content ourselves with doing nothing for any of them. Without a doubt, everyone who knew what was being done to the men in the Tuskegee study had a duty to try to stop it.

MORAL UNITY: RESPECT

Trespass. Equality. Trump. These and the other ideas that come to the surface when we review the Tuskegee study help explain human rights. Still, I could not help thinking that something was missing. There had to be a way to unify these ideas, to simplify them. That's where the idea of respect comes in.

In a general sense, the rights discussed in this chapter (life, liberty, and bodily integrity) are variations on a main theme, that theme being respect. I show my respect for you by respecting these rights in your life. You show your respect for me by doing the same thing. Respect is the main theme because treating one another with respect *just is* treating one another in ways that respect our other rights. Our most fundamental right, then, the right that unifies all our other rights, is our right to be treated with respect.

When we apply this way of thinking to the Tuskegee study, all our questions have the same answer. Did those who conducted this study show respect for the bodily integrity of the men whose health deteriorated over time? No. Did they show respect for the lives of the victims who died? No. More generally, were the participants treated with the respect to which they were entitled, as a matter of moral right? No. When, in 1997, former President Clinton, speaking for the nation, apologized to the few surviving human "guinea pigs" used in the Tuskegee study, and to the descendants of those who had died, the apology came more than sixty years too late.

LOOKING BACK, LOOKING AHEAD

What are human rights? Why do they matter? This was part of what I thought I had to "figure out" before I broached the question of animal rights. By way of summary, here is what I learned.

Our moral rights are the same regardless of our many differences. They serve to protect our most important goods: our lives, our bodies, and our liberty. Moreover, the protection they offer is not a little; it is a lot. Our rights—yours and mine, as well as those of the men abused in the Tuskegee study—should be respected even if others would reap great benefits by violating them.

To invoke our rights is different from asking for a favor. Respectful treatment is something we are owed, something we are due. When we speak the language of rights, we are demanding something, and what we demand is justice, not generosity; respect, not a favor. We make these demands not only for ourselves; we make them as well for those who lack the power or knowledge to make them for themselves. In the moral universe, nothing is more important than our right to be treated with respect—which explains why people have been willing to give their own lives or take someone else's, in defense of their rights. Without respect for someone's rights, there is no respect for the someone whose rights they are.

I was making progress. Before, "moral rights" had been an idea I appealed to, more than an idea I understood. Now I was beginning to understand it. In fact, I understood it enough to know what I did not know. There was a big gap that needed filling. To say what moral rights are and why they matter does not explain why we have the rights we do. As I muddled along this was the next question I turned to.

EXPLAINING HUMAN RIGHTS

Why do we have the rights we do? Once again, philosophers have been trying to answer this question for hundreds of years. And once again (again), I looked for ways to simplify the question, this time after the model of a proof in geometry:

Given: Human beings have moral rights.

Given: Sticks and stones lack moral rights.

Question: Why? What is there that is true of human beings, but not true of sticks and stones, that explains why we do, but they do not, have moral rights?

Whatever this "something" is, this much was clear: it would have to illuminate what makes us the same, what makes us equal, in ways that are relevant to the rights we have. So the question was (and remains), "What is this 'something'?" I set about trying to identify the most influential possibilities. Some depend on religious convictions; others do not. To be fair, I had to consider both. Historically, here are the answers that have attracted the most adherents.

Humans have rights because

1. Humans are human.
2. Humans are persons.
3. Humans are self-aware.
4. Humans use language.
5. Humans live in a moral community.
6. Humans have souls.
7. God gave them to us.

For a variety of reasons, I do not think any of these answers is satisfactory, and I want to explain why. But I also want to explain another possibility that overcomes their deficiencies.

UNSATISFACTORY ANSWERS

1. Humans Have Rights Because Humans Are Human.

Here we have an idea that is partly true but wholly irrelevant. For it is true that humans are humans, just as it is true that stones are stones. The problem is, truths like these have no moral import. All they tell us is that a given idea (human or stone) is identical with itself, and self-identity is not relevant to understanding why we have rights and stones do not.

To make this clearer, suppose I declare, "Stones have rights!" You (of course) look puzzled. "Why on earth do you believe such a thing?" you ask. I reply, "Because stones are stones." Now you look even more puzzled. "No," you say, "I mean what is there about stones that explains their rights?" "Stones are stones," I say again. "Well," you say, "believe what you will, but you haven't given me any reason for believing that stones have rights." Exactly. Just as we are not given any reason for believing that humans have rights if someone says, "Humans are humans."

Perhaps what is meant is something different. Perhaps the idea is that humans have rights because we belong to a particular species—the human species, the species *Homo sapiens*. Interpreted in this way, as a scientific (biological) assertion, answer 1 is no less partly true but also no less wholly irrelevant. Yes, human beings belong to the species *Homo sapiens*. No, we do not belong to the species *Canus lupus*. The problem again, however, is that truths like these do not help us understand why we have rights and why wolves lack them, if they do. All they tell us is that some beings (human beings) belong to one biological species while other beings (wolf beings) belong to another biological species. But who belongs to what species is not relevant to our question. If we think that wolves lack rights, this is not because they belong to the species *Canus lupus*.

2. Humans Have Rights Because Humans Are Persons.

Whether answer 2 is true obviously depends on what is meant by "persons." Among philosophers, there is universal agreement. In the relevant sense, persons are individuals who are morally responsible for their behavior, individuals concerning whom it makes sense to say, "What they did was right and praiseworthy" or "What they did was wrong and blameworthy." You and I are persons, as were all those who participated in the Tuskegee study. What answer 2 means, then, is that the people I have mentioned have rights because they are morally responsible for their behavior.

Unlike answer 1, what answer 2 says certainly seems relevant. If any humans have rights, it only makes sense to think that humans who are morally responsible for their behavior have them. Expressed another way, if *these* human beings lack rights, it would be awfully hard to understand why *any* human beings possess them.

There is a problem, though. While we may be able to understand why humans who are persons have rights, answer 2 does not say anything about the rights of humans who are not persons. And that leaves out hundreds of millions, possibly billions, of human beings. For example, humans who are soon-to-be-born, infants, and children for their first years of life are not persons in this sense. None are morally responsible for their behavior. Thus, while being a person may be relevant to understanding why some humans have the rights they do, it provides no help in understanding the rights possessed by a large segment of the human population.

3. Humans Have Rights Because Humans Are Self-Aware.

Self-awareness is a capacity we can illustrate with the following example. We look at what is in front of us. One thing we see is a book. So we are aware of a book. However, we are also capable of being aware that we are aware of a book. We can take an "outside" view of ourselves, so to speak. This higher level of awareness (being aware that we are aware of something) is at the heart of the capacity for self-awareness. I think of it this way. Not only are we aware *of* the world, we are aware of being *in* it.

Self-awareness arguably is necessary to fear death. If we are not aware of being in the world, it is difficult to understand how we could fear leaving it (that is, fear ceasing to be alive, fear dying). Because this is true, we can perhaps anticipate the next move some philosophers make. They argue that beings cannot have a right to life if they do not understand their own mortality; and since beings cannot understand their own mortality if they are not self-aware, these philosophers conclude that only self-aware beings have a right to life.

This way of thinking about human rights, even if it was satisfactory in other respects, would not take us very far. For example, it is difficult to understand how being self-aware is relevant to understanding our right to bodily integrity. As it is, however, answer 3 is not satisfactory in other respects. Psychologists tell us that children do not grasp their own mortality until they are nine or ten years old. This means that hundreds of millions, possibly even billions, of children fail to satisfy answer 3. If satisfying answer 3 is necessary for having a right to life, all these children lack this right, which is preposterous. Even if self-awareness was relevant to understanding why some humans have a right to life, it would provide no help in understanding the rights possessed by all those human beings who lack this capacity.

4. Humans Have Rights Because Humans Use Language.

As may be immediately apparent, answer 4 suffers from some of the same deficiencies as answers 2 and 3. Many human beings who fail to satisfy answers 2 and 3—human infants, for example—fail to satisfy answer 4. Accordingly, even if being able to use language was relevant to understanding why some humans have some rights, it would provide no help in understanding why those humans who lack this ability have the rights they do. But things are not this good. Unlike answers 2 and 3, answer 4 proposes a consideration (the ability to use language) that has no obvious relevance to any of the rights we have been exploring (our rights to life, to bodily integrity, and to liberty). There has to be a better answer than this one.

5. Humans Have Rights Because Humans Live in a Moral Community.

Philosophers who favor answer 5 understand "moral community" in the following way. A "moral community" is one in which the idea of moral rights is invoked and understood. Thus, all human beings are members of a moral community because all human beings are members of a community in which the idea of moral rights is invoked and understood.

The motivation that leads philosophers to favor answer 5 is not hard to find. As we have seen, several of the proposed answers are deficient because they fail to help us understand the rights of infants or young children. Answer 5 seeks to remedy this deficiency by making possession of rights independent of each individual human being's capacities (for self-awareness, say). Instead, answer 5 implies that *all* human beings have rights, whatever their individual capacities, because *all* human beings are members of a moral community.

Although the motivation behind this way of thinking may be laudatory, the thinking itself is not. The fact that an idea is invoked and understood in a community provides absolutely no explanation of the idea's veracity. Consider the idea of witches. As far as we know, this is an idea that arises among humans and humans only. Suppose this is true. And suppose we are asked whether there are any witches. No even modestly careful thinker will say, "The explanation of why there are witches is that the idea of witches is invoked and understood in our (human) community." That we have the *idea* of witches is not remotely relevant to explaining the existence (or the nonexistence) of witches. There is no reason to think of rights any differently. To say "We can understand why all humans have rights because the idea of rights is invoked and understood in our (human) community" offers no help in understanding why we have the rights we do.

6. Humans Have Rights Because Humans Have Souls.

Here we encounter the first of the two most commonly proposed religious bases of human rights. (Religious ideas are discussed at greater length in the next chapter). Many of the world's religions, both ancient and modern, teach that human beings have immortal souls. Often, it is true, the teachings differ. For example, Hindus believe in reincarnation; after our body dies, chances are our soul will be reborn in the form of some other animal. Christians, by contrast, do not believe in reincarnation; after our body dies, we are not reborn in this world ever again. Despite these differences, the root idea is the same. To say we have an immortal soul is to say we do not perish when our body dies; instead, we go on living, in one way or another.

Belief in the soul can be a comforting idea. When we face the death of a family member or close friend, our sadness can be mitigated if we believe in a life beyond the grave. It is hard to be against what helps lessen sadness in hard times, which is why, for as long as I can remember, I have always been well disposed to the idea of the soul and profoundly hope humans have one. At the same time, it has for many years been clear to me that having a soul has no relevance to understanding why we have the rights we do. Here's why I think this way.

We explain the importance of having the rights we have by noting that they serve to protect our most important goods: our lives, our bodies, and our liberty. Moreover, the protection they offer is not a little; it is a lot. Our rights should be respected even if others would reap great benefits by violating them. In the moral universe, as we have seen, our rights are trump: nothing is more important than our right to be treated with respect.

We now ask for help in understanding why we have the rights we do. Someone replies, "We have the rights we do because we have immortal souls." Clearly, that we have immortal souls, assuming that we do, is relevant to the question, "Will we go on living after our bodies die?" But no less clearly, that we have immortal souls is not the least bit relevant to the question, "Is it wrong to murder people, injure their bodies, or rob them of their freedom while they are alive in *this* world?" Expressed another way, what happens to us after we die does not help us understand why we have the rights we do while we are alive.

7. Humans Have Rights Because God Gave Them to Us.

This is the most common religious basis of human rights. The idea seems simple enough. Limited in power as we are, we cannot create moral rights. Unlimited in power as God is, God can. Indeed, not only can God do this, God actually saw fit to do it, which is why we have the rights we do.

This way of thinking will not find favor among agnostics and atheists. Given answer 7, human beings would not have rights if God did not exist to give them to us. Yet people who do not believe in God (atheists), as well as others who do not know what to believe (agnostics), believe very strongly in human rights. Are we to say that they must be mistaken, that it is impossible for us to have rights without God giving them to us? This is not something atheists and agnostics are likely to take lying down.

Dissatisfaction with this way of thinking about rights is not limited to nonbelievers by any means. Even the most devout believers have well-considered reasons for questioning answer 7. This can be explained by using Christianity as our working example.

Some Christians no doubt believe that God is the source of our rights. After all, didn't America's founding fathers (some of whom were not Christians, by the way) say we were "endowed by our Creator with certain unalienable rights"? If we can't trust the founding fathers, whom can we trust?

Whatever might be true in other regards, the founding fathers are not reliable guides in this one. Remember: these are the people whose God distributed rights with startling prejudice. Their God did not give rights to women, or to children, or to the mentally disadvantaged, or to slaves, or to Native Americans, or to citizens lacking property. Their God saw fit to distribute rights in ways that advantaged men like the founding fathers and that disadvantaged everyone else. How very convenient for the founding fathers to have God on their side! If we were asked to illustrate how prejudice operates, it would be difficult to find a better and, at the same time, a worse example. Great people are not above making great mistakes.

Simple prudence counsels that we look for wise guidance elsewhere. What better place to look (in the present context) than the Bible? When we do, here is what we find—or, rather, here is what we don't find. We don't find any place in the Bible where God gives rights to humans. In no chapter, in no verse, do we read that God said (for example): "Humans! Listen up! I am giving you rights, including the rights to life, liberty, and the pursuit of happiness!" The simple fact is, we simply do not find anything remotely like this in the Bible.

What we do find is something semantically and morally different. The Biblical ethic, especially the one we find in the New Testament, is an ethic of love (*agapē*), not an ethic of rights. Our existence is a gift of God's abundant love, and the love we are commanded to have for our neighbors is something we freely give, after the model of God's love for us, not something our neighbor is entitled to demand from us, as a matter of justice. Our obligation to love our neighbor is not based on our neighbor's right to be loved. Within the Biblical framework, my saying, "I have a right to your *agapē*!" reflects as much confusion as my telling Bill Gates, "I have a right to your money!" In Gandhi's words, "Love never claims, it ever gives." People who credit the God of the Bible with being the source of our rights are guilty of reading into the Bible what they want to be there rather than accepting what actually is said.

But suppose we assume, for the sake of argument, not only that God exists but that God in fact is the source of rights. In other words, whosoever has rights has them because God saw fit to give rights to them. Even if we make these large assumptions, we still do not know who has rights or why they have them (that is, what there is about those who have rights that led God to bestow rights on them). Moreover, as the example of the founding fathers illustrates, humans not only can be in error, we have been profoundly mistaken in the answers we have given to the question "To whom did God give rights?" The upshot is, introducing God into the equation, even making the assumptions we have, leaves many of the most important questions unanswered. (For more on God and rights, see the next chapter's discussion of objections 9–10).

AND THE ANSWER IS?

What, then, if not human biology, not our moral responsibility, not our soul, not God, not any of the possibilities we have discussed—what helps us understand why we have the rights we do? There had to be an answer out there somewhere. I resolved to keep looking. When I found what I was looking for, it felt like a discovery, it was so new to me.

Our earlier discussion in this chapter noted some of the many ways humans differ from one another—in terms of gender, race, and ethnicity, for example. Despite our many differences, there are some ways in which all humans who have rights are the same. I do not mean because we all belong to the same species (which is true but not relevant). And I do not mean because we all are persons (which may be relevant but is not true). What I mean is that we are like one another in relevant ways, ways that relate to the rights we have: our rights to life, to bodily integrity, and to liberty.

Think about it. Not only are we all in the world, we all are aware of the world and aware as well of what happens to us. Moreover, what happens to us—whether to our bodies, or our freedom, or our lives themselves—matters to us because it makes a difference to the quality and duration of our lives, as experienced by us, whether anybody else cares about this or not. Whatever our differences, these are our fundamental similarities.

We have no commonly used word that names this family of similarities. "Human being" does not do the job (a deceased human being is a human being but is not aware of the world, for example). Neither does "person" (human infants are aware of what happens to them but are not persons). Still, these similarities are important enough to warrant a verbal marker of their own. I use the expression "subject-of-a-life" to refer to them. Given this usage, the author of these words, Tom Regan, is a subject-of-a-life, and so are the people who read them.

Which humans are subjects-of-a-life? All those humans who have the family of similarities mentioned above. And who might these be? Well, somewhere in the neighborhood of *six billion* of us, regardless of where we live, how old we are, our race or gender or class, our religious or political beliefs, our level of intelligence, and so on through a very long inventory of our differences.

Why is being the subject-of-a-life an important idea? Because it succeeds where the other possibilities we have considered fail. The family of characteristics that define this idea *makes us all equal* in a way that makes sense of our moral equality. Here is what I mean.

As implied in the preceding discussion, human subjects-of-a-life differ in many ways. For example, some are geniuses and others are severely mentally disadvantaged; some are gifted in music while others cannot carry a tune; some can jump high, run fast, and throw a baseball over ninety-five miles an hour whereas the rest of us are (shall we say?) deficient when it comes to these talents. These differences are real, and they matter. If the Pittsburgh Pirates are looking for a flame-throwing stopper, they've come to the wrong place if they knock on my door.

However, when we think about the world in terms of fundamental moral equality, these differences make no difference. Morally considered, a genius who can play Chopin études with one hand tied behind her back does not have a "higher" rank than a seriously mentally impaired child who will never know what a piano is or who Chopin was. Morally, we do not carve up the world in this way, placing the Einsteins in the "superior" category, above the "inferior" Homer Simpsons of the world. The less gifted do not exist to serve the interests of the more gifted. The former are not mere things when compared to the latter, to be used as means to the latter's ends. From the moral point of view, each of us is equal because each of us is equally a somebody, not a something, the subject-of-a-life, not a life without a subject.

So why is the idea of being the subject-of-a-life important? Because it succeeds, where the other candidates we have discussed fail, in explaining our moral sameness, our moral equality:

> As subjects-of-a-life, we are all the same because we are all in the world.
>
> As subjects-of-a-life, we are all the same because we are all aware of the world.
>
> As subjects-of-a-life, we are all the same because what happens to us matters to us.
>
> As subjects-of-a-life, we are all the same because what happens to us (to our bodies, or to our freedom, or to our lives) matters to us, whether anyone cares about this or not.
>
> As subjects-of-a-life, there is no superior or inferior, no higher or lower.
>
> As subjects-of-a-life, we are all morally the same.
>
> As subjects-of-a-life, we are all morally equal.

So we return to the question with which our discussion began:

> Given: Human beings possess moral rights.
>
> Given: Sticks and stones lack moral rights.
>
> Question: Why? What is there that is true of human beings, but not true of sticks and stones, that explains why we do, but sticks and stones do not, have moral rights?

Whatever this "something" is, it was noted, it will have to illuminate what makes us the same, what makes us equal, in ways that are relevant to the rights we possess.

And the answer to our question is? It is because we are, but sticks and stones are not, subjects-of-a-life. The day I wrote these words for the first time and thought I understood their truth, I remember thinking: this must be how others feel when they say something important has been revealed to them. The sense of discovery and wonder really was this intoxicating. It remained to be seen whether what I was learning about human rights could be used to unlock the mystery of animal rights.

ANIMAL RIGHTS

What I had learned about human rights proved to be directly relevant to my thinking about animal rights. Whether any animals have rights depends on the true answer to one question: Are any animals subjects-of-a-life? This is the question that needs to be asked about animals because this is the question we need to ask about us. Logically, we cannot stand before the world and declare, "What illuminates why we have the equal rights we do is the fact that we all are equally subjects-of-a-life, but other animals, who are just like us in being subjects-of-a-life—well, *they don't* have any rights!" This would be like standing before the world and shouting, "A Volvo is not a car because a Volvo is not a Ford!" No one wants to be or to look this foolish.

So here is our question. Among the billions of nonhuman animals in the world, are there any who are aware of the world and aware of what happens to them? If there are, does what happens to them matter to them, whether anyone else cares about this or not? If any animals satisfy these requirements, they are subjects-of-a-life. And if they are subjects-of-a-life, then they have rights just as we do. Slowly but surely I realized that this is what the question about animal rights comes to.

Not surprisingly, there is no single fact, no one argument, that settles everything. Instead, a variety of relevant facts need to be considered, a family of arguments explored. The situation is akin to legal proceedings in a courtroom. Rarely is there one and only one fact or argument that decides guilt or innocence. True, sometimes crooks are caught with their hands in the proverbial cookie jar. In the vast majority of cases, however, it is the accretion of different facts (where the accused was at the time of the crime, DNA evidence, and the like) together with the relative strength of competing arguments that tip the scales of justice, one way or the other. When the relevant facts and competing arguments are weighed in the case before us, I believe their cumulative effect overwhelmingly supports a judgment in favor of only one conclusion: many nonhuman animals are subjects-of-a-life.

COMMON SENSE

In an earlier chapter I mentioned Gleco, the dog Nancy and I shared our lives with before our children were born. He was a wonderful friend, as smart a dog as we have ever known, with a pleasant disposition but also with a streak of independence. There was something of the cat in him; he was prepared to permit us to love him more than he felt the need to love us in return. You had to admire that about him.

Did Nancy and I think Gleco was a subject-of-a-life? At the time, it is true, we had never heard the expression "subject-of-a-life" so we did not think in those terms. But if someone had asked us, "Do you think Gleco is aware of the world? Aware of what happens to him? Do you think that what happens to him matters to him, whether anyone else cares about it or not?" Nancy and I would have answered, without hesitation, "Are you kidding? *Of course* Gleco is all of the above!"

What we thought about Gleco, hundreds of millions of other people think about the cats and dogs with whom they share their lives. It's just plain common sense to recognize that, behind their eyes, our animal companions are complicated psychological creatures who are no less subjects-of-a-life than we are. Granted, the parameters of their lives differ from ours in many respects. Some of us enjoy listening to hip-hop music or cruising the mall, reading history or baking bread, throwing pots or playing video games. Cats and dogs do not enjoy doing any of these things. So, yes, we will not have any trouble making up a long list of how our lives differ from theirs.

But (and this is a crucial *but*) there is a sameness amid the differences. When it comes to being subjects-of-a-life, we are on all fours (so to speak) with them. If someone told us that we are mistaken, that cats and dogs really are not aware of the world, or that they really do not care about what happens to them, we would think that (to use an old Pittsburgh expression) he must have something wrong in the head.

COMMON LANGUAGE

Imagine that one of your neighbors keeps several dogs in a small cage twenty-four hours a day. Whenever you walk by, the dogs bark and howl, they are so excited to see you. When you stop to pet them, they wag their tails and lick your hands. When you leave, they dig furiously with their paws and try to squeeze under the narrow openings created by their efforts. Your neighbor tells you to keep off his property "or else." You stand your ground. "Can't you see that the dogs want out? That they are starving for attention? That they are bored to death being confined in their cage, day in and day out?"

Does anybody have any trouble understanding what you mean? Are you using words in a way that makes what you say unintelligible? We can imagine different circumstances in which this would be true. If you told us that the ice cubes want out of the freezer or that the gravel on the driveway is starving for attention, ordinary English speakers would wonder what on earth you were talking about. But no ordinary English speaker would have the slightest difficulty in understanding what you mean when you say what you do about your neighbor's dogs. There is *somebody there*, behind those canine eyes, somebody with wants and needs, memories and frustrations.

COMMON BEHAVIOR

Part of the reason we can speak meaningfully about what dogs and other animals want is because their behavior resembles ours in relevant respects. If I am in a cage and want out, I will try to get out (for example, I will try to widen the space between the bars or push against them). If your neighbor's dogs want out of their cage, they will try to get out too (for example, by digging with their paws). We understand them and their behavior because we understand ourselves and our behavior. Just as my behavior "tells" you that I want out of my cage, without my having to say, "I want out!" so the similar behavior of the dogs "tells" us that they want out of their cage too, without their having to say so.

There are limits to what can be meaningfully ascribed to animals. If another neighbor tells you that her cat wants to study paleontology at Harvard and that her dog has decided to convert to paganism, we are right, I think, to be uncomprehending even as we remain forbearing. Without a doubt some people sometimes go too far in what they say about animals. Nevertheless, sometimes the behavior of animals, unlike the behavior of ice cubes and gravel, is so similar to our own, given similar circumstances, that we are right to infer that their experience is similar to our experience.

COMMON BODIES

If other animals all had radically different bodies than we do, it might be more difficult to see them as subjects-of-a-life. For example, suppose they all lacked all our senses (sight, smell, hearing, and the rest), all our organs (heart, lungs, kidneys, and so on), anything even vaguely resembling a central nervous system, including the barest hint of a brain. We might try to picture these animals as undifferentiated blobs of protoplasm oozing their way through the universe.

Picture such a blob confined in a cage. Could we imagine blob behavior so like our own cage behavior that we would be moved to say, and to understand, "The blob wants out of the cage?" It is entirely possible, I think, that well-informed, linguistically competent people might differ in their answers.

Whatever might be true in this theoretically possible case, the actual situation is quite different. Many species of animals have bodies like ours in many relevant respects. For example, they share our senses and have the same organs. The structural (the anatomical) similarities between humans and many other animals are both obvious and striking. In this sense, we have our bodies in common.

COMMON SYSTEMS

Here is another possibility that would make it more difficult to see other animals as subjects-of-a-life. We imagine that, while there are other animals who are structurally like us in all the relevant anatomical respects, there is this difference. When something injurious happens to our bodies, the information that gets transmitted (what makes us aware of the injury) travels along one path of nervous transmitters to our brain. By contrast, when something injurious happens to the bodies of other animals, the information that gets transmitted travels along a completely different path and goes to someplace other than the brain (to the pancreas, say). If this were true, things would be more complicated. Truly, if this were true, it would be more difficult to support the belief that animals *are aware* of what happens to them (that the transmitted information is "received," so to speak).

As it happens, the actual facts are not like this at all. The actual facts are the same in all the relevant respects. When something injurious happens to our bodies, the information that gets transmitted travels to the same destination in our case as it does in theirs. In both cases, it goes to the brain. In their case, it does not go to their pancreas. Just as the physical structures in the two cases are essentially the same in all the relevant respects, so are the nervous systems essentially the same.

COMMON ORIGINS

One final commonality should be noted. When we ask about the origin of human life, how human life began, two possibilities present themselves. First, human life might have originated because of a special creation by God; if true, our existence can be understood apart from understanding the origin and development of other forms of life, including other animals. (I will have more to say about God in the following chapter). Second, human life might have come into being after a long process of evolutionary change, which God, of course, could have been directing all along; if true, our existence should be understood in conjunction with our understanding of the origin and development of other forms of life, including other animals.

Before the publication of Charles Darwin's work on evolution, belief in special creation was compatible with our best science. Since its publication, it no longer is. Not only *that* we are but also *what* we are cannot be understood apart from the other forms of life from which we have evolved. In fact, the same is no less true of the "lower animals," by which Darwin typically means other mammals. Although the details are complicated, the main story line is simple: we share a common ancestry with these animals, the remnants of which we find in our anatomical and systemic similarities as well as in our mental powers. The minds of these animals, Darwin writes, "differ [from ours] in degree, not in kind."

What does this mean—that our mental powers "differ in degree, not in kind"? It means that the capacities that define the human mind will also be found in the "lower animals." In fact, *not* to find these capacities in these animals, as the contemporary American philosopher James Rachels notes, "would be altogether fantastic," given evolutionary theory. Writes Rachels:

> Evolutionary theory leads us to expect continuities, not sharp breaks. It implies that, if we examine nature with an unbiased eye, we will find a complex pattern of resemblances as well as differences. We will find, in humans, traces of their evolutionary past, and in other species—especially those most closely related to us by lines of evolutionary descent—traces of characteristics that may be more or less well developed in us.

When Darwin examines the behavior of other mammals "with an unbiased eye," he finds many resemblances indeed. Not only do they feel pleasure and pain, Darwin believes other mammals "experience (to greater or lesser degrees) anxiety, grief, dejection, despair, joy, love, 'tender feelings,' devotion, ill-temper, sulkiness, determination, hatred, anger, disdain, contempt, disgust, guilt, pride, helplessness, patience, surprise, astonishment, fear, horror, shame, shyness, and modesty."

I can imagine some people raising a skeptical eyebrow over some of Darwin's ideas (for example, that other animals might show disgust or modesty). However, even if a critic wants to quibble about some of the items on his list, all people of common sense, who speak common English, will agree that cats, dogs, and other mammals behave in ways that show their anxiety, joy, determination, surprise, astonishment, and fear, for example.

A second skeptical voice also can be anticipated. Many people do not believe in evolution. They believe that God created humans and animals separately, perhaps as recently as ten thousand years ago. Darwinian evolution, evolution of any kind, is fiction, not fact. For these people, the evidence for animal minds provided by evolutionary theory is no evidence at all.

Despite first impressions, rejection of evolution need not undermine the main conclusions Darwin reaches about animal minds. All of the world's religions speak with one voice when it comes to the question before us. Read the Bible, the Torah, the Koran. Study Confucianism, Buddhism, Hinduism, or Native American spiritual writings. The message is everywhere the same. Sheep and whales, goats and oxen, cats and dogs *most certainly* are aware of the world. These animals *most certainly* are aware of what happens to them. What happens to these animals *most certainly* matters to them. In these respects, all the world's religions teach the same thing.

Thus, while the argument I have given appeals to the implications of evolutionary theory, the conclusions I reach are entirely consistent with the faith-based convictions of people who believe that God created humans and animals separately. And for those who believe both in God and in evolution? Well, these people have reasons of both kinds for recognizing the mental life of other animals.

ARE ANY ANIMALS SUBJECTS-OF-A-LIFE?

So let us return to the question posed at the beginning of this chapter: Are any animals subjects-of-a-life? To answer this question wisely and well, I suggested, requires that we consider a variety of relevant facts and arguments, not just a single fact or argument apart from all others. After we have done this, but not before, we can ask which way the balance of the evidence tips the scales, whether in favor of or against an affirmative answer. Are any other-than-human animals subjects-of-a-life? For the reasons given, at least in the case of mammals, the evidence overwhelmingly supports an affirmative answer.

Common sense and the meaning of words in our common language support this answer. The behaviors that are common between us as well as our common anatomical structures support this answer. Our common neurological systems and considerations about our common origins, whether through evolution or as a separate creation by God, support this answer. If we view the question before us "with an unbiased eye," we see a world brimming with animals who not only are our biological relatives, they are our psychological kin. Like us, these animals are in the world, aware of the world, and aware of what happens to them. And, like us, what happens to these animals matters to them, whether anyone else cares about this or not. Despite our many differences, humans and other mammals are the same in this crucial, fundamental respect: we, and they, are subjects-of-a-life. Whether the same can be said of any nonmammalian animals is a question we will visit shortly.

BREAKING THE SPECIES BARRIER: MAMMAL RIGHTS

Having come to this realization in my Muddler's life, there was only one further step I could take. If I was to be consistent, I had to recognize the rights of other mammalian animals. I did not want to stand before the world and shout, "A Volvo is not a car because a Volvo is not a Ford!" If I was to be logical, if I was to render a fair and informed judgment, there was no turning back. Since what illuminates why we have the equal rights we do is our equality as subjects-of-a-life, and since other mammals are like us in being subjects-of-a-life, the conclusion was there in front of me: these animals have rights too, including the right to be treated with respect.

That animals have rights was not a conclusion I went looking for, I can assure you. Remember my profoundly original younger self, the deep thinker who classified animals as "Its," not "Thous," and placed them in the same category as other "things," like cucumbers and sack dresses? I was as surprised as anyone could be when I (former meat eater, former fisherman, former dissector, former butcher, former mink hat buyer, former defender of research on animals, former circusgoer, etc.) reached the conclusion that some other-than-human animals have rights.

LINE DRAWING

The considerations that support viewing mammalian animals as subjects-of-a-life do not exclude the possibility that the same thing is true of animals of other kinds. In particular, it is hard to understand how birds fail to qualify. Once again, common sense and the meaning of words in our common language support this judgment. The behaviors that are common between us as well as our common anatomical structures support this answer. Our common neurological systems and considerations about our common origins, whether through evolution or as a direct creation by God, support this answer. Moreover, recent studies from throughout the world demonstrate, time after time, rich, diverse avian cognitive abilities. Birds learn from experience; they can teach one another; they reason logically; they will even adjust behavior if they think other birds are watching them. For example, scrub jays will return, alone, to move food to a new place, if other scrub jays were watching where they hid it originally. (Additional corroboration of avian cognition is offered in chapter 6; this and subsequent chapters also include additional corroboration of the cognitive abilities of other animals).

Are birds in the world? Aware of the world? Aware of what happens to them? And does what happens to them matter to them, whether anyone else cares about this or not? The onus of proof must surely be borne by those who would give a negative answer to any of these questions. When St. Francis talked to the birds, he was not talking to himself.

Do birds have rights? Are we duty bound not to take their lives or deny them their freedom? Must we treat them with respect? Logically, no other conclusions are tenable. Because birds are like us in the morally relevant respects (we and they are subjects-of-a-life) and because our human equality as beings who are subjects-of-a-life illuminates why we have the equal rights we do, it follows that birds have these rights, too.

Should we go further? Should we say that all vertebrates, including fish, have a psychology? The basis for including fish is not weak by any means. Like humans, fish have a complicated physiology, anatomy, brain, and spinal cord. In addition, they have highly developed nerve endings near the surface of their bodies, especially near their mouths. In the spirit of Voltaire, would it not be an odd quirk of biology to provide fish with all the means of feeling pain and then deny the feeling? This is not runaway anthropomorphism. Thelma Lee Gross, a veterinarian summarizing current knowledge, states that "[d]irect clinical experience and scientific research has led [experts who work with fish] to realize that these animals feel pain."

Other experts have shown that fish who live in stable groups ("families") recognize each other, either by sight or sound. They can remember how conspecifics behaved in the past and alter their own behavior accordingly. The range of fish memory extends to features of the environment, including recognition of territories or home ranges. In other words, fish know where they are and where they are going. Older fish teach younger fish what to eat and what to avoid, and fish of any age can learn where to find food by observing the behavior of other fish. Moreover, fish have demonstrated what cognitive ethologists call associative reasoning or the ability to take what was learned in the past and apply it to novel situations in the future. Is there somebody there, behind those unblinking eyes? Somebody with rights?

Some people, I am sure, will think we go too far when we attribute minds and rights to fish. We will be told that their brains are too primitive, their central nervous system too rudimentary, to carry such heavy psychological baggage. Good sense should prevail. We need to "draw the line" at a place on the phylogenetic scale that excludes fish.

Well, perhaps. Then again, perhaps not. While it should be clear where my sympathies lie, for the sake of argument I am prepared to limit the conclusions for which I am arguing to the *least controversial* cases, by which I mean mammals and birds. (I say the "least controversial" because some philosophers maintain that nonhuman animals, including mammals and birds, are mindless. I respond to this view in objection 8, below). It is the rights of mammals and birds that I will be defending when I respond to objections to animal rights later in this chapter and, except for a section on fish slaughter in chapter 6, it is how these animals are treated by the major animal user industries that will concern us in the pages ahead.

EMPTY CAGES

Recognition of the rights of these animals has far-reaching consequences. The major animal user industries exploit these animals in the billions. These are the animals whose lives are taken, whose bodies are injured, and whose freedom is denied by the fur industry and by the meat industry, for example. All this emerges as morally wrong once we acknowledge their moral rights. All this emerges as something that must be stopped, not made more "humane." The task facing ARAs is daunting: we must empty the cages, not make them larger.

More than this task follows once we recognize the rights of these animals. In the previous chapter's discussion of human rights, we noted how those whose rights are violated sometimes do not understand the injustice that is done to them. This can happen in the case of children, for example. Because of their vulnerability, they are easy prey for those seeking some benefit, whether personal or public, secured by exploiting them.

What duties do we have when powerless humans are used as means to such ends? I think the answer is both clear and compelling. We have a duty to intervene, a duty to stand up and speak out in their defense. These victims are owed assistance from us; help is something they are due, not something it would be "awfully nice" to render. Arguably, the less able humans are to defend their rights, the greater is our duty to do this for them.

The same is no less true when the victims are other-than-human animals. We have a duty to intervene on their behalf, a duty to stand up and speak out in their defense. These animal victims are owed assistance from us; help is something they are due, not something it would be "awfully nice" of us to render. Their very inability to defend their rights makes our duty to help them greater, not less.

In the previous chapter I also noted that there is a limit to what we can do in the name of defending the victims of injustice. We simply cannot do everything for every victim. I also noted, however, that this limit is not zero. That we cannot do everything in defense of those who cannot defend themselves does not mean that we should content ourselves with doing nothing. What can we do? What should we do? I offer partial answers to these large questions in parts IV and V. For now, let me end the present discussion with a few final words that summarize where I had arrived in my life.

It took a long time (the better part of ten years, actually) and a lot of "figuring out," but a day dawned when, like other Muddlers who complete the journey, I looked in the mirror and could hardly recognize the person I saw there. I had arrived at a point in my moral development where my sensibilities were indistinguishable from those of DaVincians and Damascans. To my great surprise, the person I saw looking back at me was an Animal Rights Advocate. That's when the real work of my life began. There were so many questions to answer, especially ones raised by critics of animal rights.

OBJECTIONS TO ANIMAL RIGHTS

Sometimes critics of animal rights address the issues rather than content themselves with saying bad things about ARAs. Despite our reputation for being antirational extremists, ARAs prefer this kind of dialogue to name-calling. We believe our position wins, hands down, given any fair debate. Whenever critics want to voice their objections and agree to be fair, we gladly say (to use an expression favored by President Lyndon Johnson), "Come, let us reason together."

Before providing a fair hearing for the main objections raised against animal rights (representative objections raised by academic philosophers are examined in chapter 7 of *Animal Rights, Human Wrongs: An Introduction to Moral Philosophy*), I want to repeat something that was said at the beginning of this chapter, when we asked whether any animals are subjects-of-a-life. The situation we faced there was likened to legal arguments in a courtroom. In that context, it is rare that one and only one fact, one and only one argument, decides guilt or innocence. In the vast majority of cases, it is the accretion of a body of relevant facts and the cumulative strength of the accompanying arguments that tip the scales of justice, one way or the other.

The same thing can be said about animal rights. There is no one fact, no one argument that wins the day, for or against. Animal rights is a complicated issue. No one, partisan or foe, should expect a simple answer. Our guiding principle should be: let all voices be free to speak and to speak (unlike what is true of much of the media today) without interruption. After all, sometimes deciding where the truth lies takes time.

Facts and arguments that support belief in animal rights were presented earlier. Facts and arguments that dispute this belief will be considered in the rest of this chapter. Where the truth lies, readers, like jurors, will have to decide after both sides have been heard.

1. "What about Plants?"

In my experience, the objection most frequently raised against animal rights takes the form of a question: "What about plants?" If the people who raised this objection distinguished themselves by being tireless advocates of decent treatment for plants, one could perhaps understand how they might feel that plants were being treated unfairly by ARAs. In fact, the people who raise this objection do not have an especially tender place in their hearts for plants. Their point is not botanical; it is supposed to be logical.

What they think is this: If ARAs say that animals (like cats and dogs, lions and rhinos) have rights, then ARAs are logically committed to saying that plants (like tomatoes and rhubarb, kudzu and fescue) have rights too. But (so the objection goes) since it is false that rhubarb has rights, it must be false that rhinos have rights.

This objection, however well intended, is misplaced. Think about the various considerations presented in support of recognizing that the animals I have just mentioned are subjects-of-a-life. Considerations relating to common sense and common language, common bodies and common systems, for example. How does rhubarb measure up, given these considerations? Do tomatoes share our structure, anatomically and physiologically? Does kudzu have a central nervous system like ours, and a brain? If someone says, "The fescue wants to go out for a walk," do we have the foggiest idea what they mean? No, I don't think so. How ARAs argue for animal rights does not logically commit us to championing rhubarb rights.

Does it follow that ARAs must have it in for plants? That we must harbor pent-up plant hostility, believing that the only good plant is a dead plant? No, of course not. There are many reasons for treading lightly on the earth, many values we honor by trying to minimize the harm we do to all living things. The "What-about-plants?" objection does not succeed as a challenge to animal rights.

2. "Animals Are Not Human."

This certainly is true, given the standard meanings of words. Wolves and dolphins, mice and pigs are not human beings. While true, however, this fact provides no more reason for thinking that animals do not have rights than the companion claim, "Humans are humans," provides for thinking that we do.

The most charitable interpretation of the "Animals are not human" objection is that animals do not have rights because animals are not members of our species—the human species, the species *Homo sapiens*. As was noted in an earlier discussion, however, truths like this one (biological truths) have no moral import. All they tell us is that some beings (human beings) belong to one biological species, while other beings (wolf beings, for example) belong to another biological species. But who belongs to what species is not relevant to thinking about morality. If we think that humans have rights but wolves lack them, this is not just because we belong to different species.

Note this, too: Moral rights can never justifiably be denied for arbitrary, prejudicial, or morally irrelevant reasons. Race is such a reason. Gender is such a difference. In a word, *biological* differences are such reasons. How, then, can we believe that *species membership* marks a defensible boundary between those animals who do and those who do not have rights? Logically, it makes no sense. Morally, it bespeaks a prejudice *of the same kind* as racism and sexism, the prejudice known as speciesism.

3. "The Idea of Animal Rights Is Absurd!"

Sometimes critics take the offensive by making the charge of absurdity. Why is the idea of "animal rights" absurd? Often the people who make the charge do not stay around long enough to explain what they mean or why anyone should believe them.

When the basis of the charge is explained, usually it turns out that those who make it think it is silly to say that cats do (or should) have the right to vote, or that dogs do (or should) have the right to practice the religion of their choice.

And what follows? From this we are asked to infer that it is just as silly, just as absurd to think that any animal has any right.

This argument misfires. It assumes that animals do not have *any* right unless they have *every* right. No serious advocate of human rights believes this. For example, we do not believe that children must have the right to vote before they can have the right to be treated with respect. Clearly, human beings do not have to have *every* right in order to have *any* right. But if (as we come to reason together) we do not insist upon this requirement in the case of human beings (and we do not), we cannot consistently insist upon it in the case of animal beings.

4. "Animals Do Not Understand What Rights Are."

This is certainly true. No other-than-human animal understands what rights are. Consider the most intelligent among them. Nonhuman primates, for example. There is absolutely no reason to believe that great apes or bonobos understand that rights are "trump," or that to invoke a right is to make a demand rather than to ask for a favor. Without a doubt, critics are correct when they deny that animals understand what rights are.

What is supposed to follow? What inference are we supposed to make? The answer is: "No animal has rights." In other words, from the fact that animals do not understand rights, we are being asked to conclude that they do not have rights.

No one really believes this. No one really believes that before you can have something, you have to understand what it is. Consider what this way of thinking would prove. Young children do not have livers or kidneys. Why? Because they do not understand what livers and kidneys are. Billions and billions of our ancestors did not have genes or DNA. Why? Because they did not understand what genes and DNA are. And so on. Obviously, something has gone wrong here. In general, we do not require that something must first be understood before it can be possessed. Why should we accept a different standard when it comes to asking whether animals have rights? No one has ever given a satisfactory answer to this question.

Notice, too, where this way of thinking leads us when it comes to saying which humans have rights. Young children do not understand rights. In fact, it may be that many grown-ups (this certainly was true in my case for many years) do not understand what rights are. Are we to say that all these humans therefore lack rights? The question answers itself. A way of thinking that is so deficient when it comes to human rights cannot be any better when it comes to animal rights.

5. "Animals Do Not Respect Our Rights."

I call this the Serengeti Plain Objection. We are to imagine that a group of philosophers, say, just happen to be taking a walk on the Serengeti Plain when, without warning, they are attacked by a pride of hungry lions. "Hold on, there!" the philosophers say, "Don't even think about violating our rights!" Alas, their protestations have no calming effect and they end up being lunch for the lions. And the objection is? The objection is: If animals do not respect our rights, they do not have any rights for us to respect.

Many are the replies to this way of thinking. Only two will be mentioned here. We note, first, that we do not require that humans respect our rights before we acknowledge their rights. For example, we do not require this in the case of young children. Second, even if a child does something harmful to someone (for example, discharges a gun that results in someone's death), we do not say, "There, now, that's settled. This child has no rights whatsoever!" Of course we do not say this. Neither should we say anything different when the harm done is done by lions—or by any other animal for that matter.

6. "What Would Become of Us?"

This objection embroiders on the previous one. We imagine the philosophers being attacked by lions on the Serengeti. If the lions have rights, the philosophers argue, then they (the philosophers) cannot do anything to defend themselves lest they violate the lions' rights. Worse, the same must be true in general. Suppose a scourge of rats is spreading the bubonic plague throughout Paris. Surely we must permit them to do so, if we are to honor their rights. What, then, will become of us, if we cannot defend ourselves against animals? Like the philosophers on the Serengeti, we will perish, that's what.

I call this the Doom's Day Objection. It may be effective as lampoon, but it has no basis in logic. No coherent advocate of human rights believes that we must acquiesce in the face of each and every attack upon our lives, our bodies, or our freedom. On the contrary, every coherent advocate recognizes the right of self-defense, tempered by other considerations, including proportionality (that is, we are not to use more force when less force is sufficient). Thus it is that we are perfectly within our rights if we use force sufficient to injure a human attacker who violates our rights and threatens serious bodily injury.

Morally, the situation is no different if an animal being rather than a human being attacks us. No coherent advocate of animal rights does, and none must, believe that the philosophers, for example, must not lift a finger in self-defense if lions attack.

7. "Animals Do Not Respect One Another's Rights."

Sometimes critics object to animal rights because of how animals treat other animals, rather than because of how they treat us. For example, critics point out that lions eat gazelles, not just philosophers, then ask how it can be wrong if we eat steak. The most obvious difference in the two cases is that lions *have* to eat other animals in order to survive. We do not. So what a lion *must* do does not logically translate into what we *may* do.

In addition, it is worth noting how much this objection diverges from our normal practice. Most people who raise this challenge drive cars, wear clothes, use computers, and write checks. Other animals do not do any of these things. Should we therefore stop living as we live, stop doing what we do, and start imitating animals? Are the people who raise this objection prepared to go feral? I know of no critic of animal rights who advocates anything remotely like this. Why, then, place what carnivorous animals eat in a unique category as being the one and only thing they do that we should imitate? Without exception, when I have asked this question, no credible answer has been given.

8. "Animals Are Not Aware of Anything."

The French philosopher René Descartes (1596–1650) is famous for this teaching. Descartes argues that human beings have minds, which are immaterial, and bodies, which are material. By contrast, other animals have bodies only; they have no minds. For Descartes, animals are not aware of anything. Set a puppy on fire. Skin a harp seal alive. Neither feels a thing. The animals of the world are as mindless as the Energizer Bunny.

It would be a relief to say that philosophers have left Cartesianism to gather dust. Unfortunately, this is not true. Even to this day a handful of tenured philosophy professors cheerfully endorse the idea that all the "brutes" are mindless. And their argument? Invariably it comes to this: animals are not *aware* of anything because they cannot *say* anything. Or (to be more precise) animals are not aware of anything because they lack the ability to use a language like English or Italian.

Some ARAs respond to this objection by alluding to the apparent success of some animals (chimpanzees, for example) in learning how to communicate using American Sign Language for the deaf. Although a response of this type is relevant, it concedes too much. On reflection, it is obvious that awareness of the world is independent of the ability to use any language.

Consider what is involved in teaching a young child how to talk. We point to various objects and sound their names. We hold up a ball and say, "Ball." We point to the dog and say, "Dog." And so on. If awareness of the world were impossible for anyone who was unable to use a language, children could never learn to talk. Why? Because in order to learn to talk *they must first be aware* of what we say ("ball") and of what we point to (the ball). In other words, children must be *preverbally* and thus *nonverbally* aware of the world before they learn to use a language; otherwise, they could never learn to use one. However, once we acknowledge nonverbal awareness in children, the same kind of awareness cannot be summarily denied in animals. The Cartesian objection has no legs to stand on.

9. "Animals Do Not Have Souls."

Among the objections given against animal rights, some are of a religious nature. This is one of them. Like the other objections considered to this point, it cannot carry the weight proponents place on it.

If animals lack souls, there is no "life beyond the grave" for them. When their bodies die, the somebody who they were is totally annihilated. It is worth noting that not all religions agree on this point. Hinduism and many Native American traditions are obvious counterexamples; even mainstream Christian theologians (John Wesley provides one example) find Biblically based arguments in favor of the souls of animals.

But let us assume, for the sake of argument, that animals do not have immortal souls. Two points need to be made, the first logical, the second theological. Concerning the logical: Who does or does not have an immortal soul has no logical bearing on who does or does not have rights. Who does or does not have a soul is relevant to answering the question, "What happens to X after X dies?" Questions that ask who has rights, by contrast, have nothing to do with what happens after someone dies; these questions concern the moral status individuals have while they are alive. Asking who has an immortal soul is as logically irrelevant to asking who has rights as asking who has green eyes or capped teeth.

Theologically, it would be perverse to teach that, because animals do not have a life after they die, we are free to do just about anything we want to do to them while they are alive. If anything, a credible theology would teach exactly the opposite. Because animals do not have a life after they die, we should do everything in our power to ensure that this, their only life, is as long and good as possible.

Think about it. Terrible things sometimes happen to good people. Job, for example. His crops fail. His family dies. His reputation is destroyed. Even so, if he has an immortal soul, a day may come when all his earthly travails are more than compensated for by the bliss that awaits him in heaven. This can never happen to animals, if they lack immortal souls. For them, there is no heavenly bliss, no future compensation. For them, there is only this life and nothing more. Do we therefore say, "We are free to do just about anything we want to do to them while they are alive?" Or do we say, "We should do everything in our power to ensure that this, their only life, is as long and good as possible?" If the object of one's belief is a loving God, not a sadistic one, the questions answer themselves.

Rather than the "Animals-don't-have-souls" objection undermining the abolitionist goals all ARAs share, the objection's implications actually forward them. The best way to insure that animals have as long and as good a life as is within their nature to enjoy is to act in ways that respect their rights. When ARAs and others take the time to reason together, we sometimes discover that we have more in common than we realized.

10. "Well, at Least God Gave Us Dominion!"

People of a religious bent, especially Christians who take the Bible seriously, often agree that rights are not the moral currency of their faith-based ethic. You just don't find moral rights in the Bible. What you do find, very unambiguously, is that God gives us dominion over the animals, pronounced most famously in these words:

> And God said, "Let us make man in our image, after our likeness: and let them have dominion over the fish of the sea, and over the fowl of the air, and over the cattle, and over all the earth, and over every creeping thing that creepeth upon the earth." So God created man in his own image, in the image of God created he him; male and female created he them. And God blessed them, and God said unto them, "Be fruitful, and multiply, and replenish the earth, and subdue it: and have dominion over the fish of the sea, and over the fowl of the air, and over every living thing that moveth upon the earth." (Genesis 1:26–28, King James Version).

What could be clearer than that other animals were created for our use? What could be clearer than that we therefore do nothing wrong when we limit their freedom, injure their bodies, or take their lives to satisfy our needs and satiate our desires?

This is not how I read the Bible. To be given dominion by God is not to be given a blank check made out to satisfying our needs and satiating our desires. On the contrary, it is to be charged with the awesome responsibility of being the creator's agent within creation; in other words, we are called by God to be as loving and caring for what God has created as God was loving and caring in creating it. Indeed, as I understand the idea, this is what it means to be "created in God's image."

Myself, I do not know how anyone can read the opening account of creation in Genesis (one can take this seriously without taking it literally) and come away with a different understanding of God's plans for and hopes in creation. God, you may recall, creates the other animals on the same day (the sixth) as Adam and Eve. I read in this representation of the order of creation a prescient recognition of the vital kinship humans share with other animals. More than this, I find in this opening saga an even deeper, more profound message. God *did not* create animals for our use—not for our entertainment, not for our scientific curiosity, not for our sport, not even for our food. On the contrary, the nonhuman animals currently exploited in these ways were created to be just what they are: *independently good* expressions of the divine love that, in ways that are likely to remain forever mysterious to us, was expressed in God's creative activity.

"Not even for our food?" I can hear the skeptic mutter. "Is that a misprint?" To which my answer is, "No, it is not a misprint. It's what the Bible teaches." The "meat" we are given by God for our food is not the flesh of animals; here is what it is. "And God said, 'Behold, I have given you every herb bearing seed, which is upon the earth, and every tree, in which is the fruit of a tree yielding seed; to you it shall be meat'" (Genesis 1:29). The message could not be any clearer. There are no hunters, only gatherers, in Eden. In the most perfect state of creation, humans are *vegans*; we eat no animal flesh, and neither do we eat any animal products, such as milk or eggs. So if we ask what God hoped of us "in the beginning," when it comes to food the answer is not open to dispute. It wasn't Big Macs or cheese omelets.

For Christians, then, the question asked each day is a simple one. "Do I try to turn my life around and begin my journey back to Eden—back to a more loving relationship with this gift of creation? Or do I continue to live in ways that increase my distance from what God hoped for?" This is a question that is answered in many different ways, not one only. There is no argument there. But neither should we argue over whether one way Christians answer this question is with the choices they make about the food on their plate. Animals in the Garden of Eden lived in paradise *precisely because* no one violated their rights—which is what, in my opinion, Christians should want for animals today.

"Christian animal rights advocate" is not an oxymoron. Granted, love, not rights, is at the heart of the Christian ethic. Still, "Christian animal rights advocate" is a convenient way to express a faith-based advocacy that works for the same ends as ARAs work for: Empty cages, not larger cages. The same is true of Jewish animal rights advocates, Moslem animal rights advocates, Hindu animal rights advocates, Buddhist animal rights advocates, and so on. When the family portrait of ARAs is painted, people of every faith will be included. They belong there. That many people outside the animal rights community find it hard to believe that people of faith can be ARAs only goes to show how successful the major animal user industries are in creating and sustaining an erroneous picture of who we are.

11. "Let's Solve the Human Problems First!"

One final objection that should be considered does not challenge the truth of animal rights; it simply wants to put ARAs in our place, where "in our place" is shorthand for "back at the end of the line." "There are so many daunting human problems we face," so this objection goes, "from famine and war, to health care and illiteracy. *After* we solve these problems, *then* we can turn our attention to animal rights."

You don't have to be a cynic to see that this is a recipe for perpetual neglect of animal rights. If we are realistic, we know there will always be *some* human problem needing to be solved. (Is it not true, for example, that "the poor will be with us always"?) It follows (given this objection) that the day will never come when we can turn our attention to animal rights. Is it just me, or do others have the feeling that the people who raise this objection just don't want to hear what ARAs are saying?

My experience has taught me two things about people who think this way. First, almost invariably (not always, but almost always) they are not actively involved, in any serious way, in efforts to solve any human problem. Rather, they spend most of their discretionary time working on their golf game or watching *The Sopranos*. They are *faux* activists who restrict their activism to contributing money (and usually mighty little of it) to Save the Children or Oxfam. In other words, most of them, most of the time, suffer from a bad case of bad faith.

Second, ARAs do not see the issues as a disjunction: *Either* you help solve human problems *or* you help animals. We see them as a conjunction: Let's help solve the human problems *and* help the animals. For example, people can make serious efforts to help the victims of famine and practice a vegan diet, or they can help address the burdens of illiteracy and not buy fur or leather or wool. Animal rights does not have to be one's whole life in order to be part of it.

LOOKING FORWARD, LOOKING BACK

Many are the objections to animal rights. While it has not been possible to consider every one of them, it has been possible to review the main ones. (Others will be considered in subsequent chapters). Given a fair hearing, none succeeds. All are seriously flawed, for one reason or another. What, then, are we to believe about animal rights? And why are we to believe it?

Recall how our situation was likened to legal argument in the courtroom. No single fact, no one argument, is decisive—one way or the other. What we have to do is weigh the relevant facts and give fair consideration to the competing arguments;

when we do this regarding animal rights, I believe the cumulative effect over-whelmingly supports only one conclusion: billions and billions of animals, includ-ing mammals and birds (at least) have rights.

This, then, is where I had arrived in my life after a Muddler's journey of many years. The moral space I came to occupy was not something I went looking for. In fact, sometimes I think animal rights found me rather than that I found it. Re-member the sly, sarcastic smile I imagined Gandhi had when he talked to me from the pages of his autobiography? When I look back on that imaginary en-counter, I think I know what his enigmatic smile meant. So wise a man, he prob-ably knew where I was headed before I did.

One thing was clear. There was a lot of work that needed doing. I threw my-self into the cause with the zeal of the recently converted. Professionally, I wrote scores of papers and several books on every aspect of animal rights. One book in particular, *The Case for Animal Rights,* means more to me than the others. Al-though I am a compulsive rewriter (as I've told many people, many times, I've never written a sentence I could not improve, with a little tinkering here or there), it took me only ten months to finish a manuscript that became a book of more than four hundred pages. It was an amazing experience. I wrote in the morning. I wrote in the afternoon. I wrote in the evening. I wrote effortlessly, without turning back or changing direction once I had begun. For the first time in my life, the creative process took on a life of its own. The book wrote itself, taking me places I had not anticipated. The conclusions I reached at the end were at odds with the convictions I had when I started. I was like a stenographer, just along for the ride.

In addition to my writing, a variety of lecture opportunities (at universities, demonstrations, and before elected representatives, for example) began to pre-sent themselves. When my audience consisted of my philosophical peers, this sometimes provided some unforgettable experiences. Here's one example.

Philosophers all have certain benchmarks. Our first teaching appointment. Our first published paper. Our first presentation at a major international philos-ophy conference. For me, that would be the World Congress on the Philosophy of Law and Social Philosophy, held in Basel, Switzerland, more than a few years ago. In my mind it was a big deal. Here I was, rubbing elbows with famous philosophers from around the world. The conveners must have thought I had something important to say. Talk about naïveté.

I was befriended by another American philosopher. I told him I was awestruck by the conference's size and scope. He was kind enough to attempt to salve my apprehensions. He had been to many such conferences before. I should not worry too much about how my presentation would go over. The criteria used for accepting papers had deteriorated over the years. "Why," he said, "there's even a paper on animals and the law!"; his voice was a polished combination of disdain and disbelief.

I did not have the nerve to tell my well-traveled acquaintance that I was intimately familiar with the author, but from what he told me I knew I had come to the right place. Not another soul there had given a minute's thought to ideas that were beginning to dominate my life. Who better to share them with? Who better to challenge? Standing before my incredulous audience, explaining my position, fielding questions: all this was a rite of passage for me, a baptism by fire. I learned not to be afraid to say what I believed, even in a hostile environment. It is a lesson I have carried with me to this day.

As for the philosopher who tried to help me: He sat in the front row during my presentation and listened attentively. Afterward, he allowed as how he would "have to think about" what I had said. We socialized a bit and had a good laugh about his *faux pas*. Life is full of surprises. I thanked him for helping with my education.

Other parts of my learning curve saw me as observer, not agent. I knew some of the things that were being done to animals but not as much as I thought I should know. I needed to look directly at the evil I opposed in all its ugly reality. I needed to steel myself against the desire to look away. It was as if I entered into a silent compact with animals everywhere. I would immerse myself in their suffering and death in quiet homage to those who suffered and died, whether on the farm, in the wild, or at the lab, for example. Remember the older German ARA? The one who encountered the horse racing down the street, ablaze from nose to tail? "What have I ever done to deserve this?" the mare asked as she passed. "Why aren't you helping me?" I took it upon myself to learn as much as I could about the terrible things that people were doing to animals, believing then, as I believe now, that this horrible knowledge would help me help them. I sketch what I learned on this part of my journey in chapters 6–10.

Like anyone else, any time I try to explain what I think, I learn something new. The time spent writing this book is no exception. Among the many things I have learned, one stands out. It concerns the meaning of some important words, words like "humane" and "welfare," words that, depending on who is using them, can either conceal or reveal the truth. Maybe I have been too much the philosopher all these years, with my head in the proverbial clouds (or sand), believing that the animal rights debate is a battle waged in the realm of abstract ideas, not in the world of everyday facts. All along, perhaps I have been too willing to concede to people in the other camp (the spokespersons for the major animal user industries) that they speak truly when they say what these industries do.

In writing this book, I have changed my mind. I no longer make this concession. I have come to believe that these people speak falsely when they describe what these industries do. More than this, I believe that, after I illustrate the systematic disconnect between what these spokespersons say and what these industries do, Muddlers everywhere will agree with me.

SAYING AND DOING

WHAT WE LEARN
FROM ALICE

Some opponents of animal rights give credit where credit is due. They don't agree with the idea. Not at all. They wouldn't be caught dead saying "tofu" and "let's eat" in the same sentence. Nevertheless, they acknowledge that animal rights should be considered on its merits. Despite stereotypes to the contrary, ARAs do not rest our case on clever slogans, what the tea leaves say, or indecipherable haiku incantations. Fair opponents of animal rights understand that they are obliged to answer the animal rights message rather than attack the animal rights messenger.

As we have seen, the major animal user industries think they have a better idea. In their minds, attack is preferable to address. The general public needs to be encouraged to view the controversy over animal rights as a contest between sensible animal welfare moderates, who favor humane treatment and responsible care, versus "out-of-this-world" animal rights extremists, who favor no use and violent, terroristic tactics. To this end, the public relations arms of these industries feed the mass media their daily helping of positive press releases about the industries and negative stories about ARAs.

Having thus been enlisted, the mass media does its part (not always, but often) by showing and telling the outrageous or unlawful behavior of a handful of obliging animal rights advocates, then showing and telling the many (it is assumed) good things done by the industries. You don't have to be a dealer in Vegas to see that the rhetorical cards are stacked in favor of the major users. Who but irrational, misanthropic, lawbreaking, terroristic animal rights extremists can be against animal welfare, humane treatment, and responsible care?

This is not the question we should ask. The question we should ask is, "How much confidence should we place in what spokespersons for the major animal user industries say, not only about ARAs but also about their industries?" I already have addressed the first part of this question. The group portrait of ARAs painted by these spokespersons is a lot of fiction mixed with a little bit of fact. As for the second part, I hope to be able to explain why the simple one-word answer to this question is, "None."

HUMPTY DUMPTY'S ARROGANCE

Say what you will about ARAs, we don't hold anything back. What we say is what we mean, and vice versa. We are forthright, if nothing else. Even people who disagree with us do not have any trouble understanding what we think. We think the major animal user industries are doing something terribly wrong. We think the only adequate response to what they are doing is to put them all out of business. Empty cages, not larger cages. It's hard for anyone to misunderstand that.

The same cannot be said for those who speak for the industries. When it comes to the meaning of words, these people apparently take their inspiration from Humpty Dumpty. Recall his famous exchange with Alice, in Lewis Carroll's *Through the Looking Glass*:

> "I don't know what you mean by 'glory'," Alice said.
>
> Humpty Dumpty smiled contemptuously. "Of course you don't—until I tell you. I meant [by 'glory'] 'a nice knockdown argument for you'!"
>
> "But 'glory' doesn't mean 'a nice knockdown argument for you'," Alice objected.
>
> "When *I* use a word," Humpty Dumpty said in a rather scornful tone, "it means just what I choose it to mean—neither more nor less."

When industry spokespersons use words like *animal welfare, humane treatment, and responsible care,* they must be thinking that, like Humpty Dumpty, they can make these words mean anything they choose. In fact, as Alice could have told them, they can't.

Consider the word *humane.* Like other words, it does not have a vaporous meaning that is just hanging around, like an empty parking place, waiting for people to fill it with a self-serving definition of their choosing. *Webster's Unabridged Dictionary* defines it this way: "marked by compassion, sympathy, or consideration for other human beings or animals." The *American College Dictionary's* definition differs somewhat; *humane* is defined as "characterized by kindness, mercy, or compassion." When spokespersons for the major animal user industries tell us that they treat their animals humanely, we should expect to find industry practices that show compassion, sympathy, consideration, kindness, and mercy. Why? Because (unless you're Humpty Dumpty) this is what *humane* means.

Again, think about what it means to act in ways that pay due regard to another's welfare. *The Random House College Dictionary* defines *welfare* in terms of "good fortune, health, happiness." To this list the *American Heritage Collegiate Dictionary* adds "well being." No one who speaks common English will have any difficulty in applying these ideas to animals.

For example, if I tell you I treat my cat and dog with due regard for their welfare, you will have reasonable expectations about my behavior. You will expect to see me making sure that their basic needs (for food, water, shelter, and exercise) are satisfied, and you will not expect to see me deliberately do anything to harm them—like break their legs or burn their eyes out. If spokespersons for the major animal user industries say they treat animals with due regard for their welfare, we should have the same expectations. Why? Because (unless you're Humpty Dumpty) this is what "concern for animal welfare" means.

The next five chapters will describe some of the conditions in which animals are raised, as well as some of the other treatment they routinely receive, in the hands of the major animal user industries. As we work our way through these chapters, we will see how industry spokespersons describe the conditions and treatment as "humane" and profess their commitment to "animal welfare." Given what these words mean, we know what to expect: conditions and treatment that reflect compassion, sympathy, and mercy, for example; conditions and treatment that aim to forward the animals' good fortune, health, happiness, and well-being. In fact, nothing could be further from the truth. These spokespersons talk a good game when it comes to "humane treatment" and "animal welfare" (and the same can be said in the case of "responsible care"), but *what they do does not match what they say.*

It will be useful to give a name to the idea expressed by the words I have just italicized. I will call it the Disconnect Dictum. Whenever we find a disconnect between what the major animal industries say and what they do, I will say, "Remember the Disconnect Dictum" or "No clearer example of the Disconnect Dictum can be imagined," and so on. The Dictum's importance to the animal rights debate will become clearer as we proceed. Even at this early juncture, however, its role should be clear.

Like a red flag, the Disconnect Dictum functions to call attention to something important we might otherwise miss, in this case the rhetoric employed by the major animal user industries. These people never tire of saying how they treat animals humanely, responsibly, with due regard for their welfare, and so on. But (like Alice in her exchange with Humpty-Dumpty) fair-minded people will understand that spokespersons for these industries can't just make up what these words mean.

"SADISTIC NAZI LIAR SCUM"

Whenever ARAs criticize spokespersons for the major animal user industries, we are asking for trouble. These people have a lot of power and influence, which they believe is well deserved. They view themselves as experts and ARAs who criticize them as . . . well, as less than their equals. ARAs need to be prepared for a lot of verbal roughing up if we dare to raise doubts about people who think they know way, way more than we do. Over the years, I have experienced this (to be charitable) lack of hospitality many times.

By way of example: On one occasion, I was invited to give a public lecture at an American university, which shall remain nameless. Faculty who did research on animals were enraged. Letters of protest were circulated in which I was described as a dangerous zealot, a firebrand, and a rabble-rousing demagogue. The researchers likened me to Hermann Göring and to monomaniacal mental patients who think they are Jesus Christ or Napoleon; one spokesperson even went so far as to call me the Jim Jones of the animal rights movement.

As for my public lectures, the researchers accused me of advocating violence; spreading lies; of being antiscience, antirational, and anti-intellectual; of asserting that I have the right to impose by violent means my notion of ethics on others; and of inflaming my audiences to commit unlawful acts.

Warming to the occasion, other faculty chimed in by asserting that I was the "point man" for laboratory break-ins (I visited a campus, gave a talk, packed my bags, and the next day the Animal Liberation Front trashed a lab and liberated the animals). Oh, and then there was the "suggestion" that the invitation should be revoked because I was a prime suspect in the recent murder of a researcher, shot dead in his driveway. There is more, but I'm sure you get the drift. Let's just say these folks were not laying out the welcome mat.

Not a word of what they said is true; all of it is pure fiction. Why, then, mention it? Because it illustrates the lengths to which experts who don't like the idea of animal rights sometimes will go in their attempt to discredit those who would dare to disagree with them. So, yes, as I say, ARAs need to be prepared for a lot of verbal roughing up if we challenge the ideas of people who think they know way, way more than we do. Because I don't want to be roughed up for the wrong reasons, let me take a moment to clarify the nature of the criticism embodied in the Disconnect Dictum.

In general, whenever we say something false, there are two possibilities. Either we know it is false, or we do not. If the former alternative is true, we are insincere in what we say, and we tell a lie when we say it; if the latter, we are sincere in what we say and just happen to be mistaken. When major animal user spokespersons say what is false, the same alternatives present themselves. Either they are lying, or they are mistaken.

Many ARAs believe the former. Many believe that these spokespersons know full well that their industries do not treat animals the way they say they do. After all, these people are the experts, and one thing experts know is what simple words like *humane* and *welfare* mean. We're not talking rocket science here—which is why many ARAs believe industry spokespersons are lying through their teeth when they say what these industries do. Why, then, would they say it? For two reasons. First, they need to make a show of conforming to federal laws, which require "humane" treatment; second, they need to reassure a trusting public that "everything is fine" in those places to which the public has no easy access.

These are harsh judgments. If true, they cast serious doubt on the moral character of industry spokespersons. If true, these experts are not to be trusted. If true, these experts lie.

Whether this is true or not, I leave for others to decide. The criticism I am making is different; it includes no "firebrand" message, no negative assessments of character. (I am not saying, for example, that industry spokespersons are "sadistic Nazi liar scum.") I am willing to assume that industry spokespersons all sincerely believe that their respective industries do what they say they do: treat animals humanely, with due regard for their welfare. This sincerity granted, my criticism comes to this: As I hope to demonstrate in the following chapters, when these spokespersons say these things, what they say is not just sometimes false; it is always false.

People of good will who are not ARAs will find this hard to believe, I know. Aren't there laws on the books to protect animals? Aren't there inspectors galore to make sure the laws are being followed to the letter? And don't we have veterinarians out there to make sure animals receive decent treatment? Besides, the major animal user industries very rarely are charged with violating the law. Things cannot be as bad for the animals as I am suggesting.

Let me make just three points at this juncture. First, when spokespersons for the major animal user industries speak in the language of "humane care," they are mouthing the words the government has told them to say. The first two provisions of the Congressional Statement of Policy in the federal Animal Welfare

Act are "(1) to insure that animals intended for use in research facilities or for exhibition purposes or for use as pets are provided humane care and treatment" and "(2) to assure the humane treatment of animals during transportation in commerce." It is no accident that spokespersons for the major animal user industries all talk the same way. They all say the same thing because this is what the government wants to hear.

Second, it is true that major animal user industries are very rarely found in violation of the Animal Welfare Act. In 1990, for example, a not untypical year, 13,050 inspections were conducted and only 27 complaints were issued. That works out to a compliance rate of approximately 98 percent. Don't these impressive statistics show that the major animal user industries really are doing a good job of providing animals with "humane care and treatment"?

Readers will have to judge for themselves. As I hope to be able to explain, the kind of legal protection animals receive is part of the problem, not part of the solution. The fact that there are so few violations of operative law shows not that animals are treated well, but that the legal standards for "humane" treatment are too minimal, their enforcement, pitiful. With few exceptions, which will be duly noted, the treatment of animals I will be describing in the next five chapters *is entirely legal*, thus *entirely in keeping with the provision of "humane care and treatment*," a true celebration of compassion and kindness, sympathy and mercy. To say this would be laughable if it were not so cruelly false. But, as I say, readers will have to decide where the truth lies, whether in what industry representatives never tire of saying or in what I have just written.

Last, the role of veterinarians in the legitimization of standard practices in the major animal user industries is an unspeakable tragedy, their betrayal to the animals is so great. With few exceptions, which will be duly noted, the animal abuse I will be describing in the next five chapters is perfectly consistent with policies endorsed by (of all people) The American Veterinary Medical Association.

The public's image of vets is of people who love animals. This is why they became vets in the first place. They would never stand idly by and tolerate animal abuse. Aren't they all members of the animal rights movement? Well, frankly, no. In fact, the American Veterinarian Medical Association (AVMA) vigorously distances itself from animal rights, stating that it "cannot endorse the philosophical views and personal values of animal rights advocates when they are incompatible with the responsible use of animals for human purposes, such as food and fiber, and for research conducted to benefit humans and animals." However, animal welfare is another animal. "[T]he AVMA's commitment to animal welfare is unsurpassed," we are told, because of its "long standing concern and commitment to the welfare, humane treatment and care of animals."

Let's see. "[C]ommitment to the welfare, humane treatment and care of animals." "Responsible use." It sounds familiar. Hard as it is for the general public to believe, the rhetoric of the national organization that represents most veterinarians in America—not all vets, by any means, and certainly not the members of the Association of Veterinarians for Animal Rights (AVAR)—is the same as that used by the major animal user industries. With friends like this, animals don't need any enemies.

THE METAMORPHOSES

TURNING ANIMALS
INTO FOOD

For most of us, just thinking about giving up meat is hard; actually giving it up may seem impossible. DaVincians see things differently. Because they don't eat their friends and because animals are their friends, they don't eat meat (unless their parents make them). Damascans, too, can make the transition to vegetarianism without thinking about their gains and losses. Rebekah Harp, a special education teacher in Jacksonville, Florida, provides an example. Although she had always thought of herself "as a person who was compassionate towards animals," she had been a lifelong meat eater. Then something happened a few years ago. She writes:

> I was enjoying a steak dinner in a nice restaurant, and I looked around at the people in the room. When I recall the event, I always remember it in slow motion, like a scene from an Oliver Stone film. The sounds of the knives sawing through the slabs of cow became magnified, and the rivulets of blood and grease pooling on the plates made me sick. An image of terrified cows awaiting their slaughter flashed through my mind—and that was the last piece of meat I ever ate. Those cows were no different from my dogs or cats, so how could I justify eating any animal?

A change in perception occurred. A Damascan moment. Rebekah Harp, lifelong meat eater, became Rebekah Harp, vegetarian. Just like that.

Something similar happened to Gary and Gillian Cutick (Gary is a physical therapist, Gillian an architect, living in Raleigh). They found themselves stuck in traffic directly behind a large truck that was densely packed with hogs headed for slaughter. The truck had oval holes cut in its metal exterior to let air pass through. The hogs in the rear of the truck looked out of the openings, some standing on their hind legs to get a better view. So there, directly in front of Gary and Gillian, were ten, maybe more, pairs of eyes looking down at them. And there were Gary and Gillian, with no means of escape, looking back. A perfect place for a change in perception. What before they had always seen as "something that comes wrapped in cellophane" became "someone who was going to be killed." Without either of them saying a word to the other, both decided then and there that they would never eat pork again. It was, as Gary describes it, "a small thing to do, to make things better." Later, when they did discuss what had happened, they agreed that stopping with pork was arbitrary. Other animals were headed to the place from which no animal returns. There was a lot in their freezer they got rid of when they got home. A rare Damascan "twofer" for the animals.

In contrast to Damascans, Muddlers have a lot to "figure out" before we are prepared to give up our meat. For one thing we have a hard time imagining what eating would be like without it. Let's see: Here's the steak. Here's the baked potato. Here's the salad. Take away the steak and what's left? A baked potato and some salad. No wonder Muddlers initially think that becoming a vegetarian is like taking a vow of culinary abstinence mixed with voluntary poverty.

Of course, in time Muddlers discover that there is an incredibly delicious, colorful, and nutritious animal-free cuisine out there to be discovered, a menu of possibilities that includes foods from every nation and ethnicity in the world. It is the great new food we gain, not the customary old food we lose, that is the real surprise, something all of us have to discover for ourselves. It is not something anyone can teach us.

One thing we can learn from others is how the animals who are raised to be eaten are treated. Learning this made an important contribution to my expanding animal consciousness. As an urban dweller, I had very little direct contact with farmed animals and, before I read Gandhi, no interest in learning anything about them. Once Gandhi got under my skin, I understood that I had to try to make the invisible visible. I had to go inside the barn, so to speak, to see what was happening. I wish I could say that what I found was bright and cheerful. Regretfully, it was anything but. A solitary black cow still casts shadows in my memory.

The farm was located in eastern North Carolina, about an hour's drive from Raleigh, where I live. The family who operated the farm relied mainly on income from tobacco, but they also ran a small-scale slaughter operation. Local farmers would bring their cow, or hog, or sheep in the morning, then pick up their butchered and packaged meat later in the day. That's how I met the black cow, the only animal to find death on that farm, on this day.

By the time I arrived (I had phoned the farmer a week before and arranged a visit, explaining that I was a "university professor doing some research"), the cow was in a stall, adjacent to a roofed enclosure where he would be dismembered. The farmer pressed a small caliber rifle against the cow's forehead. A single shot echoed across the flat landscape. Without uttering a sound, the cow fell in a heap, not gradually, but all at once, like a collapsed folding chair. The farmer's helper then inserted a stiff wire into the hole in the cow's head, turning it vigorously ("scrambling its brains" is how he described what he was doing). After this he fastened a chain around a rear leg, hoisted the cow to his eye level, and plunged a well-used knife into the animal's throat, pulling down and across with great force.

Then the blood began to flow. And flow. And flow. I was not prepared for the gallons of blood that pulsed from the still breathing cow, as if a fire hydrant had been opened, except it was not water that was coming out. The animals I had butchered years before didn't bleed; by the time they met my knife or saw, they had been long dead, not recently alive. And when does life end, anyhow? Even after the cow was skinned and cut into quarters, the molted white and blue flesh quivered.

After thanking the farmer, I drove home, trying to process what I had seen. In the weeks ahead, I would visit other, larger slaughterhouses and watch as hundreds of pigs and thousands of chickens breathed their last mortal breath in large-scale disassembly lines of death, like the hog operations I will describe later in this chapter. The people who worked in these places actually likened what they did to "assembly lines running in reverse." Poultry processors boasted that the only thing they didn't use was "the cluck." The story differed slightly at plants where hogs went to their death; there the only thing that wasn't used was "the oink." I will never forget the carnage I witnessed, in numbers I could never have imagined. Most of all, though, I will never forget that solitary cow. Young, he was, and black all over. So trusting, his large mercurial eyes had no fear in them. Only when he collapsed into himself might he have sensed the finality of his betrayal.

One final introductory note. Photos like the ones available at the website mentioned in the prologue, as stark and disturbing as some of them are, do not adequately convey what life is like for animals raised on factory farms, an idea explained below. What we see is their lives observed from the outside. What we do not see, and what only our imagination can provide, is their lives viewed from the inside, by the subject living it. The plain fact is, the vast majority of these animals, literally *billions* of them, suffer every waking minute they are alive. Physically, they are sick, plagued by chronic, debilitating diseases. Psychologically, they are ill, weighed down by the cumulative effects of disorientation and depression. Viewed at a distance they may look like the animals all of us read about in the picture books of our childhood. Viewed inwardly, in their present circumstances, they are tragic, pathetic shadows of their more robust ancestors. Remarkably, however, the fullness of their being remains, waiting to be set free. Sanctuaries for farmed animals, described near the end of this chapter, teach us that.

THE VEAL INDUSTRY

Veal, especially so-called pink or milk-fed veal, is the centerpiece in what some people regard as the finest dishes, prepared by the finest chefs, and served in the finest restaurants, especially French and Italian restaurants. Famous for its tenderness, milk-fed veal can be cut with a fork. No gristle. No muscle. Just soft, unresisting flesh that melts in your mouth. When it comes to good eating, some people find it hard to imagine how it can get any better than this.

The situation is different for the calves who end up as veal. Veal calves (or "special-fed veal," as they are also known) are surplus calves, most of them bull calves, born to Holstein dairy herds. While the majority of the surplus calves, both male and female, are raised and sold as beef, approximately eight hundred thousand annually enter and exit an American market of their own. That market is the special-fed or milk-fed veal industry.

Calves who enter this industry are taken from their mothers hours or days (less than seven days is the industry's recommendation) after they are born, then sold at auction or delivered to contract vealers. Throughout most of history, demand for pink veal outstripped supply. Calves were slaughtered when they were very young, before they consumed too much iron-rich food, like their mother's milk or grass, which would turn their flesh from pink to red and reduce consumer demand.

Understandably, these animals were not large, weighing in at only about ninety pounds. Because they were so small, the supply of their tender, pink flesh was limited and the price per pound high. Predictably, premium veal found its way onto the dinner plates only of the wealthy. In time things changed, first in Europe in the 1950s, then in the 1960s in the United States. A new production system was introduced that enabled veal calves to live four or five months, during which time they more than tripled their birth weight, without the calves' flesh losing its desired pale color and tenderness. With the advent of larger calves, the industry offered milk-fed veal to an expanded market by selling it at a more affordable price.

For the system to work, milk-fed veal calves are permanently confined in individual stalls. Recommended stall dimensions in the United States are 24 inches wide by 65 inches long. Veal production systems can range from 50 to more than 3,000 stalls, with 200 the average. Of the approximately 1,400 systems in the United States, most are found in Indiana, Michigan, New York, Pennsylvania, and Wisconsin. Approximately 450 are located in Pennsylvania alone.

Because calves lick their surroundings, because metal box stalls contain iron, and because extra iron can help turn their flesh red, the stalls are made of wood. *The Stall Street Journal*, a now defunct veal industry newsletter, explains: "Color of veal is one of the primary factors involved in obtaining 'top dollar' returns from the fancy veal markets. . . . 'Light color' veal is a premium item much in demand at better clubs, hotels and restaurants. 'Light color' or pink veal is partly associated with the amount of iron in the muscle of calves."

Of course, if iron is totally eliminated from their diet, the calves' lives could be placed in jeopardy, as would the farmers' financial interests. So *some* iron is included in the total liquid diet (a combination of nonfat powdered milk, vitamins, minerals, sugar, antibiotics, and growth-enhancing drugs) the calves are fed twice a day, throughout the duration of their short lives. This, not their mother's milk, is the dietary history of so-called milk-fed veal.

To withhold real milk and other plentiful sources of iron from veal calves makes perfectly good sense to veal producers. In the words of *The Stall Street Journal*, "the dual aims of veal production are firstly, to produce a calf of the greatest weight in the shortest possible time and, secondly, to keep its meat as light colored as possible to fulfill the consumer's requirement." For calves, this means being raised in a chronically iron-deficient (that is to say, a chronically anemic) condition.

When the calves are small and able to turn around in their stalls, a metal or plastic tether prevents them from doing so. Later, when they are three or four hundred pounds and too large to turn around in their narrow enclosures, the tether may be removed. Whether tethered or not, the animals are all but immobilized. Calves are notorious for their friskiness. We all have seen these boisterous youngsters gamboling across spacious pastures, their tender muscles firming up to support their increasing weight. Not so the calves raised in veal crates. The conditions of their confinement ensure that their muscles will remain limp so their flesh retains the degree of tenderness that, according to the *Journal*, "fulfill(s) the customers' requirement."

The stalls in which individual calves are confined have slatted floors made either of wood or metal covered with plastic. In theory, the openings between the slats prevent urine and excrement from collecting. The theory does not work well in practice. When the animals lie down, they lie in their own waste. When they stand, their footing is unsure on the slippery slats. Unable to turn around, the calves cannot clean themselves. Unable to move without the prospect of slipping, they learn to stand in one place for long periods of time, a passive adjustment to their surroundings that takes its toll on their anatomy, especially their knees, which often are discernibly swollen and painful.

Independent scientific observers have confirmed what people of plain common sense already know. Veal calves suffer, both physically and psychologically. Physically, they suffer because the majority of these animals endure the pain and discomfort of swollen joints, digestive disorders, and chronic diarrhea. Psychologically, they suffer because their lives of solitary confinement are characterized by abject deprivation. Throughout their lives they are denied the opportunity to suckle and graze; denied the opportunity to stretch their legs; denied the fresh air and sunlight they naturally enjoy.

In a word, calves raised in veal crates are denied virtually everything that answers to their nature. That they display behavioral patterns (for example, repetitive movements and tongue rolling) associated with psychological maladjustment should surprise no one. These animals are not well, not in body, not in mind. When the day arrives for them to go to their foreordained slaughter, not as the frolicsome creatures they might have been, but as the stunted "fancy" meat machines their producers and consumers have made them, death arguably offers these forlorn animals a better bargain than the lives they have known.

Not surprisingly, the veal industry drapes itself in the mantle of humane concern for animal welfare. "Because veal farmers recognize that their livelihood depends upon the health and well-being of their animals," states the American Veal Industry, "the humane production of veal calves is a top industry priority." "The humane production of veal calves." This is what it says. I am not making it up. We are being asked to believe that vealers treat the animals in their care compassionately, with mercy and kindness, with genuine concern for their well-being. Remember the Disconnect Dictum? What these industries do does not match what they say. A clearer example of the Dictum is hard to imagine. "Humane treatment" is just a rhetorical tool used by veal industry spokespersons. It has no basis in fact. Regrettably, too many people are too trusting and believe it. After all, if anything was wrong, government inspectors and spokespersons for the American Veterinary Medical Association would tell us, wouldn't they? And yet nothing I have described violates any law. And nothing I have described runs counter to the AVMA's breast-beating support of "humane" treatment of veal calves. That must be because everything is just fine.

FACTORY FARMING

Compared with the other animals raised for human consumption, the total number of milk-fed veal calves who end up on America's dinner plates is small— some eight hundred thousand of the approximately *ten billion* farmed animals slaughtered annually, more than twenty-seven million every day, in excess of a million every hour. A million every hour, just in the United States. But while their number is small, the lifeway of "milk-fed" veal calves is a microcosm of the larger reality of commercial animal agriculture as it is practiced today.

The myth of Old McDonald's Farm dies hard. Whatever the reasons, and in the face of years of ARA efforts to educate the general public, many people persist in believing that farm animals live in bucolic conditions. The truth is another matter. The vast majority of animals who enter and exit through the doors of today's commercial animal industry live lives not very different from those of veal calves. Intensive rearing systems ("factory farms") are the rule, not the exception. As highlighted below, hogs, chickens, cattle, and other animals raised for human consumption, not just veal calves, have become so many biological machines.

The reasons behind the ascendancy of factory farming are not hard to find. The profit motive, aided by government subsidies and price supports, drives the industry. Animal agriculture is a business, after all, whose object is to maximize financial return while minimizing financial investment. The key to financial success is a variation on the main theme found in veal production.

Factory farming requires that animals be taken off the land and raised indoors. This is important. Indoor farming enables a comparatively few people to raise hundreds, sometimes (as is true in the case of laying hens and broiler chickens) hundreds of thousands of animals, something that would be impossible if the animals were free to roam.

Next, farmers must do whatever is necessary to bring the animals to market in the shortest possible time. Measures that might be taken include limiting the animals' mobility, manipulating their appetite so that they eat more than they would in natural conditions, and stimulating their weight gain by including growth-enhancing hormones in their feed. In the words of *The Stall Street Journal*, it is essential "to produce a calf [or a chicken or a hog, for example] of the greatest weight in the shortest possible time." Those farmers who fail the test fail in the marketplace of commercial animal agriculture. And many do. Unable to compete with their large corporate neighbors, powerless against the economies of scale and massive government assistance enjoyed by the multinationals, Old McDonalds' Farms are an endangered species. As is true of farming in America in general, when it comes to raising animals for human consumption, agribusiness has replaced agriculture.

Others have written in detail about factory-farming practices. Readers looking for this level of information will find it in the relevant books referenced in the accompanying notes and at the website given in the prologue. Especially recommended (because very little is said on these matters here) are studies that document the incredible costs factory farming exacts on human health and environmental quality. Here it will suffice to summarize, like so many snapshots, examples of how other factory-farmed animals are treated. The recurring theme is a retelling of the misery endured by calves destined for the veal trade. Because farmed animals are seen as commodities, they have no right to respectful treatment. Because they lack this right, their pain and deprivation need no justification. And because their pain and deprivation need no justification, pain and deprivation are heaped upon them in amounts beyond human calculation.

THE HOG INDUSTRY

Approximately one hundred million hogs are slaughtered annually in the United States. Most spend the four to six months of their lives standing and sleeping on surfaces of wire mesh, when they are born, and on metal or concrete slats soon thereafter. Foot and leg injuries as well as skin abrasions and bruises are standard and go untreated. Dysentery, cholera, trichinosis, and other diseases are common. Newborn hogs have their tails removed and ears notched without the benefit of anesthetic. In their overcrowded conditions, these normally docile animals sometimes resort to cannibalism.

Piglets who do not grow fast enough (the "runts" of the litter) are killed by having their heads "thumped" against the concrete floor. Because of the dust, dander, and ammonia that fill the air, most hogs suffer from respiratory disease; for example, it is estimated that 70 percent have pneumonia at slaughter.

Breeder sows, weighing as much as four hundred pounds, are confined to two-foot-wide stalls for most of their breeding lives, which can be as long as four years. Tethering the animals to the front of their stalls lessens mobility further. A Dutch animal behaviorist describes the sows' response, writing that they "threw themselves violently backward, straining against the tether. Sows thrashed their heads about as they twisted and turned in their struggle to free themselves. Often loud screams were emitted and occasionally individuals crashed bodily against the side[s] . . . of the tether stalls. This sometimes resulted in sows collapsing to the floor."

As Matthew Scully discovered, things are even worse for sows in America. A speechwriter for President George W. Bush, Scully describes the conditions he found in one of the better hog operations in North Carolina:

> Sores, tumors, ulcers, pus pockets, lesions, cysts, bruises, torn ears, swollen legs everywhere. Roaring, groaning, tail biting, fighting and other "vices," as they're called in the industry. Frenzied chewing on bars and chains, stereotypical "vacuum" chewing on nothing at all, stereotypical rooting and nest building with imaginary straw. And "social defeat," lots of it, every third or fourth stall some completely broken being you know is alive only because she blinks and stares up at you . . . creatures beyond the power of pity to help or indifference to make more miserable, dead to the world except as heaps of flesh.

The plant's owner assured Scully that the hogs were treated "humanely." In fact, when asked what the hogs thought, the owner's enthusiastic reply was, "They love it!"

Compare these wretched circumstances with the kind of life that even factory-farmed pigs are capable of having. Two Scottish scientists released a group of intensively raised pigs in a small park, then stepped back and watched how they got on with their lives. Bernard Rollin describes what they saw:

> It was found that pigs built a series of communal nests in a cooperative way. These nests displayed certain common features, including walls to protect the animals against prevailing winds and a wide view that allowed the pigs to see what was approaching. The nests were far from the feeding sites. Before retiring to the nests, the animals brought additional nesting materials for the walls and rearranged the nests. On arising in the morning, the animals walked at least 7 meters before urinating and defecating. . . .
>
> The pigs formed complex social bonds between certain animals, and new animals introduced to the area took a long time to be assimilated. Some formed special relationships—for example, a pair of sows would join together after farrowing, and forage and sleep together. Members of the litter of the same sex tended to stay together and to pay attention to one another's exploratory behavior. Young males also attended to the behavior of older males. Juveniles of both sexes exhibited manipulative play. In autumn, 51 percent of the day was devoted to rooting.
>
> Pregnant sows would choose a nest site several hours before giving birth, a significant distance from the communal nest (6 kilometers in one case). Nests were built, sometimes even with log walls. The sow would not allow other pigs to intrude for several days but might eventually allow another sow with a litter, with which she had previously established a bond, to share the nest. . . . Piglets began exploring the environment at about 5 days of age.

Commenting on these findings, Scully speaks for humane humans everywhere when he observes that "[these] pigs, in short, bear an amazing resemblance to pigs. . . . They remain, miraculously, living creatures with a nature of their own."

Evidently, the conditions Scully found on that hog farm in North Carolina are required by (or at least they must be compatible with) "humane care for swine." States the National Pork Producers Council in its Position Statement, "Research and Production Issues": "Pork producers have always recognized their moral obligation to provide humane care for their animals." What was true in the past remains true today, as "pork producers strive to provide humane care for swine." It's those "animal rights and vegetarian activists" who are the ones who cannot be trusted; they are the ones who are "mislead[ing] well meaning people who care about animals." Thank heavens we have "legislation that will protect [pork producers] from animal rights violence." And thank heavens as well that we have the NPPC to "strong[ly] resist any effort to adopt animal-rights inspired regulations or legislation."

Turning pigs into commodities, the deliberate reduction of them into mere things, characterizes the mindset of the industry. "The breeding sow should be thought of, and treated as, a valuable piece of machinery," advises a corporate manager of Wall's Meat Company, "whose function is to pump out baby pigs like a sausage machine." Say what you will, the hog industry is mighty good at this.

THE POULTRY INDUSTRY

The poultry industry is more than chickens. It includes ducks, geese, guinea fowl, pheasants, pigeons, quail, and turkeys. Still, chickens are numerically the largest population, whether they are raised for their meat ("broilers") or their eggs ("layers"). The treatment they receive is representative of other factory-farmed poultry.

Broilers

Approximately nine billion chickens are slaughtered annually in the United States. Characteristically, these animals are raised on open floors in low-slung metal sheds, some containing as many as thirty thousand birds. Average space is less than one square foot per each mature animal. As a result of selective breeding, broilers today are almost twice as heavy at slaughter as their ancestors. However, because the animals' skeletal system has remained the same, vertebra injuries, broken bones, and inflamed joints are common. Moreover, because of the added weight, cardiovascular systems are strained and heart attacks are an everyday occurrence. Hundreds of millions of broilers die annually because of the environments in which they live.

The oppressive smell of ammonia permeating broiler operations comes from decomposing droppings. The ammonia fumes assault the animals' immune systems and respiratory tracts; diseases of the eye, even blindness, are not unusual.

On average, male broilers live six weeks, females seven, before being transported to slaughter. Given their natural life span (chickens can live healthy lives of twelve to fifteen years, and sometimes longer), broilers at slaughter are mere babies. What small proportion of life they have is characterized by chronic deprivation and acute suffering.

Layers

Approximately three hundred million hens are laying eggs on any given day in America. Average annual egg production per bird? Approximately 250. Average length of life? Two years.

The vast majority of layers are packed into batteries, metal cages arranged in tiers. The hens below live in a steady stream of excrement produced by those above. Whatever their position in the industry's pecking order, living conditions are cramped. As many as ten (the industry average is between seven and eight) hens share a space roughly equivalent to the size of a file drawer.

Layers are not anatomically adapted to standing on wire for years. Almost half the birds have leg or claw abnormalities. Most have sores and abrasions from rubbing against their enclosure. All endure the pain and trauma of debeaking.

"Forced molting" is a common practice. In order to "encourage" another laying cycle, layers are denied food for ten to fourteen days, during which time they can lose as much as 25 percent of their body weight. As many as 10 percent of layers die during the molting period.

Like male calves born on a dairy farm, male chicks born on egg farms are in the wrong place. Since this happens 50 percent of the time, each year some 150 million male chicks are killed the same day they are born. The means used vary. Sometimes the newborns are (literally) thrown into garbage cans, the ones on the bottom suffocating to death; at other times they are ground alive. Analgesics are never used.

Not surprisingly, the poultry industry is solidly in favor of animal welfare and opposed to animal cruelty. In its "Animal Care/Well-Being Guidelines," the U.S. Poultry and Eggs Association (USPOULTRY) states that "[a]buse of animals should not be tolerated under any circumstances." In fact, USPOULTRY "has always supported humane treatment of animals." And what might such treatment look like? Well, it just happens to look like what is being done. The current system is "consistent with the generally accepted criteria of humane treatment." This includes forced molting, which "benefit[s] both the producer and the animals."

As is true in general, so in this case: The Disconnect Dictum rules. What poultry industry spokespersons say does not match what the poultry industry does. I believe that anyone who views, with an unbiased eye, the practices of the industry cannot help but see the tragic falsehoods endemic to how the industry's wordsmiths describe these practices.

THE CATTLE INDUSTRY

Dairy Cattle

At least half of America's dairy cattle are raised permanently indoors, almost always on concrete, a kind of flooring to which they are not anatomically adapted. As a result, the majority of these animals find it painful to rise and stand. A large percentage of cattle not housed indoors are raised on "dry lots," barren enclosures without a blade of grass on which to graze or a bed of straw on which to rest.

On average, dairy cattle are impregnated once a year for three or four years, after which many are sold for cheaper beef products. (Fully 40 percent of the hamburger sold in stores and restaurants comes from the flesh of discarded dairy cows). As a result of genetic manipulation and selective breeding, some dairy cattle produce as much as one hundred pounds of milk a day, ten times their normal capacity. This excess weight strains the udder and aggravates leg and hip injuries. Fully 20 percent of these animals suffer from mastitis, an inflammation of the udder. Healthy dairy cattle, in a supportive environment, can live to be twenty-five.

Beef Cattle

Cattle sold for beef (upwards of thirty-five million annually, just in the United States) are branded, dehorned, and in the case of males, castrated, all without the benefit of anesthetic. It is not uncommon for these animals to be born in one state, raised in a second, and slaughtered in a third. Water, food, and veterinary care are not provided even during hundreds of miles of transport.

Most beef cattle spend much of their lives at feed lots. Some of the larger ones are hundreds of acres and house more than one hundred thousand animals. The cattle live permanently out of doors without protection or anything for bedding except dirt, mud, and manure. By nature, these animals are ruminants, preferring grasses and roughage. At feed lots, their diet is almost exclusively grain, which (along with heavy doses of growth stimulants) accelerates weight gain and gives their flesh the white "marbling" characteristic of more expensive cuts of beef.

Lest anyone else might be tempted to keep burgers off their plate and out of their bodies because of how beef cattle are treated, the National Cattlemen's Beef Association wants to assure us that "[c]attlemen are committed to providing the utmost in humane care for their livestock." In fact, they have "a moral responsibility" to do so.

"HUMANE" SLAUGHTER

Everyone should go to at least one slaughterhouse, at least once. It is an unforgettable experience. I know I still carry the memory of a solitary black cow with me. The larger operations are more anonymous, filled with the noise of the animals when they are off-loaded, the bellowing of the cows, the hysterical squeals of the pigs. Many of the workers say the animals know why they are there, and many of the animals strenuously resist being forced into the chute from which there is no return. Those animals who resist the most are punished the most, with electric prods or chains or swift kicks. The helplessness of the animals— and the helplessness I felt in the face of this engine of death, wanting to make it stop but unable to do so—is one of every ARA's nightmares. By the time the animals are off-loaded, it is way too late to do anything to help them.

Hog slaughter represents a variation on the main theme of the meatpacking industry. Hogs are driven up a narrow restrainer where the "stunner" gives them an electric shock that is supposed to render them unconscious, as required by the Humane Slaughter Act (HSA), passed in 1958. (Remarkably, poultry, far and away the most numerous farmed animals slaughtered, are explicitly excluded from the Act's provisions). After being rendered unconscious, hogs are then shackled with chains attached to their rear legs, hoisted so that they dangle upside down, and placed on a conveyor belt where they meet the "sticker," whose job is to slit the animals' throats. After being bled to death, the pigs are submerged in a tank of scalding water, then eviscerated, having never regained consciousness. At least this is the way things are supposed to work in theory. In practice, as Gail Eisnitz found in her undercover investigation of America's slaughter industry, things frequently do not work out this way.

As Americans, we pride ourselves in being decent people. We all want to think animals, even animals in slaughterhouses, get a fair deal. Surely the HSA is vigorously enforced for the animals' sake. Although they have spent their lives in misery and deprivation, surely their death must be painless. It might have been possible to believe this in the past; since the publication of Eisnitz's book, it no longer is. Among the deficiencies Eisnitz documents are the following:

1. People working in slaughterhouses sometimes are unaware that there is such a thing as the Humane Slaughter Act.
2. Inspectors charged with enforcing the HSA are not expected to be present in those areas where animals are slaughtered.
3. Inspectors who observe unlawful activity in these areas can be charged with "neglect of duty." The reasoning goes like this: If they saw what was happening, they were where they were not supposed to be. If they were where they were not supposed to be, they were neglecting their duty. Therefore, they were neglecting their duty.
4. Inspectors who try to stop the "line" (of animals heading for slaughter) because of a violation of the HSA "have been reprimanded, reassigned, physically attacked by plant employees [then] disciplined for being in fights, had their performance appraisals lowered, been placed under criminal investigation, fired or been subjected to other forms of retaliation that were necessary to 'neutralize' them."
5. It is a commonplace for hogs to enter the scalding tank while fully conscious. As one worker says, "Happens all the time."

When it comes to enforcement of the HSA, Eisnitz puts the question to someone who should know. Roberto Macias has spent his entire adult life in the meatpacking industry. The former chairman of the National Joint Council of Food Inspection Locals, Macias states flatly that "The Humane Slaughter Act is not being enforced." In fact, things are so bad inside America's twenty-seven hundred slaughterhouses that Macias estimates that "as many as 90 percent of the vets [are] not effectively enforcing even meat safety regulations. And [he says, chillingly] I can't conceive an inspector stopping the line for humane violations." In other words, any thought of "humane treatment" in the slaughterhouse goes out the window once the animals are inside.

Symbolic of the "humane" treatment animals receive at slaughterhouses is the plight of so-called downers. These are animals who are so sick or so badly injured they cannot stand up or walk. Depending on conditions at the plant, downers can lie on the ground for a day or more, without water, food, or veterinary care. Whether dead or alive, eventually they are pulled inside the slaughterhouse by chains or hoisted by a forklift. A Zogby America poll found that 79 percent of the adults interviewed opposed the slaughter of downers.

Not the dairy industry, which lobbied vigorously to delete legislation before the Congress in 2001 that aspired to ban the sale of downers. Why would the dairy industry oppose such minimal legislation? Because "most . . . downed animals are dairy cows that can be slaughtered for their meat after they no longer can produce milk."

The meatpacking industry also vigorously opposed the proposed downer legislation. Why waste an animal? According to the American Meat Institute, "A common theme among all [religious] faiths has been a respect for animals, avoidance of animal suffering, and appreciation of the nourishment that they provide. These themes permeate the practices of the meatpacking industry. Regardless of their religious backgrounds, those who work in packing plants are concerned about livestock well-being and increasingly recognize the many benefits of humane handling and stunning." When the treatment downers receive qualifies as "humane," we know we are in Disconnect Dictum country. Whatever it is that explains why they say what they do, industry spokespersons are not to be believed when they say it.

FISH SLAUGHTER

Whether fish are subjects-of-a-life was an issue we tabled in chapter 4. Are they aware of the world? Aware of what happens to them? Does what happens to them matter to them, whether anybody else cares or not? I think yes is the correct answer to each question. Suppose this is true. If it is, then a minimal moral requirement demands that we forgo killing them for their flesh. Unfortunately for fish, many people have a different idea.

The American fish industry kills approximately seven billion fish (this figure excludes shellfish) annually. The minimal protection afforded by the Animal Welfare Act (AWA) does not apply to them; fish are explicitly excluded when it comes to how they are raised, caught, used in research, or slaughtered. How are they killed? Joan Dunayer describes some of the methods used to kill fish on fish farms:

> At slaughter, most trout [from trout farms] are dumped into a mix of water and ice. Struggling to breathe, they suffer until, after about ten minutes, lack of oxygen renders them unconscious. . . . Most salmon are dumped into water infused with

carbon dioxide, which is painful to breathe. The carbon dioxide paralyses them, but most still are conscious when their gill arches are slit for bleeding. Standardly, catfishes are paralyzed when electricity surges through their holding tanks. Because the current isn't directed through their brain, they feel a shock. If the current is too weak, they're conscious when a band saw or other blade cuts off their head.

Although fish are exempt from the protection ostensibly provided by the federal legislation, the fish flesh industry wants everyone to know that they kill fish humanely. In the case of trout farms in England, for example, the Humane Slaughter Association proudly informs readers that electrical fish-killing machines are being developed "that [will harvest] fish in a humane manner, whilst retaining the speed and efficiency of current methods." Just because the industry kills fish fast does not mean it kills them inhumanely. Right?

Americans who kill fish for "sport" (245 million deaths annually) also advocate "humane" methods of killing, including the following:

Priest

A priest is a small cosh for dispatching fish. These can be bought or fashioned at home from a piece of piping. The fish is hit quickly and sharply behind the eyes resulting in instant death. This method requires a bit of practice to get the aim right. If the blow is too soft the fish may simply become stunned and recover later; tales of fish suddenly resurrecting in the kitchen abound. If in doubt hit twice. If done properly this method is humane and is one of the most common techniques used by anglers.

Banging Head on Hard Surface

The fish is held upside down and its head is hit on a rock, rail, tackle box etc. This is effective with small fish such as whiting and mackerel but awkward with large species.

When behavior like this counts as humane, we know we are in the vicinity of the Disconnect Dictum. Sometimes the most damning things that can be said about people are the things they say about themselves. None of this should be happening, if fish have rights. However, for reasons already given, I will not press this issue beyond saying the following: The reasons for viewing fish as subjects-of-a-life are so plausible, that I personally would rather err on the side of moral caution and give them the benefit of the doubt—which is why I think we should think and act *as if* fish have rights. The days of the *pesce* vegetarian are numbered. At least they should be.

FARMED-ANIMAL SANCTUARIES

Part of the *Random House College Dictionary*'s definition of "sanctuary" includes the words "any place providing refuge." Farmed-animal sanctuaries do this for farmed animals: they offer them refuge in a safe environment where they are free to be who they are, usually for the first time in their lives. It is hard to believe the differences in appearance, behavior, and health of farmed animals after they have been rescued from the horrors of factory farming. Karen Davis, of United Poultry Concerns (Karen has been a one-person army in her defense of chickens and other birds), tells the following not untypical story about two hens at her sanctuary:

> Penny and Sweet Pea had a terrible life before they came to United Poultry Concerns. They spent their entire lives stuffed in a tiny wire cage [on a factory farm] . . . They weren't allowed to do anything but lay eggs and eat powdery food to be turned into more eggs. Penny and Sweet Pea never even saw the sun until they were rescued one day in March. Three months later in June, these sad little hens were completely changed. In March, their feathers were scraggly, their combs were sickly, and their eyes were murky. They had never walked or spread their wings. They could hardly stand up, let alone fly!
>
> Now they run around the yard on their strong little legs with snowy feathers, red combs, and bright eyes. They dart around like dancers.

Among the notable farmed-animal sanctuaries are Animal Place and Suwanna Ranch, both in California, the latter operated by Humane Farming Association. Farm Sanctuary, a pioneer in the field, with two sanctuaries (one in Watkins Glen, New York, the other in Orland, California), describes the growing phenomenon of farmed-animal refuges in these words. "The farm animal sanctuary movement provides life-long shelter for victims of 'food animal' production and educates the public about the animal suffering associated with meat, dairy, egg, and poultry production. Through its rescue and education efforts, the movement is playing a key role in changing the way society views and treats 'food animals.'"

Our culture teaches us *not* to see hens like Penny and Sweat Pea as distinct individuals. The same is true of pigs. As befits the prejudicial glasses through which our culture sees them, most of us probably believe that if we've seen one pig, we've seen them all. But then most of us (and I include myself in this group) have probably never really known a pig.

My favorite pig story dissolves this prejudice. It takes place when Sue Coe, who has done more through her paintings and prints to help animals than any other artist in history, meets Lorri Bauston, cofounder with her husband, Gene, of Farm Sanctuary. The setting: an exhibition of some of Sue's work. Sue had executed one of her prints using a photograph of a pig. There were quite a few pigs represented in this print, but just one that was based on this particular photograph.

When Lorri saw the print hanging on the wall, she burst into tears. "There's Hope!" she cried. "Yes, yes," Sue said, "There is always hope." "No," Lorri insisted, "I mean, there's Hope!" "Yes, yes," Sue repeated, reassuringly, "There is always hope." "No," Lorri insisted even more emphatically, in tears, this time pointing to the pig in the picture, the one based on the photograph. "I mean *the pig in the picture:* her name is Hope. She lives with us!" And so it was. When the photo was traced to its origins, that was Hope in Sue's print all right. Out of the many millions of pigs in the world, Lorri recognized a friend when she saw her. The moral of the story? If we ever *really* see a pig, we'll know, as Lorri Bauston knows, that we haven't seen them all.

"But why did Lorri cry?" I am always asked when I relate this story. "She cried," I answer, "because, in Sue's print, Hope was shown on her way to slaughter."

I say nothing new when I note that we tend to underestimate the intelligence of farmed animals. Probably everyone has heard that pigs are just as smart (if not smarter) than dogs. What may come as a surprise are results from studies showing that pigs can develop some behaviors that put them on a par with nonhuman primates. For example, like chimps, pigs can use their knowledge of what other pigs believe to mislead them, the better to obtain food for themselves.

So, yes, pigs are intelligent, highly social creatures. But intelligent sheep? If we ask the people who study these animals, the answer is yes. Sheep have been shown to have remarkable memories. Not only do they quickly learn to recognize faces (both sheep and human), they are able to remember them even after they have not seen them for more than two years. The person who reported these findings, Dr. Keith Kendrick of the Babraham Institute in Great Britain, said that "the sophisticated face recognition abilities imply sheep value social interactions with flock-mates and some humans." When interviewed Dr. Kendrick allowed that, although he was "not a vegetarian," he had "not eaten lamb in a while." A Muddler in the making if I ever saw one.

Do cows remember? Is there something going on there, behind those big brown eyes? In another film made by James LaVeck and Jenny Stein (this one called *The Peaceable Kingdom*), we meet Harold, a young man who grew up on a farm and with other members of his family, raised, cared for, and slaughtered animals. After hearing a talk by Gene Bauston, Harold decides to adopt a young cow named Snickers. Harold visits Farm Sanctuary, spends time with Snickers, then leaves, feeling that he and Snickers have a special bond. A year passes and Harold returns to Farm Sanctuary. Here is how he describes what happened:

> All the cows were up in the barn, and Snickers is over in the far corner, and of course it's been about a year since I've seen him. So I walk about halfway to him and I look at him and I say, "Snickers!" and I put out my arms. And it was unbelievable. He ran over to me, as much as a cow can run. He runs over to me and he puts his head right on my chest, he just thumps me right in the chest with his forehead, and he just stands there leaning against me.

Not a scientific study, to be sure, but Snickers had never behaved this way with anyone else before. If we reason to the best explanation, the conclusion is obvious. Snickers remembered Harold and was glad to see him.

Then there are those proverbial "bird brains" of the barnyard, chickens, surely the most maligned and abused animal on the face of the earth, and—just as surely—among the brightest, most social birds we'll find anywhere. Recent studies confirm what Karen Davis and the Baustons knew already: Chickens not only are capable of learning, they are also capable of teaching one another. It turns out that chickens are not as dumb as popular mythology makes them out to be.

ARAs might be forgiven for hoping that the increasing recognition of the cognitive abilities of farmed animals will hasten the day when their cages are empty. Unfortunately, the farmed-animal industry sees things differently. Commenting on the findings showing that pigs are equal to nonhuman primates in some tests of intelligence, the director of the study, Dr. Mike Mendel, told reporters that "[a] better understanding of animal intelligence could help farmers tackle problems such as aggression in pigs, which causes death and injuries and accounts for an estimated 20 million pounds ($30 million) each year in lost revenue in Britain." In other words, rather than these new insights into the cognitive abilities of pigs giving their exploiters reason to ponder the morality of what they are doing to them, they hope to use this new knowledge to exploit them more efficiently. For them, there are only vases, not faces (or vice versa).

CONCLUSION

For most of my life I had no direct contact with farmed animals and, before reading Gandhi, no interest in learning anything about them. It was his vegetarian challenge that motivated me to go to factory farms and slaughterhouses, to see for myself what was happening. I wanted to know whether the government's and the AVMA's assurances that "all is well" were credible. What I saw and learned had a profound impact on the future direction of my life. Some of what I saw and learned I have shared in these pages. It does not make for pleasant reading. Unfortunately, sometimes the truth is like that.

When it comes to the ethical question of turning animals into food, the ARA position is both simple and clear. We ought to stop eating the bodies of animals ("meat"), just as we ought to stop eating "animal products," such as milk, cheese, and eggs. Commercial animal agriculture is not possible without the violation of the rights of farmed animals, including violations of their right to life. More fundamentally, commercial animal agriculture violates the right of animals to be treated with respect. We are never justified in injuring the bodies, limiting the freedom, or taking the lives of animals because human beings will benefit, even assuming that we do.

To eat in ways that show respect for animals, though it is unusual at this point in American history and while it may cause some inconvenience now and again, is no great hardship. As I mentioned at the beginning of this chapter, there is an incredibly delicious, colorful, and nutritious animal-free cuisine out there to be discovered, a menu of possibilities that includes foods from every place and ethnicity in the world. For Nancy and me, discovering this cuisine, trying it, and enjoying it, taught us more about the diversity of the world than anything we ever learned in classes in history or cultural anthropology. I said this before, but let me say it again: It is the great new food we gain, not the customary old food we lose, that is the real vegan surprise.

As for the estimated ten billion farmed animals who will be raised and slaughtered this year, just in America, it is hard to find the words adequately to describe the institutionalized cruelty they must endure, every minute of every day, even including the last moments of their lives. Among the many memorable things Gandhi says, one seems especially appropriate here. "The greatness of a nation and its moral progress," he writes, "can be judged by how its animals are treated." I am sorry to say that America, the nation I love above all others, does not fare well given this simple standard.

TURNING ANIMALS
INTO CLOTHES

The most common justification of meat eating is that it is necessary. Every red-blooded American knows that we have to eat meat. Without three or more ample portions a day, we won't get enough protein. And without enough protein, we'll end up either sick or dead, take your pick. That is certainly what I was taught while I was growing up, and what I continued to believe well into young adulthood.

The protein myth (you have to eat meat to get your protein) once enjoyed wide currency among the general public. Times have changed. Today, more and more people are beginning to understand that all the protein humans need for optimal health can be obtained without eating meat (a vegetarian diet) and without eating meat or any other food derived from animals, including milk, cheese, and eggs (a vegan diet). Even the Food and Drug Administration, no friend of vegetarianism in the past, today waves a dietary flag of truce. In its most recent assessment, the FDA acknowledges that vegetarianism and veganism offer positive, healthful dietary options.

Still, one thing meat eating historically has had in its favor is its presumed necessity for achieving two very important human goods: health and survival. The same is not true in the case of another ongoing chapter in the history of human exploitation of nonhuman animals: taking their skin, or fleece, or fur off their backs to make something for humans to wear. True, wearing fur might be necessary for health and survival if we are Inuits who choose to remain in the far North. But in the case of people on the streets of New York? The shopping malls of Chicago or Atlanta? The ski lodges of Aspen? No, neither health nor survival explains wearing fur in these places. The reason is *fashion*. And, truth to tell, when it comes to making a fashion statement, in some circles nothing speaks louder than fur—which was why, those many years ago, I bought Nancy that smart looking mink hat. She was *in style!*

As for clothes or accessories made from the skin or fleece of animals, these are as ho-hum as leather shoes and belts, wool jackets and sweaters, standard items of clothing for most Americans. I mean, who can possibly be against buying and wearing leather or wool? I wore both for most of my life. If someone had told me back then that I was doing something wrong, I would have thought they had a screw loose somewhere. The only problem was, this was before I knew the price animals pay to "give" us the fleece or skin off their backs.

The present chapter reviews some of the ways animals are exploited for their fur, skin, or fleece. It begins with a description of the kind of fur that originates in America. This section also includes a description of the annual slaughter of harp seals in the Northwest Atlantic (conducted in Canada and Greenland), information about fur from karakul (Persian) lambs, and facts about the international market in cat and dog fur. In addition to fur, other industries discussed are leather and wool. The chapter concludes with a general ARA statement regarding the ethics of turning animals into clothes and offers some suggestions (from a nonsartorial expert, to be sure) on what to look for the next time we go shopping for new clothes.

THE AMERICAN FUR INDUSTRY

The number of animals utilized by the fur industry has varied over time. Approximately 4.5 million animals were killed for fur in the United States in 2001. Mink is the most common source, accounting for roughly 80 percent of all retail fur sales.

Where does fur originate? In the not too distant past, trappers were the primary source of fur pelts, but recent years have seen a major shift in methods of procurement. Today, the majority of animals destined for the fur trade (2.5 million) are raised on what the industry calls "ranches," a word that conjures up bucolic images associated with Old McDonald's Farm, only this time for mink and other fur-bearing animals. As it happens, a "fur ranch" is as close to an actual ranch as a veal stall is to a pasture. A more appropriate name is "fur mill," since these operations produce fur-bearing animals the way steel mills produce girders.

Fur Mill Fur

Fur mills throughout the world share the same basic architecture. They consist of long rows of wire mesh cages raised several feet off the ground. The cages have a roof overhead, and the entire structure is surrounded by a fence. (The fence ensures that any animals who happen to fall through or free themselves from their cage will not escape.) A fur mill might contain as few as one hundred or as many as one hundred thousand animals. Among the fur bearers raised are mink, chinchilla, raccoon, lynx, and foxes. For 2001 the U.S. Department of Agriculture gave 324 as the number of fur mills operating throughout the country.

Mink breeder cages, which house mothers and their kits, can contain as many as eight animals. Except for the tracks they leave behind, mink in the wild, with a home territory up to two and one-half miles in length, are rarely seen. Nocturnal creatures, they spend most of their time in water, and their reputation for being excellent swimmers is well deserved. Confined in cages, mink are like fish out of water. Much of their waking hours finds them pacing, back and forth, back and forth, the boundaries of their diminished lives defined by the path they repeat, over and over again, in their wire mesh world.

As was noted in the discussion of veal calves, repetitive behavior of this sort is a classic symptom of psychological maladjustment. Other forms of repetitive motions (for example, jumping up the sides of cages and rotating their heads) attest to the same thing. Unnaturally confined as they are and denied an environment in which they can express their natural desires to roam and swim, fur mill mink (and we find the same behaviors in all caged fur bearers) give every appearance of being neurotic at best, psychotic at worst.

Whatever its severity, the mental state of animals in fur mills is of no direct economic concern to those who raise them. By contrast, the condition of an animal's coat is, and necessary steps are taken to preserve the coat's integrity. For example, under the stress of close confinement, foxes in breeder cages will sometimes attack one another. Cannibalism among foxes, unknown in the wild, is not unheard of in fur mills. Proprietors respond by reducing cage density from eight to four or even two. In the worst cases, "problem" animals are destroyed.

The premium placed on not spoiling the coat carries over to the methods of killing. No throat slitting here, as is true in the case of the slaughter of veal calves. Noninvasive methods, none of which involves the use of anesthetics, are the rule. In the case of small fur bearers, mink and chinchilla in particular, a common practice is to break the animal's neck. However, because this method is labor-intensive, even these small animals, as is true of many of the larger ones, frequently are asphyxiated through the use of carbon dioxide or carbon monoxide.

In some cases, anal electrocution may be the method of choice. It works this way. First a metal clamp is fastened around the animal's muzzle. Next, one end of an electrified metal rod is shoved up the fox's anus. Then a switch is turned on and the animal is electrocuted to death, "fried" from the inside out. Sometimes the procedure has to be repeated several times before the animal dies. When properly done, these methods yield unblemished pelts. The Chinchilla Industry Council, speaking for chinchilla mills throughout the country, would have us believe that the industry "practice[s] humane conduct toward domestic animals and [seeks] to prevent avoidable suffering at all stages of their lives." Which must explain why the Council regards neck breaking and electrocution as acceptable methods of killing.

In 2002 Scotland joined England and Wales in prohibiting raising mink and other animals solely or primarily for their fur. American lawmakers don't see the need to change. The view from Washington is that fur mills are the very personification of humaneness. Representatives of fur ranchers say so themselves. "In the animal welfare view," states Fur Commission USA, "social traditions and the body of existing law with respect to our use of animals are based on the premise that man's right to use animals for human benefit carries with it the responsibility to do so humanely." Indeed, "[t]oday's farm-raised furbearers are among the world's best cared-for livestock."

I am not making this up. This really is the way Fur Commission USA describes how animals are treated in fur mills. They are treated "humanely," meaning with compassion, kindness, and mercy. In fact, they are "the best cared-for livestock" in the world, a statement that, tragically, just might be true. Compared with veal calves, hogs, and chickens raised in confinement, those lucky mink who spend their waking hours pacing back and forth, jumping up the sides of cages, and rotating their heads are leading a country club existence. May God forgive us.

Trapped Fur

Whereas damaged pelts do not pose a serious problem for fur mill entrepreneurs, they can be a nightmare for those who trap fur-bearing animals in the wild. The fur of these animals can be so bloody and gnarled that it is economically useless. Sometimes this "wastage" (as it is called) results because a trapped animal is attacked by a natural predator. At other times potential pelts are ruined because of the frenzied efforts of the trapped animals, as they attempt to free themselves. In other cases trapped animals chew through their trapped leg ("wring off" in the language of trappers) before crawling away, leaving no pelt at all. Friends of Animals, which has for many years aggressively campaigned against fur, estimates that a quarter of those animals trapped for their fur (roughly 625,000) are lost to wring off. FOA literature would give us to believe that trapped animals certainly have enough time to chew themselves apart. Whatever the species, FOA estimates that these animals can spend up to a week (fifteen hours is given as the average) before they die or are killed by a trapper tending the lines.

In the United States, the steel-jawed and conibear are the most widely used traps. The conibear entraps animals by their head, neck, or upper body; the steel-jawed, by a leg. The design of the latter is simplicity itself. The steel jaws of the trap are held apart by a spring. A pressure-sensitive weight pan is baited. When the animal reaches for the bait, the spring is released and the trap slams shut.

The physical trauma a trapped animal experiences has been likened to slamming a car door on a finger. According to the animal behaviorist Desmond Morris, the shock experienced by trapped animals "is difficult for us to conceive, because it is a shock of total lack of understanding of what has happened to them. They are held, they cannot escape, their response very often is to bite at the metal with their teeth, break their teeth in the process and sometimes even chew through the leg that is being held in the trap." The trap is so barbaric that even the AVMA has spoken out against it. To date, however, legislative efforts to prohibit its use on federally owned lands have been unsuccessful.

Various attempts have been made to design a more "humane" trap, an idea that makes as much sense as "humane slaughter." In place of steel jaws, for example, traps with padded jaws have been tried. None of these alternatives has caught on in the United States, and the steel-jawed leghold trap continues to be used (how often is unclear) by America's estimated 100,000 to 135,000 trappers, this despite the fact that even the AVMA has been moved to condemn the trap for its cruelty. In the fifteen nations that compose the European Union, by contrast, use of the steel-jawed leghold trap became illegal in 1995. Two years later, European Union nations, Canada, and Russia entered into an Agreement on International Humane Trapping Standards, a pact whose true purpose, despite all the rhetoric about "humane traps," is to promote the moral fiction that some traps are kind, compassionate, and merciful, while others are not. Here (again) we have a classic application of the Disconnect Dictum. When people take the platform to tell us about "humane traps," we should politely interrupt to say, "You may be fooling yourself, but you're not fooling us."

Whatever the type of trap used, the device itself obviously cannot distinguish between fur-bearing and so-called nontarget animals, including ducks, birds of prey, and companion animals. Trappers (showing their compassion) refer to these unintended casualties as "trash animals." Because trappers are not required to collect and report such data, hard numbers concerning "trash animals" are hard to come by. FOA estimates the total number of nontarget animals that die in traps at between four and six million annually. If we split the difference and say the number is five million, that works out to approximately fourteen thousand a day, just about ten "trash animals" every minute.

Semiaquatic animals, including mink and beavers, also are trapped in the wild. In their case underwater traps are common. Mink can struggle to free themselves for up to four minutes; beavers, over twenty. Eventually, the trapped animals drown. Comparatively speaking, there is very little wring off or wastage in the case of animals trapped underwater.

Whether made from milled or trapped fur bearers, fur coats require a lot of dead animals—the smaller the animals, the more required. FOA estimates that a forty-inch fur coat, depending on the type, requires 16 coyotes, 18 lynx, 60 mink, 45 opossums, 20 otters, 42 red foxes, 40 raccoon, 50 sables, 8 seals, 50 muskrat, or 15 beavers. Of course, the suffering and death of *trapped* animals used to make fur coats is only part of the story. The number of nontarget animals needs to be added; and the time trapped land animals suffer before dying (fifteen hours, as we have seen, is the FOA estimate) also should be factored in. When the necessary computations are made, a forty-inch fur coat made from coyotes, for example, equals sixteen dead coyotes, *plus* an unknown number of dead nontarget animals, *plus* more than two hundred hours of animal suffering. Similar calculations can be made for the remaining target animals. As is true of many things in life, when it comes to fur coats, there's more than meets the eye.

You wouldn't know the truth about animal suffering if you listened to Marshall Cohen, copresident of NPD Fashionworld, specialists in the analysis of retail trends, with offices in Port Washington, New York. There are wealthy Americans who want to "show the world that the difficult [economic] times haven't affected them. . . . With fur you're saying, 'Everyone is suffering but I'm not.'" Perhaps money would make narcissists of us all. It seems to have had this effect on Robert Verdi, the host of cable television's *Full Frontal Fashion.* "Once I happened upon anti-fur protesters on Fifth Avenue in my raccoon coat," he told a *New York Daily News* reporter. "They started holding up the pictures and screaming at me, 'They used to be cute!' I said, 'Yeah, they used to be cute, and now they're gorgeous!'" And lest anyone be concerned about the history of Verdi's fur, the Fur Information Council of America's Keith Kaplan is standing by to assure everyone that "[o]ur industry is committed to the humane treatment of animals."

THE INTERNATIONAL FUR MARKET: THREE EXAMPLES

The Northwest Atlantic Seal Hunts

Other forms of massive slaughter of wildlife also find outlets for the products of their predation in the fur industry. None is more ignominious than the annual slaughter of harp seals in the Northwest Atlantic.

Long before Europeans settled in what today are Canada and Greenland, the original inhabitants depended for their survival on the seals in these waters. Subsistence hunters, they killed only what they needed to survive. It did not take long for the new settlers to begin to change things. Parts of a dead seal could be sold even if you did not need the seal for reasons of survival, even if you threw the carcass away. (Seal flesh is notoriously bad tasting). The real market was and remains seal pelts. In time, the seal industry replaced aboriginal hunters. Today, the number of seals killed annually in Canada and Greenland (500,000 is a conservative estimate, 350,000 in Canada alone in 2003) represents far and away the largest destruction of marine mammals anywhere in the world. Plans call for increasing quotas in both countries for 2003.

Most of the fatalities (approximately 95 percent) are harp seals, whether newly born (pups), juveniles (beaters), or adults. Of those killed, independent observers estimate that approximately 80 percent are between twelve days and one year old. No law requires that the whole seal (that is, both the pelt and the body) be taken, and it is not unusual for hunters to take only the pelt.

Of course, to refer to these annual events as "hunts" is creative semantics. Picture this: There are the seals, many newly born, lying on the ice; not the speediest sprinters in the world, they are so many defenseless pods of sheer innocence. There are the brave "hunters," beating them to death with hakipiks (wooden clubs with a metal hook at one end) or shooting them. Does anyone see anything remotely resembling a hunt here? Shades of Humpty Dumpty. Following this usage, I go "hunting for pickles" whenever I remove a pickle from a jar.

Like other controversies, people often disagree about the facts relating to the seal hunts. For example, people disagree about how many "hunters" participate. They also disagree about how important the annual hunt is to the economies of Canada and Greenland.

These debates are aired in the notes for this chapter. I believe unbiased readers will find that comparatively few (approximately a third of the fifteen thousand commercial interests and individuals that obtain the required license) actually take part in the hunt. I also believe readers will find that, when all the relevant costs (including direct government subsidies and other indirect forms of assistance) are totaled, the annual seal hunts, in both Canada and Greenland, probably end up losing money. The explanation for why the hunts continue is political, not economic.

The hunts continue because too few elected representatives are willing to go up against the powerful commercial sealing interests and their even more powerful allies in the fishing industry. Newfoundland's Minister of Fisheries and Agriculture, John Efford, speaks for these interests when he says, "I would like to see the 6 million seals, or whatever the number there is out there, killed or sold, destroyed or burned. I do not care what happens to them . . . the more they kill the better I will love it." As long as politicians like Efford continue to hold office and exercise control over government policy, massive numbers of seals will continue to be slaughtered. It really is that simple.

Beginning in the 1960s, an aroused public began to call for an end to the hunts. Few who have seen the photos and videos released at the time will forget the images: Dark-clad hunters clubbing defenseless, big-eyed whitecoats to death, their innocent blood flowing over the ice. In response to the public outcry, Canadian legislators made it illegal to kill a pup younger than two weeks (the age when they begin to molt and lose their white hair). Like other laws that purport to regulate the hunt, however, this restriction may be more honored in the breach than it is in the observance. Government inspection of the Canadian hunt is spotty at best. At least Greenland is honest enough to disassociate itself from Canadian hypocrisy. In Greenland, no crime is committed when whitecoats are bludgeoned or shot to death. To think otherwise (according to Greenland's Supreme Court) would be unconstitutional.

From 1983 forward the countries composing the European Economic Community have banned the importation of whitecoat pelts. The United States has a similar prohibition, set forth in its Marine Mammal Protection Act of 1972. The cumulative effect of these embargoes was not hard to predict: the market for whitecoats dropped dramatically. Today, most "quality" seal pelts are exported to Norway (a non-ECC country) for their fur and leather while the bad taste of seal flesh is "enhanced" in Canada (with support from hefty government subsidies) by chemicals that are supposed to make it taste like salami or bologna. The political power of so inane a position should never be underestimated. In 1994, the Canadian seal industry was all but bottoms-up; in 1995, after instituting "meat subsidies," the hunt was back to 1975 levels. In February 2003 Canadian Fisheries Minister Robert Thibault announced a three-year harvest of 975,000 harp seals, with no more than 350,000 for any given year.

Another factor that helped rejuvenate the Canadian seal hunt was the market for seal penises. Especially in Asia, tonics containing capsules made from these organs are consumed for their alleged aphrodisiac powers. Need a good erection? Seal penis is the answer. In the not too distant past, whole seal penises sold for upwards of five hundred dollars. With the introduction of Viagra as a treatment for male sexual dysfunction, the market for seal penises is less than a fourth of what it was just a few years ago.

The task of enforcing applicable regulations for the Canadian hunt falls to the Department of Fisheries and Oceans. Among the regulations: hunters are required to do a "blink test" to confirm that an animal is dead before skinning. The test consists of hitting seals in their eyes to see if they blink. If they do, they are presumed to be alive; if not, they are presumed to be dead. DFO officials insist that regulations are "strictly enforced." Their assurance is unfounded, as the independent findings of Mary Roberts, DVM, attests:

> I have now reviewed new video evidence obtained by IFAW [International Federation for Animal Welfare] during the 1998 commercial seal hunt. Even though a full year has passed since the 1997 footage was released, it is clear that the DFO, which is responsible for monitoring this hunt, and the Canadian Sealers' Association, which promotes this hunt as well-regulated, have done nothing to ensure that seals are not suffering and that the relevant provisions of the Marine Mammal Regulations and the Criminal Code of Canada are upheld.

Dr. Roberts is no animal rights radical. She is in fact a highly respected professional who has served as Chair of the Animal Care Review Board for the Solicitor General of Ontario and as Director of Animal Welfare for the Ontario Veterinary Medical Association. If asked whom to trust, a spokesperson from DFO or Dr. Roberts, it is hard to imagine how any fair-minded person could choose the former.

The suffering to which Dr. Roberts refers is both real and tragic. Some of the seals are beaten with clubs. Some are shot and die slow, agonizing deaths. Others, wounded and still conscious, are dragged across the ice. Despite official assurances to the contrary, many seals are skinned while still alive. It would be a relief to learn that this happens rarely, though of course it should not happen at all. The bad news is, it happens a lot. An independent scientific study, conducted in 2001 by a team of veterinarians, concluded that fully 42 percent of the seals were skinned alive. That works out to approximately 130,000.

Numbers can be numbing. Sometimes they can make things less rather than more real. People who have followed the annual slaughter have for many years known that things are bad. However, it was not until the publication of Mickey J. Dwyer's *Over the Side, Mickey: A Sealer's First-Hand Account of the Newfoundland Seal Hunt* that readers learned how bad. Things actually are much worse than had been imagined. Surrounded by a supportive culture of cruelty, hunters sink to depths where no human being should go. Here's one example Dwyer experienced himself:

> I had heard the anti-sealing protesters say that sealers were barbarians. They were right. You have to be a barbarian to survive it! . . . How barbaric one became depended on how long one was subjected to it. Once, after only a short time into the Hunt, I had saved up ten heads that we used for two hours to play "head-ball." It

was like hockey but instead of using sticks, we used our hakipiks to try to shoot the head between two twitching carcasses we used as goal posts. We all took turns in the net. By the time it was over, eyeballs, teeth, fragments of skull bone and lower jawbones were scattered all over the rink. Darrell [Dwyer's friend] won but we all had a great bit of fun.

Unless we suppose that other sealers are somehow immune to finding similar ways to have "a great bit of fun" we will refuse to believe Canadian Fisheries Minister Thibault when he assures us that "Canadians place a high value on humane hunting practices. As minister, I intend to uphold this value, and ensure that the seal hunt is conducted humanely and in accordance with all proper regulations."

To speak of "humane" methods and treatment in this context is worse than dishonest. Even the Canadian government must know this. They are so confident that the seals are treated "humanely" they have made it a crime for any "unauthorized" person to take pictures or videotape the hunt. They have nothing to hide. Nothing at all. Rebecca Aldworth, of the International Fund for Animal Welfare–Canada was not deterred. Among the things she saw during the 2003 slaughter:

> The killing methods were cruel. The sealer would club a seal, and it would lie still. He would begin to cut it open, but all too often, it would start to move. The sealer would react by clubbing the animal again. It would lie still, and the sealer would resume skinning. Again the seal would move. Usually the sealer would give up and finish skinning the still thrashing animal.

As for the required blink test, Aldworth reports that "almost none of the sealers [used] it."

In a classic case of blaming the victim, harp seals are being blamed for the dwindling supply of cod in the Northwest Atlantic. Too many seals are eating too many of "our" fish, which is why it is "necessary" to cull the seal population. This is the mindset of people like Newfoundland's Minister of Fisheries and Agriculture, whatever the facts say to the contrary. And the facts are to the contrary. As recently as November 1999, marine biologists showed that "the number of seals being killed by humans . . . exceeds the levels that would be permitted by a truly 'precautionary' management model by as much as two (2) to six (6) times." It is not the overabundance of seals that explains the precipitous decline of cod in the region; the explanation lies in the rapacious overfishing by the fishing industry.

It is said that Christian missionaries faced a daunting challenge when they used the image of the "lamb of God" in their attempts to convert Eskimos. Having never seen a lamb, the image did not resonate. In its place, the missionaries chose *kotik*, which means "young seal." It is difficult to imagine a better choice.

As Wilfred Grenfell observes, "This animal, with its perfect whiteness as it lies in the cradle of ice, its gentle, helpless nature, and its pathetic innocent eyes, is probably as apt a substitute . . . as nature offers." So why don't we kill several hundred thousand of them each year? Such a piece of work is man.

Why does the seal slaughter continue? The bottom line is money. People sell the pelts, after all, and someone cashes a check with each transaction. If other people stopped buying the products fashioned out of seal skin, seal flesh, and seal oil, that would be the end of the matter. That's all it would take. Just a small change of behavior on the part of a comparatively small number of people. Short of that, if elected politicians had the courage to stand up against the entrenched interests of the captains of the sealing, fishing, and fur industries, the annual slaughter could come to an end. Viewed within a political context, the fate of animals depends on whom we elect, and whom we don't.

Persian Lambs

Not to go unmentioned in our discussion of fur are the coats and other garments that are made or trimmed with fur imported from Central Asian nations, including Afghanistan and Uzbekistan. The pelts come from unborn or newly born karakul lambs (also called "Persian lambs"). The older the lambs grow, the more their tight, smooth curls begin to unravel. Since premium prices are paid for the tightest, smoothest curls, the lambs are killed anywhere from one to three days after they are born and up to fifteen days before. This latter procedure requires the death of the pregnant mother, which at first is hard to understand. Why would anyone in this line of work kill a female, a breeder?

The answer is money. A coat made from aborted karakul lambs sells for twice as much as a coat of comparable size made from those newly born, as much as twelve thousand dollars for the latter but more than twenty-five thousand dollars for the former. Ralph Lauren and Karl Lagerfeld are among the designers who use Persian lamb, and Fendi and Neiman Marcus are among the stores that carry it.

The website of the Humane Society of the United States (HSUS) has video taken by an undercover investigator in March 2000. The graphic video "shows a pregnant ewe held down, her throat slit and her stomach slashed wide so that a worker could remove the developing fetus—the 'raw material' for fur coats, vests, and other [articles of] fashion." Once skinned, the remains of the lambs are discarded. The Dutch animal rights group Bont voor Dieren gives four million as the number of Persian lambs killed annually. The fur from sixty lambs will make one standard-sized coat.

Cat and Dog Fur

If people in China eat cats and dogs, it should not be surprising that they would also find some use for their fur. Americans do essentially the same thing when cows are raised for their meat and skinned for their leather. Why think the Chinese would be any different?

Annually, two million dogs and cats (this is the estimate given by HSUS) have their fur taken off their back in China and other Southeast Asian countries. These pelts find their way into merchandise that is exported throughout Asia, Europe, and North America. The products can vary from stuffed animals to the fur trim on a parka. Full-length coats require the fur of more than twenty cats or as many as twelve dogs, more if the fur is obtained from puppies or kittens.

Most operations are small (a few hundred animals, at most), but the cruel deprivation is massive. Because of the fullness of their coat, short-haired cats and German shepherds are preferred. The animals are housed in deplorable conditions with no regard for their quality of life.

Methods of slaughter are horrific. Cats are sometimes strangled to death by their owners; at other times they are killed by hanging or, while being hung, by forcing water down their throats to drown them. Dogs are hung using a metal wire that cuts into their neck as they vainly struggle to free themselves; or, while being hung, they are stabbed with a sharp knife and bled to death. Skinning occurs quickly, sometimes before the animals have died. In these barbaric circumstances, there is no thought of anesthesia. To their credit, at least the Chinese (and the same is true of the people who slaughter Persian lambs for their fur) do not say they care about the welfare of their animals or that they treat them humanely.

Beginning in 1997, Americans were outraged when HSUS exposed the international trade in cat and dog fur, especially when they learned that garments in American stores were trimmed or lined with fur from these animals but labeled as something else (China or Asian wolf, for example). Cats and dogs should not have their fur stolen from them, Americans protested. It's *their* fur; it *belongs to them, not to us.* To kill cats and dogs for their fur is both uncivilized and unethical. ARAs could not agree more. It's just that we think the same is true when the fur is stolen from any animal.

Cat and dog fur. For all of us, the opportunity for a change in perception in this context is very great. It is as simple (and as difficult) as coming to see that the moral status of beavers and coyotes, of mink and seals is no different from that of cats and dogs. Granted, many of us have close relationships with the latter that we do not have with the former. Cats and dogs live with us, as members of our households. In a very real sense, they are family. Wild animals are not.

Still, there is a basic sameness, if only we will see it. *There is somebody there*, behind the eyes of a beaver or a seal, just as *there is somebody there*, behind the eyes of a cat or a dog. As animal consciousness expands, as our perception changes, we see the one just as surely as we see the other.

LEATHER

While all Americans (one hopes) repudiate garments made from cat and dog fur and comparatively few buy garments made from the fur of other animals, wearing leather is as common as having a morning cup of coffee. And not just cowhide. America's leather inventory includes the skin of pigs, goats, lambs, horses, snakes, boars, deer, frogs, sharks, bison, zebras, kangaroos, alligators, lizards, eels, and elephants. That said, the hide from cows, their skin, dwarfs other types of leather by a large margin.

The countries composing the European Union are the largest suppliers of leather to the world market, with Italy by far the major producer, followed by Spain. Other leather-exporting countries include China, South Korea, Brazil, Pakistan, Thailand, India, Canada, and the United States. As the effects of globalization continue to be felt, leather production is beginning to find a niche in new places throughout Asia and South America.

How is leather made? What are the steps between the slaughterhouse and the clothing store? Elliot Gang offers the following summary:

> The basic process involves stripping the hide from the carcass, cleaning it with a salt and bactericide solution, and soaking it for cleaning and rehydration. Then sulfides and calcium hydroxide are used to remove the hair and make removing all the flesh easier. The hide is then treated with more chemicals (and sulfides), neutralized, and pickled (usually with a sulfuric acid solution) to allow tanning agents to penetrate the skin. Then it is tanned using chromium salts and wrung out to dry before being sorted and further processed based on its ultimate use.

If that sounds like a lot of chemicals, this is because it is. And therein lies the basis for the legitimate worker safety and environmental concerns that have been raised in connection with leather production, concerns that are more than adequately addressed in the notes for this chapter. All those chemicals are not any better for the people who work with them than they are for the streams and rivers into which their waste eventually flows. You do not have to be an animal rights advocate to find something wrong with leather. But you most certainly will find something wrong with it if you are.

Many people seem to think that purchasing leather is a moral free ride. After all, leather comes from animals who were killed for their flesh. If we buy something made of leather, all we are doing is purchasing some of the skin ("hide") that was taken from a dead animal. What could possibly be wrong with that? Let's take a look.

Here is a good test case for how little many of us know about leather (and, believe me, I thought I knew everything there is to know about leather before I learned what I am about to describe). If asked to identify the country where cows are treated *really well*, chances are most of us would say India. Most of us would be wrong.

An undercover video made by People for the Ethical Treatment of Animals-India shows old, sick, and lame cattle being forced to march hundreds of miles or being crammed into trucks that rattle over unpaved roads. Many cattle die in transit. Many more are injured. Some are so exhausted they collapse, and like other downers, must be dragged into the slaughterhouse. Those who are still ambulatory are pushed and prodded to meet their death; to keep them moving, workers rub their eyes with chili pepper and break their tails. Like karakul lambs in Afghanistan, who are slaughtered for their fur, not their flesh, the cows shown in the video—gaunt, emaciated, little more than skin and bones—are slaughtered for their hide, not their meat. All this in a country in which the cow is supposed to be sacred. If Gandhi could see how his beloved cows are treated in India today, he would look away in horror and disgust.

India's special brand of cruelty to one side, farmers and economists alike know that the leather industry provides a necessary revenue stream for people who farm cattle. Raising animals is not cheap, and producers cannot afford to do without the 10 percent of their income that comes from animal "by-products," leather chief among them. As Gang notes, "[g]overnment and industry figures put the worth of the hide at about 6–7 percent of the value of the live animal, just over $2 billion a year in the United States." With the average rancher's margin of profitability at 2 percent, many ranchers would be forced out of business if consumers boycotted the market in leather. Whenever we purchase leather goods, therefore, we lend our support (at a minimum) to the animal abuse that is inseparable from the mass production of animals on factory farms today. The cows and pigs used to make shoes, belts, jackets, and other articles of clothing are the same ones who were raised in the deplorable conditions described in chapter 6. Morally, buying leather is no free ride.

WOOL

Merino wool is ubiquitous throughout American clothing stores. Gloves, scarves, vests, sweaters, coats: whatever the type of clothing, we'll find merino products on the shelf or hanging from the rack. Whether many consumers know where merino wool comes from, beyond knowing that it originates in Australia, is another matter.

Merino sheep are the wool industry's answer to a vexing economic question: How can we maximize the amount of wool produced per sheep? The industry's answer: By increasing the amount of skin per sheep. This is not a misprint. The industry's answer really is: By increasing the amount of skin per sheep. It's simple arithmetic. Smooth skin gives you x amount of surface for wool to grow on; but wrinkled skin, skin that folds into itself, like beds of coral in the ocean, gives you $x + y$ amount of surface. And $x + y$ amount of skin gives you more wool per sheep.

"Having wrinkled skin" describes merino sheep. The product of years of intensive selective breeding, merino sheep have the skin they do because generations of Australian sheep ranchers have selectively bred them to have it. Having sheep with wrinkled skin may be good for the ranchers, who believe they maximize production per sheep raised. It certainly is not good for the sheep.

When merino sheep urinate or defecate, the wrinkles collect urine and feces. Looking for a moist place to lay their eggs, blowflies deposit them in the folds of the skin. In less than a day, the eggs hatch and the larvae, now maggots, look for the nearest source of nourishment, which happens to be the sheep. Left untreated (an invasion of this sort is called "fly-strike"), the voracious larvae can spread to other parts of their hosts and (literally) kill them in a matter of days. Goats, even dogs, especially if they are incontinent, can be the victims of fly-strike. Cause of death? Loss of fluids and blood proteins.

Over time, the sheep industry has fashioned a response. The response is called "mulesing," named after its inventor, J. H. W. Mules, a twentieth-century Australian sheep farmer. Using a sharp knife, ranchers cut large areas of sheep skin from the crotch area, the idea being that, once the wound heals, the wrinkles will be gone and, with the wrinkles gone, the potential for fly-strike will be gone too. In other words, in order to address the problem of fly-strike, the ranchers attempt to undo (at least in part) the very skin condition for which they have been selectively breeding merino sheep for generations.

Of course, the festering wound, which takes from three to five weeks to heal, itself offers a tempting moist environment for blowflies, so there is some question whether mulesing is an effective preventative, judged from the rancher's point of view. As for how the sheep respond, here is one description: "After mulesing, lambs can be seen writhing and scuttling side-ways like crabs, trying to escape the pain."

Mulesing is part of the genealogy of merino wool. So is tooth grinding, a procedure that ranchers claim extends a sheep's life. The procedure goes like this.

Grinders or disk-cutters are used either to grind teeth to the nubs or cut them off just above the gums; in either case, the procedure permanently exposes the nerves. Just like the Dustin Hoffman character in the movie *Marathon Man,* the sheep receive no anesthetic during the procedure. And just like the experience they had when they were subjected to mulesing, the sheep receive no postoperative relief either.

Merino sheep are subjected to other forms of direct physical assault, including ear notching (for identification), tail docking, and, in the case of males, castration. All these procedures are carried out when the sheep are only a few days old, without any attempt to minimize or alleviate their pain. Castration takes one of three forms: it can be done by using a knife, by using a device that crushes the spermatic cord, or by tightening a rubber ring around the scrotum.

If all these attacks on the bodily integrity sound like they are cruel, that is because they are. According to Australian Law Reform Chairman, M. D. Kirby, sheep in Australia are annually subjected to *fifty million* invasive procedures that would be classified as acts of cruelty if they were done to cats or dogs. All these procedures, each one of which violates the animals' rights to bodily integrity, are perfectly legal when sheep are the victims. The suffering of animals makes no difference to the law or to the merino ranchers. And why should it? From the ranchers' point of view, the main thing is to maximize production of wool per animal; since animal pain does not figure in the economic equation, there is no need to consider it.

Indifference to what the animals experience carries over to the process of shearing itself. City folks that most of us are, we picture lambs being gently lifted and carried to get their haircut, as when we go to the barber or hair stylist. We should think again. Gentleness is not part of the bargain. Jennifer Greenbaum tells us why:

> The sheep are thrown on their backs and restrained while a razor is run over their bodies. Whether sheared manually or mechanically, cuts in the skin are very common. Careless shearing can injure teats, pizzles, other appendages, and ligaments. Sheep are held in restraints with tight clamps on their faces when they're mechanically sheared. . . . Death can occur when the shearer is rough and twists the sheep into an organ-damaging position, when the health of the sheep already is poor, or when being stripped of wool is a shock to the sheep's system. . . . [After shearing] [n]aked to the world, sheep are put back out to pasture where they can suffer severe sunburn or freeze as the heat is drawn from their bodies.

One last consideration: There comes a time in a merino sheep's life when the animal no longer produces quality wool. For an estimated seven million sheep annually, this means they are destined for the mutton market in the Middle East. The sheep are pushed and prodded onto large tiered ships, some capable of transporting 125,000 animals. There they spend three weeks at sea, sometimes longer, crammed together in spaces that make ordinary physical movement impossible. Once at their destination, assuming they have survived (many do not), they are off-loaded and pushed and prodded some more until they meet their bloody, terrifying end at the hands of a ritual slaughterer in Iraq or Iran. If truth in labeling really were truth in labeling, the gruesome final days of merino sheep would be included. Here is the label I propose: "This wool comes from sheep who have spent their entire grazing lives being abused because some humans want to make money and others want to be fashionable, only to be mercilessly transported and ruthlessly killed because other humans want to make money and eat them." Who wants to wear *that*?

The sheep industry in America, as elsewhere in the world, represents a variation on the main themes illustrated by the sheep industry in Australia. Some of the particulars might vary, but the general story is always the same. Sheep are raised for food and fiber with a view to turning a profit, the bigger the profit, the better the investment. The cultural paradigm (animals exist to satisfy human desires and needs) reigns supreme. Given this paradigm, sheep, like other farmed animals, have only two reasons for being: to be eaten and to be worn by human beings.

CONCLUSION

Nobody had to tell me how sensational Nancy looked in her mink hat. That's why mink existed. They were "Its," not "Thous." They were things, occupying the same moral category as cucumbers and sack dresses. Back then, if someone had told me that I should not buy leather shoes or wear a wool sweater, I would have felt sorry for their poor mental health. But this is ancient history. This was before I knew where fur and wool and leather really come from. Once you know this, it can make a difference. It helps some Muddlers see the world differently.

Animal rights advocates find no justification for raising fur-bearing animals on "ranches," trapping them in the wild, clubbing them to death on the ice, or killing them before they are born. The way most Americans feel about cat and dog fur, ARAs feel about all fur. Similarly, ARAs find no justification for turning an animal's skin or fleece into an article of clothing. The treatment these animals receive from human hands is not "humane," and those furriers and hunters who say they "support animal welfare" are paradigm examples of the Disconnect Dictum. When they say they treat animals this way, our response should be, "No, you do not. What you say is false."

To attempt to justify how these animals are treated by claiming economic benefits for humans is illogical. The money someone makes by violating another's rights is never moral reason enough for doing so. Considerations of the same kind apply to other claimed benefits attributed to commerce in fur, skin, and wool. A woman's pleasure in having a luxurious looking coat or a man's in having a leather jacket evidently make life more enjoyable for the people who have them. But the pleasures derived do not come remotely close to justifying the violation of anyone's rights, human or otherwise. The only proper place for animal fur or skin is on the animal whose fur or skin it is.

ARAs do not dress in sackcloth and ashes. There are wonderful clothing options out there that do not require that anyone deliberately kill any animal. For example, many shoes, belts, purses, and other nonleather products are on the market, often found in major retail chains as well as through mail order companies. (Some are listed on the website mentioned in the prologue.) When it comes to clothing, the old standbys, cotton and cotton flannel, are widely available. But also be on the lookout for the new synthetics, including synthetic shearling and Tensel, a fabric that is the equal of wool in every respect. Moreover, today's synthetic coats are warmer than fur, and leather's fabled protection against the cold (for bikers, for example) is surpassed by the warmth provided by lighter, less restrictive new "pleather" fashions. And for those who can't give up the look and feel of fur? Faux fur is now widely available, is much cheaper, and is becoming far more fashionable. Even in Aspen.

TURNING ANIMALS INTO PERFORMERS

Animals have been used in the name of human entertainment for thousands of years. Wherever it exists, whenever it occurs, the basic logic is the same. Humans train animals to perform various tricks or routines that audiences find entertaining. Sometimes there is a close connection between entertainment and sport. Rodeo, for example, is promoted as a sport, as is horse racing ("the sport of kings"). At the same time rodeos and horse races are places people go to be entertained. However, the two (entertainment and sport) differ in one crucial respect. In general, sports involve an element of competition where there are winners and losers; other forms of entertainment (think rock concerts or ballet) do not. But some sporting events (football and hockey games, for example) are also considered a form of entertainment. Some people think the same is true when animals are involved. For example, they view bullfights and greyhound racing both as sports and as forms of entertainment. Why this is not true will be explained in chapter 9.

The present chapter explores some ways wild animals are used for purposes of entertainment, in contexts in which there are no winners and losers, at least not in any conventional sense. The plight of some wild animals that perform in circuses and marine parks will serve to illustrate the conflict between training them to entertain us, on the one hand, and respecting their rights, on the other.

THE TRADITIONAL CIRCUS

Some circuses include animal acts; some do not. Among the best known that do are the Ringling Brothers and Barnum and Bailey Circus, and the Clyde Beatty-Cole

Brothers Circus. Among the best known that do not are Cirque du Soleil, and the New Pickle Family Circus. Unless otherwise indicated, our discussion is limited to circuses (often referred to as "traditional" or "classic" circuses) that include wild-animal acts.

Traditional circuses put on a happy face. The decorations are colorful. The music, gay. The costumes, sequined and gaudy. Everything that can be done is done to make sure "children of all ages" enjoy themselves. And many of us do, including many parents and their children. The Regan family always had a good time. In today's world, it is not hard to understand why. Two hours with no foul language, no blood, no guts, no sex. Two hours during which parents are mercifully relieved of the need to shield their children from so much that they are too young to need to know. No wonder that circuses are synonymous in the minds of many people with wholesome family entertainment or that ARAs who criticize them are seen as antifamily and anti-American, moralistic busybodies determined to take both fun and free choice away from everybody else.

As it happens, there is much to criticize. Behind the traditional circus happy face, there lies a hidden world of systematic animal deprivation, a world where, in the name of "animal training," documented cruelty is no stranger, and a world where the existence of animal welfare laws and inspectors offers false assurance that "everything is just fine."

DIMENSIONS OF DEPRIVATION

That wild animals in circuses are systematically deprived is inherent in the very nature of the enterprise. Wild animals do not belong in circuses; they belong in environments where they are free to express who they are, both individually and (in the case of elephants, for example) as members of a mobile social group, something no circus environment can possibly provide. Limitations of space, loss of social structure, and abnormal behavior help chart the dimensions of their deprivation.

Limitations of Space

It does not take the knowledge of a Jane Goodall to understand that circuses do not approximate the natural habitat of wild animals. It is not unusual for circuses to be on the road forty-eight to fifty weeks a year. While en route from one venue to the next, the animals are packed into trucks or train cars. Once at their destination, they face further confinement—lions and tigers in cages, elephants tethered by chains.

Relevant federal regulations concerning cage size are worse than vague; they are dishonest. Section 3.128 of Title 9 of the Code of Federal Regulations, entitled "Space requirements," states: "Enclosures shall be constructed and maintained so as to provide sufficient space to allow each animal to make normal postural and social adjustments with adequate freedom of movement." What counts as "sufficient space" or "adequate freedom of movement" is not specified; this is why the regulations are vague. The dishonesty arises because the regulations imply that cages having "sufficient space" *can* satisfy these requirements. This is preposterous.

An opportunity to expand our animal consciousness presents itself if we look behind the eyes of wild animals trained to perform in circuses. In the wild, the home range for lions varies from 8 to 156 square miles; for male tigers, from 8 to 60 square miles (in India) and up to 400 square miles (in Siberia). For the sake of comparison, consider that San Francisco and Boston occupy 47 and 48 square miles, respectively; Chicago, 227; New York City, including all five boroughs, 309 square miles.

No sensible person can believe that circuses provide lions and tigers with a caged environment of "sufficient space," one that offers the animals "adequate freedom of movement." In a gesture more designed for public relations than for the animals themselves, the Ringling Brothers circus boasts of having cages with "fold-out sections (known as 'verandas') much like those used on newer house trailers. When fully opened each cage measures thirty-six feet long and provides ample room for the seven to nine animals housed in it to walk about, interact, and exercise." To suppose that a thirty-six-foot-long cage provides lions and tigers with "ample room" to be the animals they are is absurd on its face, something even honest circus people understand. Paul Binder, of the Big Apple Circus, explains why he has "never presented a cat or caged animal act"; it is "because he is unable to provide the kind of accommodations such animals would require."

What is true of lions and tigers is no less true of elephants. Home range varies from 5 square miles in a groundwater forest to over 1350 square miles in an arid savanna, an area more than four times the size of New York City. It is not uncommon for elephants to walk 50 miles in a day. "Sufficient space." "Adequate freedom of movement." Humpty Dumpty could not describe things any better.

Loss of Social Structure

Once in the circus any semblance of social structure for the "big cats" is nonexistent. In their natural habitat tiger cubs stay with their mothers for years. As mentors, mothers teach survival skills. When a new litter is born, the older tigers strike out on their own. Although males tend to lead a solitary existence, they sometimes cooperate with one another when hunting.

Lions are social creatures who live in groups called prides. Prides consist of as many as a dozen females, all of whom are related, and their offspring. The young are raised communally, but the bond between mothers and daughters is especially close and lasts a lifetime. At the head of each pride is a dominant male or, sometimes, a group of males. In lion culture females tend to be the hunters; males, the protectors. In some cases, males form a group of their own, living together for years.

Confined in their spacious verandas, Ringling's tigers and lions have no place to go and nothing to teach. Any sense of enduring community, any opportunity to participate in cooperative activities, is absent here. The lions and tigers who perform in circuses may *look* like their wild cousins, but for all intents and purposes, their wildness has been drained out of them, a day at a time.

And then there are the elephants. Everyone knows something about their complicated matriarchal social structure. Elephants live in groups (herds) numbering anywhere from eight to fifteen, with a dominant female in charge. Males leave at puberty, but daughters remain with their mothers for life. Groups related to one another ("kin groups") tend to remain in the same general area and frequently communicate with one another. In times of danger, they join forces, up to two hundred strong, in common defense. With a home range for African elephants extending five hundred miles, the herd's migratory routes are not known "instinctively" but must be taught by the elders.

None of this makes any sense in a circus environment. There are no matriarchs, no kin groups, no migratory routes, nothing that even suggests the lifeway of these majestic animals. "A circus must have clowns," writes circus enthusiast Earl Chapin May, "peanuts and elephants—but the greatest of these are elephants." Unfortunately for the elephants, what May says is all too true. Die-hard supporters of the traditional circus, like Ringling Brothers, would rather forgo their peanuts than surrender "their" elephants.

Abnormal Behavior

Lacking a common verbal language, humans and animals communicate with one another through observed behavior. Anyone who watches how performing circus animals behave will learn something about what is going on behind their eyes. What we see is the same kind of stereotypical behavior we find in caged animals on factory farms and in fur mills. Lions and tigers pacing, back and forth, back and forth, back and forth, never deviating from their circumscribed path. Elephants swaying back and forth, back and forth, back and forth, or bobbing their heads, now this way, now that, over and over and over again. Sometimes behavior speaks louder than words. These are mentally ill, psychologically defeated animal beings. And for what? So that tigers can jump through flaming hoops and elephants can do "hand stands" on their front legs. What have we come to?

Seeing an elephant—actually *seeing* an elephant—was what turned Gary Yourofsky's life around. Gary was twenty-three at the time. His stepfather, who performed as a clown, was able to take Gary backstage when the circus came to town. That's where Gary saw a solitary elephant, chained to a post, swaying back and forth, back and forth, back and forth. More important, the elephant saw Gary. I mean he took in the whole of Gary's being—just pierced Gary's mind and heart with his doleful eyes, overflowing with sadness and helplessness. As Gary describes the encounter, nothing else existed, just the elephant's gaze and his awareness that the elephant was looking at him, looking through him. It was as if this mammoth creature was asking Gary, in words we have heard before, "What have I done to deserve this? Why aren't you helping me?" A Damascan moment. By the time he said goodbye to that elephant, Gary Yourofsky had a new identity, a new reason for being in the world. There, on that spot, he became an ARA. Thanks to that elephant, Gary today (as he tells anyone within earshot) is among the most committed spokespersons for the rights of all animals.

In an earlier draft of this chapter, I compared the living conditions of circus animals to criminals behind bars. "It is a cruel joke," I wrote, "to say that human prisoners confined to six-by-eight-feet cells have 'ample room' to be human. In fact, limited space is meant to be a deprivation for human prisoners, part of the punishment for crimes committed. For cats or caged animal acts in circuses, limited space is no less a deprivation; only in their case no crime has been committed."

When a helpful ARA critic read this, he took me to task. He had spent more than three years in prison. What is done to circus animals, he wrote, "is infinitely worse" than how prisoners are treated. "The worst they can do to prisoners is put them in 'solitary confinement,' but even here, they are legally required to give an hour of exercise per day, and you still have a cell large enough to do exercise, you have a TV and books, and so on . . . [E]ven Tim McVeigh and the Unabomber were allowed to hang out together for an hour each day." So, yes, let me caution others not to make the same mistake I did. The living conditions for lions and tigers, bears and elephants in circuses are much worse than those we provide for even our most violent criminals.

NO PAIN, NO TRAIN

Wild animals cannot be trained to perform tricks without assaulting their integrity as the wild creatures they are. To the extent that the training succeeds, a part of the animal's wild nature is lost. No serious advocate of animal rights can accept this loss; all will step forward and shout, if shout we must, "Stop it! What are you doing? Stop it!"

To make matters worse, trainers physically assault and intimidate these animals while wrapping themselves in the mantle of "professionals." The tools of the trade today are much the same as the tools used by trainers in the past: whips, bullhooks, metal bars, chains, electric prods, muzzles, human fists.

No one denies that wild-animal trainers treated animals cruelly in the past. Spokespersons for today's circus would have us believe that kindness is the rule today. Contemporary training methods, we are told, take their inspiration from Clyde Beatty. "No jungle animal can be trained successfully by cruelty," Beatty avers; rather, trainers must have "a kindly approach and a capacity for taking pains, plus a reasonably cheerful disposition." This sounds reassuring, as if trainers persuade tigers to jump through flaming hoops by whispering sweet entreaties in their ears. The harsh truth is another matter.

"Don't Touch 'Em! Hurt 'Em!"

The Carson and Barnes Circus has toured North America for four generations, offering (in their words) "the finest big top show in America." In addition to elephants, lions, tigers, and horses, the circus also touts "a huge zoo on the midway."

Readers who explore the Carson and Barnes website will read that the elephants "are only trained through positive reinforcement. It is important that both the animals and trainers have a mutual trust. . . . A relationship is formed between the animals and the caretakers, which is very important in the training process. You have to have trust between the two or panic will arise. If an animal is in a panic stage it is most likely that the animal will not be trainable. It is important to be calm, patient, and only use positive reinforcement." Sounds reassuring. Sounds humane enough. There is only one problem: we have to remember who is saying it. Not surprisingly, Carson and Barnes's record does not match its rhetoric.

Tim Frisco serves as Carson and Barnes's director of animal care. Frisco's training methods are on view in an undercover video produced by People for the Ethical Treatment of Animals (PETA). They are anything but "only positive reinforcement." Words cannot adequately describe what we watch. That said, it would be difficult to improve on the narrative accompanying the video. It reads:

> [Frisco] is seen screaming obscenities at, viciously attacking, and electroshocking endangered Asian elephants. The elephants emit agonizing screams as they try to escape the assaults. Frisco instructs other trainers how to beat the elephants using both hands and sink a sharp metal bullhorn into their flesh until they scream in pain. He tells them that the beatings have to be effective behind the scenes, for they, the trainers, cannot do any of this "in front of a thousand people."

In a particularly chilling exchange, Frisco tells his students, "Don't touch 'em! Hurt 'em! If you're scared to hurt 'em, don't come in this barn!"

Barbara Byrd, one of the owners of Carson and Barnes, told the Associated Press that Frisco's language was "horrible, terrible." But not, apparently, his other behavior. Ms. Byrd denies that the tape "proves that we have ever injured an elephant." Though he is still employed by Carson and Barnes, Frisco has been relieved of his duties as an elephant trainer.

How common is training like that shown on the tape? Is Frisco the rule? Or is he the exception? Regretfully, he is not the latter. In October 2002 David A. Creech, an elephant handler with the Sterling and Reid Brothers Circus, was found guilty of three counts of cruelty to animals in the General District Court of Norfolk, Virginia. Witnesses testified that they saw Creech repeatedly hit Joy, a twenty-three-year-old elephant, with an ankus, a steel rod with a hook at one end. A veterinarian who inspected Joy testified that he detected three fresh wounds on one leg.

So, no, Frisco evidently is not the exception. Without easy access to training sessions, which are shrouded in secrecy and normally off-limits to the public, who can say how often animals in circuses are abused? In face of the gross disparity between what circuses say and what some handlers do, the burden of proof clearly must be borne by circuses, not their ARA critics.

LEGAL ILLUSIONS

Enforcement of the Animal Welfare Act, together with relevant federal regulations, falls to the Animal and Plant Health Inspection Service (APHIS), an agency of the U.S. Department of Agriculture (USDA). In the case of circuses, APHIS is responsible for enforcing standards for the handling, care, and transportation of animals. Once again, this sounds more reassuring than the facts warrant. Peggy Larson, a veterinarian, former bareback bronco rider in the rodeo, and a former APHIS supervisor, highlights the chronic failures of government inspection in her testimony presented in support of a Riverside County (California) ban of displaying elephants for public entertainment or amusement:

> Circus animals are poorly inspected under the Animal Welfare Act for several reasons. When a problem with a circus is found, paperwork must be generated and a compliance officer needs to visit the circus. Often by the time this is completed, the exhibitor is in another state and in another USDA veterinarian's jurisdiction. If that veterinarian happens to inspect that circus, the procedure is repeated and the exhibitor moves on without the problem being solved.
>
> Veterinarians working for USDA do not receive training in diseases that affect animals performing in circuses and exhibition. They do not know how to diagnose diseases and do not know if the elephant or any other circus animal has a disease that infects humans. USDA veterinarians do not know how to restrain elephants or other circus animals and, furthermore, do not have the drugs necessary to do proper restraint. Proper restraint is necessary to take blood samples or tissue samples to send to a diagnostic laboratory. So the USDA veterinarians do not do diagnostic workups on circus animals. USDA veterinarians are more concerned with housing and husbandry than diseases.
>
> Furthermore, USDA veterinarians must work with state agricultural officials who have the ultimate control over what the USDA veterinarian does or does not do. Many state agricultural officials know less than the USDA veterinarian about circus animal diseases. Often state political interests interfere with the USDA veterinarian's conducting a proper inspection. . . . Unfortunately, USDA veterinarians do not work with the state Department of Health officials. These officials have a greater knowledge of zoonoses [diseases that animals can transmit to humans] than agricultural officials do but they seldom learn of a problem with a circus animal. They are "out of the loop."

Lack of time. Inadequate medical education and training. Conflicting political interests. The initial sense of assurance that "everything is fine" at the circus, that "all the animals are being protected" because "we have laws," withers in the face of hard facts. There simply is no good reason to believe that government inspectors adequately protect circus animals from abuse and cruelty. How could they? In 2001 there were nine thousand USDA licensed facilities, ranging from roadside zoos to state-of-the-art research laboratories. And the number of inspectors? The total number of inspectors, for the whole country, charged with inspecting all nine thousand licensed facilities, was . . . one hundred. With rare instances to the contrary, "legal protection" of animals in America is an illusion.

"Radical Views"

In an effort to shore up the status quo, some traditional circuses have adopted the proactive strategy first fashioned by the AMA. Ringling Brothers is a leader in this effort. If ARA groups can distribute leaflets critical of their circus, Ringling can turn the tables and distribute leaflets critical of their critics. And who are their critics? Not the decent people who support animal welfare. No, the critics are animal rights radicals. To quote from Ringling's leaflet ("Don't Be Fooled by the Demonstrators"): "The 'animal rights' groups appeal to your love of animals, when, in fact, they are trying to raise money to promote their radical views—'total liberation' of all animals from 'human custody.' . . . Don't confuse their radical views with animal 'welfare,' or the ethical, responsible and humane treatment and care of animals."

Let's see: "Animal welfare." "Responsible and humane treatment." Haven't we heard this before? And look who is saying it: another leader of a major animal user industry. If ever there was a situation in which the Disconnect Dictum applies, this is it. The first thing people who truly, sincerely, genuinely care about the welfare of animals in circuses would do is ask, "How can we get them out of here?" And the second thing? The second thing they would do is to try to make it happen.

"No 'Boutique Circuses' for Me."

Traditionalists cannot imagine circuses (they call them "boutique circuses") without performing animals. Writes the chairman of the board of Big Apple Circus, Alan Slifka: "I believe that a circus without animals is a contradiction of terms: a virtual rain forest without trees, a true asphalt jungle. In a world becoming increasingly modern, those rituals which connect us to our essence, such as Circus, need to be understood."

Even if we ignore the new-age talk of "connect[ing] . . . to our essence," Slifka's logic is mired in the status quo. Not too many years ago, people were saying it was "a contradiction of terms" to have a circus without having sideshows on the midway exhibiting the deformed and disabled: Alligator Woman, Dog-face Girl, Lobster Boy, Legless Acrobat, Four-Legged Man, Two-Headed Baby, and (a real crowd favorite) Siamese Twins. Thankfully, a new sensibility has taken root and is flourishing, one that finds such exhibitions morally obscene and demeaning. Having a "freak show" as part of the circus was a tradition; that and nothing more. When circuses stopped having them, that was a good thing, both for circuses and for those who support them. Having performing animals in circuses is a tradition; that and nothing more. When circuses stop using performing animals, that will be a good thing too.

People who only know the traditional circus might find Slifka's logic appealing for a different reason. They might think that attending a circus without performing animals cannot be any fun. Others, who have tried the alternative, think differently. Reviewing a July 26, 2002, performance of Cirque du Soleil, the *Boston Herald* comments: "Gone are the animals . . . With these changes, Cirque has redefined the circus for the 21st century . . . the [n]ew . . . Barnum and Bailey. And Cirque creates an entertainment that can be enjoyed equally by adults and children." Even Slifka would agree. When in January, 2003 our local paper ran a story about Cirque coming to town, the Greater Raleigh Convention and Visitors Bureau said, "It adds to [Raleigh's] luster as a top entertainment destination to have Cirque come to our market for the first time ever." They never said this about Ringling Brothers—and it has been coming to Raleigh for more than thirty years. (By the way, Cirque's Raleigh performance ran for three solid weeks, with two shows on the weekends. Capacity audiences crowded into the big top. The night Nancy and I attended, everyone stood as one and applauded after the finale, still wondering if all that we had seen had really happened. It was magical!)

Some forward-looking people are not waiting for circuses to change. Brazil, Costa Rica, Finland, Israel, Singapore, and Sweden are among the nations that have passed legislation prohibiting the use of performing animals in circuses. Eighteen counties and municipalities in the United States, including Boulder (Colorado), Hollywood (Florida), Newport Beach (California), and Orange County (North Carolina), have ordinances that ban wild or exotic animal displays. The same is true of many jurisdictions throughout four Canadian provinces. Thankfully, signs are that *another* new sensibility is beginning to take root and flourish in our new world.

MARINE MAMMAL DISPLAY

A variety of marine and other mammals are exhibited or perform at marine parks throughout the world. For example, Sea World–San Diego features orcas (killer whales), beluga whales, walruses, polar bears, penguins, and arctic foxes. Among the animal shows described on Sea World–San Diego's website are the following:

> [Listed under] Fools with Tools: [Two sea lions, Clyde and Seamore, offer] a hilarious episode of their very own "Fools with Tools," a TV home-repair show where mischievous mayhem rules the airwaves! . . . Clyde and Seamore will en-

tertain you as they show such basic home repairs as fixing a doorknob, wallpapering, plumbing and electrical work.

[Listed under] Shamu Adventure: The Shamu Adventure features the world-famous killer whale, Shamu, performing along with Baby Shamu and Namu. . . . They'll delight you as they interact with one another and their trainers.

[Listed under] Dolphin Discovery: Dolphin Discovery showcases bottlenose dolphins in a splashy, high energy show with some surprising comic moments. It's a fast-paced show featuring tailwalks, spinning jumps, and backflips.

Like other industries that depend on wild animals for their revenues, the "dolphin captivity industry," to use Ric O'Barry's words (we will have more to say about him and his wife, Helene, later), emphasizes its roles as educators and conservationists. What conservationist contribution they make is limited at best; no endangered species are protected by these parks. And as for education: No doubt *something* is learned by the children and adults who watch two trained sea lions fix doorknobs and hang wallpaper. The question concerns what this is. That sea lions like to yuck it up? That dolphins will do just about anything to get a dead fish? Or is it (to quote syndicated columnist Dave Barry) how dolphins "naturally behave when they live in concrete pools and perform tricks all day?" Besides, it is hard to square the promotional talk about education and conservation with what the folks at Sea World–San Diego themselves say about the animal shows. The real purpose, as we have seen, is "mischievous mayhem," a performance that "delight[s]," "a splashy, high energy show." The real purpose is good old-fashioned entertainment.

The use made of bottlenose dolphins in shows like Dolphin Discovery is representative of shows of a similar kind. All the considerations that are relevant to morally assessing what is done to these captive animals in particular apply with equal force to assessing what is done to captive marine mammals in general.

Dolphins in Their Element

Bottlenose dolphins (or dolphins, for short) occupied a special place among the ancient Greeks. Anyone convicted of killing a dolphin was guilty of an offense against the gods that was punishable by death. Aristotle recognized that dolphins are mammals, not fish, and many Greeks believed in a strong spiritual, biological kinship between humans and their "marine cousins." Numerous stories and frescoes depict the playfulness and courage of dolphins as they took children for rides on their backs and rescued drowning sailors. So venerated was the dolphin in the Greek mind that the Oracle who spoke at Delphi, the one deity who was able to communicate between Zeus and mere mortals, was none other than the dolphin god Apollo Delphinos.

Today, we perhaps understand dolphins better even as we appreciate them less. We know that they evolved over millions of years. With large, highly developed brains, these marine mammals are among the most intelligent animals in the world. They are also among the most active. Dolphins swim up to forty miles a day. Even when they are "sleeping," they are moving, left or right, up or down. Able to hold their breath for twenty minutes, with little effort dolphins can plunge to depths of more than sixteen hundred feet.

The social aspects of dolphins are no less remarkable. These are not solitary creatures. Rather, they live in groups of varying sizes, called pods. Newborns stay with their mother for four or five years. Most females never leave; young males in time form their own pods. Throughout their early years both males and females learn from their elders: how to ride the current, where to find food, the identity of predators. Old and young swim together, look for food together, and play together. Their normal life span in nature is twenty to fifty years.

Dolphins who leave a pod sometimes return, meaning that at any given time generations of dolphins from the same family can be living together, an extended aquatic family. The social ties are so close that each pod has unique forms of communication, understandable only to that pod's members. Not surprisingly, therefore, to remove a dolphin from a pod is a momentous event, both for the one removed and for those left behind.

Dolphin Capture

Much has been written about the brutalities of dolphin capture, and rightly so. Boats pursue a pod until the members are too exhausted to try to escape. A net is lowered, the pod is trapped, and the dolphins are dumped on board. Thrashing and protesting (emitting clicks and whistles), the most desirable specimens (usually between the ages of two and four) are kept; the others are thrown back into the sea. Some drop dead on the deck, from shock. Many are injured. The pod's social unity is permanently impaired. Every one of the estimated one thousand dolphins presently held in captivity throughout the world today has a genealogy that includes capture at sea.

Dolphin Welfare

Voices that speak for the captive dolphin industry insist that they do everything they can to promote the welfare of their animals. For example, major marine parks will have a veterinarian on staff, the animals will get plenty to eat, their water will be clean, and the temperature will be just right. What more could one ask for?

The depravity of this logic takes one's breath away. One wants to say, "You cannot be serious! If you were—if you really were concerned about the welfare of these animals—you would not have them here in the first place! Just who is it that you think you are fooling?"

Lest this seem overly harsh, overly opinionated, consider the following: Dolphins swim up to forty miles a day and can dive to depths of more than a quarter of a mile. In their natural environment, they live in extended social groups and find their way around in an ever changing, challenging environment via echolocation. (They "see" by hearing.) Once in captivity, these same animals are confined in concrete tanks (sometimes measuring as little as twenty-four feet long by twenty-four feet wide by six feet deep) or in small sea-cages. There are no pods here. Nothing changes in any significant way in this desolate world. No natural challenges are faced. Nothing naturally interesting is found because there is nothing naturally interesting to be found.

To speak candidly, it is worse than disingenuous; ARAs believe it is shameful that anyone would stand before us and say, "We really and truly care about the welfare of our dolphins," animals who have nothing to locate, no family to be with, no place to dive, no miles to swim. As Professor Giorgio Pilleri, the Director of the Brain Anatomy Institute at Berne University, observes, "[w]hatever efforts are deployed, the keeping of cetaceans in captivity will [face] . . . the inherent contradiction on which it is based; the keeping in cramped conditions of creatures which are accustomed to vast spaces . . . . Even the standards themselves [for housing captive cetaceans]," Professor Pilleri laments, "have been formulated with human ignorance as their foundation."

A Powerless Predicament

Ric O'Barry, who I quoted earlier, is a former dolphin trainer; in fact, he probably is the most famous dolphin trainer ever, having been responsible for training the dolphins who performed in the hugely successful television series *Flipper*. There was a time when O'Barry favored keeping dolphins in captivity. In fact, when he worked at the Miami Seaquarium, he not only trained dolphins, he participated in capturing dolphins at sea.

The person Ric O'Barry is today is not the person Ric O'Barry was back then. His Damascan moment happened in 1970 when Cathy, a dolphin he had trained for the television program, died in his arms. When he looked at Cathy, dead in the water, he entered an expanded animal consciousness. A change in perception occurred. He saw what dolphins are and what he was doing to them.

From that moment forward, Ric O'Barry's reason for being in the world was to liberate every dolphin in captivity.

O'Barry and his wife, Helene, head The Dolphin Project. Helene knows first-hand how dolphins are trained. She describes the animals' situation as a "powerless predicament" because "[the dolphins] depend totally on their keepers to be fed. Once the hungry dolphins have surrendered to eating dead fish, the trainer teaches them that only when they perform a desired behavior . . . do they receive their reward: a fish. This is how abnormal behaviors are enforced in a dolphin." With this kind of power, trainers can induce behaviors that the paying public enjoys.

Quoting Helene again (and at length, because of the importance of what she writes):

> Disguising food control as communication is obviously an essential part of the captive-dolphin spectacle, and it's ironic how the very tricks the dolphins are encoded to perform become the most convincing basis of the illusion. Just a few examples: When the dolphins "walk" on their tail and "play" basketball, the spectators predictably interpret the dolphins' behavior as fun-loving playfulness. And when the dolphins "kiss" their trainers, applaud at their own tricks with their pectoral fins, and eagerly nod their heads in agreement to questions like "are we having fun?" it adds very human-like traits to the dolphins, leaving the audience with the false notion that there does indeed exist a common language between the dolphins and their trainers. To the performing dolphins, of course, the trained behaviors hold no other meaning than that of being the key to obtaining a fish.

To speak of the "illusion" here is accurate. These animals do not "enjoy playing basketball." They do not have the foggiest idea about the game. In fact, to think that they do contradicts one of Sea World's most important educational lessons. "When we study animal behavior," their trainers warn on Sea World's website, "*we may mistakenly attribute human characteristics or motivations to animals.* Attributing human characteristics to animals is called anthropomorphizing. Beware of these inaccurate assumptions when you observe animal behavior! (italics added)" But how else are the children and adults in the audience supposed to understand the "fun-loving playfulness" of the performing animals *except* by "attributing human characteristics" to them? Isn't that the whole point of the act, the reason for the illusion? The success of the performance contradicts the stated reasons for having it.

It is difficult to say which is the most demeaning: that captive dolphins are trained to act like clowns, that people are paid to train them to do so, or that the people making the money tell us that we will learn something important about dolphins by watching them act the fool. Even the best-of-the-best marine parks (roadside and other dolphin exhibits, all perfectly legal, are even worse) are concrete prisons for these animals, the prisoners in them sentenced to a life of deprivation made to look like "fun." These prisons serve no legitimate educational purpose and no legitimate conservation purpose either. What purpose they serve is economic. As Jean-Michael Cousteau observes, marine parks are nothing more than "lucrative commercial ventures—circuses of the sea."

CONCLUSION

Various animals are trained to perform various "tricks" or "routines" for purposes of entertainment. This chapter has described the plight of only a few performing animals in circuses and marine parks. Many people, especially parents and their children, enjoy watching these performances. The animals make us laugh and sometimes "ooh" and "aah." You have to marvel at what they can do and applaud the skill of their trainers. For most people, it is hard to see what could be wrong with this.

Having once counted myself among "most people," I understand this point of view. Without a change in perception, most people will never see anything wrong with performing animals. How could we? If we think lions, tigers, elephants, and dolphins *belong* in circuses or marine parks, how could we possibly see anything wrong when they *perform*? Why else would they be there?

ARAs do not view things this way. Our perception sees wild animals as wild, not wild animals as performers. They should never be in circuses or marine parks in the first place; to train them to perform various "tricks" only compounds the injury. The rights of animals should never be violated so that some people can have a good time or because others make a comfortable living from doing so. Benefits for us, even if they happen to accrue, and regardless of the amount, never justify turning wild animals into performing animals. From an ARA's perspective, only when all the cages, and all the tanks, are empty—only when all the "performing" animals are free—will justice be done. We really are extremists on this issue.

From Boulder to Brazil, some people are taking steps to prohibit performances of wild or exotic animals. The same sort of process is underway in opposition to captive marine mammal shows. The good folks in England are a model for the rest of us, in this as in so many other respects. They became so disenchanted with marine parks that they stopped patronizing them, one prospective patron at a time. They simply stopped going. Real animal rights terrorists, the Brits. The result? Collectively, they put every English marine park out of business.

And then there are the good folks of South Carolina. The legislature there had the vision and courage (despite being located on the Atlantic coast, with all the lucrative possibilities this made possible) to pass a law that prohibits all exhibits or displays of whales and dolphins anywhere in the Palmetto State.

When dramatic abolitionist change can occur in such different places, with such different heritages, and using such different approaches, one cannot help believing that, with the right combination of good strategy and hard work, ARAs can bring about comparable change anywhere.

TURNING ANIMALS
INTO COMPETITORS

No one knows the exact date when a human being for the first time engaged in an activity involving animals and called it "sport." We do know that the Olympics, as far back as 680 BCE, featured chariot races and that nomadic tribesmen in Central Asia raced horses as early as 4500 BCE. But when and where humans began to use animals in sports, whether in human competitions or as competitors themselves, remains unknown.

Whenever it started, uncounted hundreds of millions of animals are exploited in sports today. That most of these animals are injured or killed does not seem to trouble those sportsmen (and sportswomen) who participate. Granted, as we shall see, they are eager to talk about "animal welfare" and their responsibility to treat animals "humanely." The seriousness of this concern can be fairly measured, I think, by asking when those participating in any sport have ever stopped or modified what they are doing because of concerns over animal welfare. The answer says a lot about the depth and sincerity of their professed concern. To the best of my knowledge (and I stand to be corrected, if I am mistaken), the one-word answer is, never.

As is true of other forms of animal exploitation, the full story of the violation of animal rights in the name of sport cannot be told in these pages. Our conversation can cover only a few sentences from a few chapters of a much larger story. Even so, the sports discussed (hunting, rodeo, and greyhound racing) are representative and should help explain why ARAs are extremists when it comes to turning animals into competitors, in one sport or another, in one way or another. ARAs really are against this, all the time.

HUNTING

People who hunt for sport are a dwindling breed. Today fewer than 5 percent of Americans have hunting licenses, half the number who bought them as recently as the 1970s, significantly fewer than the number who hunted back when I envied the older boys in my neighborhood who got to go hunting. Still, sport hunting remains big business. The Fund for Animals estimates total annual outlay for all costs (guns, ammunition, clothing, etc.) for 2000 at $21 billion. Money in that amount translates into a lot of dead animals. The Fund places the figure at 134 million animals killed annually, just in America, including 35 million mourning doves, 13 million rabbits, 26.5 million squirrels, 12 million quail, 7 million pheasants, and 16.5 million ducks.

While sports hunters always want to frame the "hunting debate" in terms of deer hunting (the Fund puts the total of deer killed at six million), the vast majority of the animals hunters kill are not related to Bambi. Regulated species (wildlife that can only be killed at certain times) include waterfowl, upland birds, and mourning doves, while unregulated species (wildlife that can be killed at any time, in any amount) include coyotes, porcupines, crows, and prairie dogs.

One reason sport hunting is declining in popularity is simple: most of us cannot see the sport in it. Traditionally defended on the grounds of fair chase, we are to imagine today's brave hunters, armed with their superior knowledge and skills, out in the woods, there to outwit their prey, in a setting that offers the animals, using their knowledge and skills, ample opportunity to escape. Never mind that hunters today are outfitted with hundreds, even thousands, of dollars' worth of weaponry and technology—turkey, deer, duck, or Lonesome Cow Elk Calls; Silver Top Gel Paste Doe Estrus Deer Lure; Doe-in-Rut Buck Lure; scent blocker clothing; a Garmin GPS V Deluxe Horizontal/Vertical GPS Unit with Routing Capabilities; or (my personal favorite) the Shaggie 3-D Cover System (the latter from Rancho Safari www.rancho.safari.com). If going out in the woods wearing a Shaggie doesn't get you shot at, it is hard to understand why not. As for the ferocious geese and ducks, squirrels and mourning doves, deer and other animals: what are they armed with? Just their senses. Still, they have plenty of means of escape, which is why trying to kill them is a sport.

Humpty Dumpty Redux

To think that having a means of escape makes hunting a sport distorts the truth; it does not describe it. As Humpty Dumpty says, people can say a word means anything they want it to mean. They can say "glory" means "a nice knockdown argument for you!" But (obviously) words do not change their meaning just because someone says they do.

What "sport" means is no exception. "Fair chase" alone does not a sport make. No matter what hunters say to the contrary (and the same applies to those who refer to fishing, rodeo, and greyhound or horse racing as "sports"), to participate in a sport in its true sense requires voluntary participation on the part of those who compete. This is why baseball, soccer, and golf are sports and why (in part) the bloodbath of Christians in the Coliseum was not.

Sport hunting is not like baseball, soccer, and golf. It is like the "games" played in Rome. The Christians who were forced to face the lions in the Coliseum did not volunteer to compete in an episode of *Survivor*; neither do the millions of animals who annually are killed by hunters in America. Call it "recreational hunting" if you will, but "sport" hunting is no sport.

"Humane" Hunting

Hunters do not like to be thought of as cruel. On the contrary, they see themselves as among the most humane people in the world. Ann S. Causey explains why:

> The genuine sport hunter due to his earnest respect for his prey is usually highly sensitive to the animal's pain and suffering and makes every effort to minimize both. Proper weaponry and hunter training can minimize trauma to the animal. In terms of overall humaneness, a life free of confinement and a quick death at the hands of a skilled sport hunter beat anything the livestock industry can offer and certainly beat most of the death scenes Mother Nature directs.

So there we have it. People who blow a squirrel or coyote's brains out are paragons of humaneness, displaying their mercy, compassion, sympathy, consideration, and kindness. At least they do better in these respects than factory farmers, not to mention other animals.

Comparisons like this prove nothing. Hunters do not demonstrate their humaneness by pointing out that some people treat animals worse than they do. Logically, what Causey says is fully comparable to saying that rapists who only assault unconscious women (and thus are "sensitive to their victim's pain and suffering," doing what they can to "minimize trauma") are "more humane" than rapists who like to hurt their victims. One would have thought that "humane rapist" is a cruel contradiction. Apologists for sport hunting, like Causey, offer no reason for thinking that "humane hunter" is any different.

CHAPTER 9

List Hunters

Topping the chart of "humane hunters" are so-called list hunters. List hunters collect the heads of dead animals the way other people collect stamps or comic books. Different hunters try to complete different lists. The African Big Five includes leopard, lion, elephant, rhinoceros, and cape buffalo. The Arctic Grand Slam consists of caribou, musk ox, polar bear, and walrus. For most of the twentieth century, walrus were a protected species. That changed in 1994; since then an increasing stream of list hunters has been willing to pay $6,000–$6,500 for the privilege of completing the Arctic Grand Slam.

New York Times reporter C. J. Chivers describes one such hunt, this one conducted by Peter Studwell, a successful businessman from Connecticut. Inuit guides escorted Studwell out to the ice where a pair of bull walrus rested. As the men approached, the walrus regarded them more out of curiosity than fear. When they were within fifteen feet, the lead guide told Studwell to shoot. Studwell fired. The animal was killed with a single shot.

By his own account, Studwell has killed 45 different species of animals, including 11 bears, 10 elks, 6 caribou, 3 moose, 2 musk oxen, a bison, a cougar, and perhaps as many as 300 deer. The walls of his living room display 147 of his trophies. The walrus will make that 148. Studwell could not be prouder. "It's the biggest thing I've ever killed," he said. "That or the bison."

Ever the observer, Chivers puts Studwell's hunt in perspective. "It is an achievement that is not surprising, considering that walrus hunting, under Inuit supervision, is the approximate equivalent of a long boat ride to shoot a very large beanbag chair." Except, of course, beanbag chairs are not alive and cannot be killed for "sport."

Canned Hunts

Comparatively few hunters (fewer than one thousand, Chivers estimates) have added a walrus to their Arctic Grand Slam. Many more (no one knows the exact number) enthusiastically participate in an even less demanding equivalent of shooting very large beanbag chairs.

Estimates place the number of facilities offering canned hunts in America at about one thousand. Found in most states (only fourteen states ban canned hunts), these operations frequently are advertised as "game" or "hunting preserves."

The animals "hunted" in canned hunts include Asian and African antelope, bison, bears, zebras, and elks. The animals, many of whom have been raised by humans and who have come to trust us, are confined in fenced enclosures. After deciding which animal to kill, patrons either walk or are driven to the appropriate location. As they approach, the animals are not perturbed; just another human visitor. But then the hunters aim their weapon and kill their prey.

"Fair chase" is pure fiction here. Canned hunts are like shooting fish in a barrel, created for the convenience of "sport" hunters who want a trophy for their den but don't want to go to the time or trouble of actually tramping through the woods to get it. The following is a description of a canned hunt that was captured on video by undercover investigators for the Humane Society of the United States:

> The Corsican ram stopped cold in his tracks, raised his head to sniff the breeze, and tried to peer through the foliage. The hunter, covered head to toe in camouflage, slowly raised to shoulder level a modern techno-marvel of levers, wheels, and pulleys and released his arrow. At the twang of the string, the ram jerked his head around—just as the razor-sharp broadhead sliced into his left flank. Letting out a bellow of pain and terror, he lunged forward into the wire fence that held him captive. The hunter, no more than twenty yards away, reloaded and shot. Another strike in the flank and another bellow as once again the ram hurled himself against the fence. A third arrow struck him in the side, a fourth high up on the back. The hunter was deliberately aiming away from the head and shoulders to avoid any risk of spoiling his trophy. "If you fall," he yelled at the ram, "fall the right way. I don't want you bending my arrow." The slowly dying animal huddled against the bottom of the fence. After six arrows, the guide put the doomed animal out of his agony with a bullet.

At $350 per animal, Corsican rams are among the cheaper choices. Taking down a rhinoceros, for example, will cost you $20,000. And that does not include travel, accommodations, meals, and the services of a taxidermist.

"The Animals Come from Where?"

Where do these animals come from? After all, African antelope and rhinoceroses are not exactly indigenous to the United States. How do they end up on "hunting preserves" in Texas, say? Well, sometimes they come from private breeders, who are in the business of supplying trophy animals and who have very little to say about "animal welfare" and "humane and responsible care." But sometimes trophy animals come from two of America's loudest backers of these values. I mean circuses and zoos, including some of the best known.

The role played by zoos is especially instructive. The best zoos in the country belong to the American Zoo and Aquarium Association, which has a written policy that explicitly prohibits the direct sale of "surplus" zoo animals (animals who have been bred at a zoo but for whom there is no room). However, nothing prevents zoos from selling their surplus animals to animal dealers, who in turn sell them to canned hunt operations. After a two-year investigation, the *San Jose Mercury News* learned that "of the 19,361 mammals that left the nation's accredited zoos from 1992 through mid-1998, 7,420—or 38 percent—went to dealers, auctions, hunting ranches, unidentified individuals or unaccredited zoos or game farms." Remarkably, many of the "trophy animals" (gazelles, zebras, even rhinoceroses) that attract the "humane" hunters who frequent canned hunts once called a circus or a zoo home. The hypocrisy of zoo (and of circus) administrators is shameful beyond words.

"Real" Hunters

Some hunters (they think of themselves as "real" hunters) repudiate canned hunts as well as list hunts like Studwell's. To shoot a caged animal or a walrus half dozing on the ice is as far from real hunting as buying salmon at the fish counter is from real fishing. It is hard to fault their logic. On this point, "real" hunters are right. Where they go wrong is in thinking that what they do is a sport. At least this is where they go wrong conceptually: there is no true sport where there is no volunteering.

"Real" hunters not only believe they have a right to hunt; they believe hunting is right. Why? "Real" hunters are not the least bit reticent when it comes to trying to justify what they do. On the contrary, they obviously feel a need to explain themselves, as well they should. On examination, I believe their attempts at justification are best understood as so many stories, so many pieces of fiction they tell one another and us, while all the while the real truth goes unspoken. We can listen only to some of the main stories here. (Others are more than adequately addressed in the online resources available at the website listed in the preface.)

1. "My Genes Made Me Do It."

"The reason humans hunt is genetic. It's human nature. To kill other animals is part of what it is to be human." Probably everyone has heard this explanation, at one time or another. If the only hunters who spun this tale were backwoods folks like the ones Burt Reynolds meets in the movie *Deliverance*, we perhaps could brush it aside. In fact, however, sport hunting's intellectual heavyweights (Aldo Leopold, Ortega y Gasset, Ted Nugent) line up behind this way of thinking.

Consider Leopold, a visionary, influential forester, famous for his *A Sand County Almanac*. Leopold would have us believe that "[the] hunting fever is endemic in the race." Ortega y Gasset goes further, declaring that the desire to hunt "is a deep and permanent yearning in the human condition," something that is "bred into every fiber of the human race."

There's just one problem with this genetic hypothesis. The evidence is strongly against it. How explain the 95 percent of Americans (and comparable statistics for many other countries) who do not hunt? Are we missing a gene somewhere? In particular, are ARAs repressing our natural urge to kill animals every time we stalk the salad bar? It is difficult to take such thinking seriously. People who hunt cannot blame it on their genes.

2. *"Love Made Me Do It."*

Another prohunting justification has orgiastic overtones. Ortega actually writes in these terms. Blood (others', preferably) has "unequaled orgiastic power." Those who would substitute wildlife photography for hunting, in Ortega's view, might just as well substitute platonic love for the real thing. As Randall Eaton (a strident advocate of sport hunting) declares, "the hunter's feeling for his prey is one of deep passion [and] ecstasy. . . . The hunter loves the animal he kills."

Something has gone wrong here. I love Nancy and my children. I am happy to say that they love me too. Yet we do not make it a practice of trying to kill one another. In this, I cannot believe that the Regan family is in any way exceptional. True, there are tragic cases where, because of a wayward psychopathology, this sort of thing happens; for example, a woman drowns her children because, she says, "I loved them so." But everyone recognizes such occurrences for what they are: tragic aberrations involving people who do not understand their own actions. Why think any differently when sport hunters tell us they love the dead animals in the back of their pickup truck? Why, indeed?

3. *"It's a Spiritual Thing."*

Many are the spiritual encomiums written in celebration of hunting. By killing animals, we are to believe, a door is opened to the divine. In David Petersen's words, hunting "is the closest thing I've known to a spiritual experience." James A. Swan describes the situation in greater detail. "Anyone can declare an animal to be special, even sacred. But a thing can become truly sacred only if a person knows in his or her heart that the object or creature can somehow serve as a conduit to a realm of existence that transcends the temporal." That's what dead wild animals are for: they serve as (or at least they can serve as) "a conduit [for the hunter] to a realm of existence that transcends the temporal."

It is difficult to know what to say about these musings. Jim Motavalli, editor of *E Magazine*, just shakes his head when he hears (these are his words) "this spiritual mumbo jumbo." Perhaps this is all that needs to be said, all that should be said. But perhaps it is worth trying to draw an analogy to make a logical point. So suppose someone were to say the following: "Anyone can declare a *human being* to be special, even sacred. But a thing can become truly sacred only if a person knows in his or her heart that the object or creature can somehow serve as a conduit to a realm of existence that transcends the temporal."

If we adopt a certain way of looking at the world, it would be hard to quarrel with some of what is said here. There is no reason to think it is impossible that human beings can be "special, even sacred." But if in the next breath we are told that *killing human beings* can serve as "a conduit to a realm of existence that transcends the temporal," all of us (one must hope) will demur. We don't justify killing one another because doing so is a source of spiritual uplift. But (and here we come to the logical point) if killing humans for "spiritual" reasons is wrong, how can it be right to kill wildlife for reasons of the same kind? Those who rest their hunting ethic on things spiritual have a lot of explaining to do.

4. "We're Doing Them a Favor."

One of the favorite stories hunters tell pictures them as the best friend dead wildlife ever had. The plot goes like this. Winter is very hard on animals. Many will die either because of the elements or from starvation; both are slow, agonizing ways to return to the earth. Fortunately for the animals, hunters are on hand and eager to help. Animals shot by expert marksmen are the lucky ones. They die quickly, without feeling a thing. When it comes to being humane, to promoting animal welfare, it's hard to get much better than this.

"Hypocrisy" is the best thing that can be said about this story, as the following reasons explain. First, the vast majority of animals killed by hunters do not belong to species facing the prospect of freezing or starving to death during the winter; this includes the 50 million mourning doves, 25 million rabbits and squirrels, 25 million quail, 20 million pheasant, and 10 million ducks, to mention only some of the most obvious examples.

Second, among those animals who do face this prospect, it is the young, the old, the sick, and the lame who are most at risk. Third, if hunters really mean it when they say that, by killing animals, they are trying to prevent them from dying in misery, the animals they would kill would be . . . the young, the old, the sick, and the lame. But, fourth, these are precisely *not* the animals hunters want to bring home after a day of hunting. The animals they want to bring home are the biggest and healthiest, the very ones who have the best chance of surviving through the winter. So, yes, "hypocrisy" is the best thing that can be said about this story.

5. "It's Fun!"

Underneath all the talk about love and spirituality there is one simple, incontrovertible fact. Sports hunters enjoy hunting. They like hiking through the woods, sitting for hours in a tree stand, or watching their breath in the chill of a duck blind. Plus it's fun being out with the guys or gals, communing with nature. All true, no doubt. But when all the rhetorical dust settles, the real rush for the sport hunter comes from the kill. Any doubt about this, just look through any of the hunting magazines on the rack at the local newsstand. The hunters pictured in those pages, displaying their dead wares, smiling from ear to ear, could not be happier. If we asked them to pose with beanbag chairs, it just wouldn't be the same.

Here, I think, is the true explanation of why hunters hunt. *The mere possibility of killing animals* is exciting. A study conducted at Michigan's William Beaumont Hospital found that "[t]he heart rate of some hunters would almost double upon seeing a deer, even though they [the hunters] were standing still." Imagine the rush of enjoyment they must experience when they actually kill (and don't just see) an animal, something which, when you stop to think about it, is a pretty awful thing to say about oneself. Imagine saying, "Yeah, I'm planning on having a really good time this weekend killing me some animals!" Maybe there are some hunters who would not have trouble saying this, but my guess is that most would. Which is why they tell the stories they do, about why hunting is in the genes or why animals should be grateful when hunters are kind enough to blow their brains out. The stories function to divert attention from the truth. To enjoy killing anyone is not something in which any humane person can take pride. Who among us wants to insist, "Call me anything, but don't you dare call me humane!"?

"Send in the Vandals!"

Prohunting organizations like the National Rifle Association are none too happy whenever the violence-prone anti-American ARAs get in a snit over hunting. The NRA's response is predictable. "Our hunting heritage is under attack by uninformed, misguided people who wish to impose their values on society by any means possible. Anti-hunting activists attack hunting through deceptive publicity campaigns, disguised educational programs in schools, physical harassment of law-abiding sportsmen and women, and vandalism of personal property."

I hope it is clear that the NRA fails to address the animal rights message and instead resorts to the all too familiar tactic of attacking the animal rights messenger. Such tactics, though lacking in logic, are not lacking in power. In American politics the NRA is the tail that wags the dog. ARAs understand this. We know the influence money can buy. But we also believe that the great majority of Americans will think beyond the bad things others say about us. All that ARAs want, in the present context, is the chance to have a conversation, to reason together. Not even the NRA can prevent that from happening.

In his *New York Times* story about walrus hunting, C. J. Chivers tells of overhearing one young Inuit guide talking to another. "Sometimes I don't know why they call it sport hunting," the guide said. "We take them out, and they sit there. We find them the walrus, and we drive up to it and tell them when to shoot. We butcher it and carry it to the boat. Then they get to shore, and say: 'I got one! I got one!'"

There is wisdom in these words. In this hunt there is no sport. Nor in any other. I understand now why I should never have envied the older boys in my neighborhood, the ones who got to go hunting. When my parents said no, they raised me well.

RODEO

The Professional Rodeo Cowboys Association (PRCA) takes its stand for animal welfare and against animal rights. The philosophy of animal rights means we have to stop using animals in rodeos, and much else. PRCA wants none of that. By contrast, the philosophy of animal welfare is "based on principles of humane care and use. Organizations [like PRCA] who support animal welfare principles seek to improve the treatment and well being of animals. Supporting animal welfare premises means believing humans have the right to use animals, but along with that right comes the responsibility to provide proper and humane care and treatment." PRCA presents itself as doing all the above and more. Not only do they have strict rules concerning animal welfare, they require that a veterinarian be on site at all their sponsored contests.

PRCA-sponsored contests are just the tip of the rodeo iceberg. Of the estimated five thousand rodeos held each year in America, 85 percent are not sponsored by PRCA; for these rodeos, PRCA rules do not apply and no on-site veterinarian is required. Even if it were true that rodeos associated with PRCA were above reproach, it would not follow that the same is true of the overwhelming majority of rodeos.

Rodeo is billed as a "sport" and rodeos themselves as "contests" that pit the courage and skill of human contestants (almost always men) against the strength and speed of animals. Cash and other prizes are awarded to those who earn the highest score in the individual events and overall. Rodeo's popularity is growing. Upwards of twenty-five million people attended a rodeo in the past year. Wrangler, the "other" jean maker, was the corporate sponsor of the 2002 national championships. Other major sponsors include Coors beer, Dodge trucks, and Jack Daniels whiskey. Since 2001 the national championships have been televised nationally by ESPN.

Rodeo is even less a sport than sport hunting. Most of the time the animals killed by hunters at least have some opportunity to escape. Not so the calves and bulls (and sometimes the horses) used in rodeos. The only way these animals escape is when they die in the ring or are shipped to slaughter.

"Why Do Those Horses Buck?"

Saddle bronc riding is rodeo's "classic" event, one that PRCA traces back to a time when cowboys would compete among themselves to see who could display the best style while riding unbroken horses. Today's riders are required to spur their horses, and receive points for how skillfully they do so. Other factors scored concern length of ride, control, and the effort of the horse. In fact, fully 50 percent of possible points are awarded on the basis of how hard the horse (or the bull, in bull bucking) bucks. Understandably, contestants and event organizers can go to great lengths to encourage bucking behavior.

The horses who participate in these contests are not unbroken. They are veteran performers who are hauled from show to show. Left to their own devices, there is not much buck in them. This behavior is induced by a variety of human interventions, including the use of electric prods administered just as the horse leaves the holding chute and the tightening of a flank strap, a leather strap cinched behind the rib cage where there is no rib cage protection. Tightened near the large and small intestines and other vital organs, some critics charge that the belt pinches the groin and genitals.

Peggy Larson, the large-animal vet and former bareback bronc rodeo rider, thinks most of the pain is caused by spurring. "It is deceptive of PRCA to require spurs to be blunt . . . so the horse will not be cut. Cutting is not the problem. Tissue damage is caused by repeated blunt injury. Usually the horse is bucked again before the bruises heal, so the damage is compounded. Common sense will tell you that when steel meets flesh, flesh loses."

So, why do horses buck? Because they are frightened and in pain. Why do some buck more than others? Because they are more frightened and in greater pain. Such is the perverse logic of the "sport" that points are awarded commensurate with the amount of a horse's fear and pain.

Roping Babies

In addition to the riding events, other staples are calf roping and steer wrestling. PRCA again traces the origins of calf roping to the Old West, when cowboys roped calves who needed veterinary care.

Calf roping does not last long. After the calf is given a head start, the horse and rider set off in hot pursuit. Once roped, the animal must first stand, then be flanked (thrown to the ground), then have any three legs tied. As soon as this is completed, the cowboy raises his hands, then mounts his horse, the rope going slack. If a calf becomes free before six seconds elapses, the run does not count. Participants put in hours of practice to sharpen their skills—sharpen their skills, that is, going through their routine, often on the same calf, over and over and over, beyond the reach of any law.

Like the other animals used in rodeos, calves have no say in the proceedings. They *will* perform whether they want to or not. And they *will* be subject to the same tactics of fear and pain (a twisting of the tail here, the use of an electric prod there) that other animals endure. In the case of the calves, however, there is a special kind of insult.

Calves can reach speeds up to thirty miles an hour before they are lassoed ("clotheslined"); often they are jerked over backward and slammed to the ground. (Though this outcome is technically illegal, penalties are seldom meted out.) The faster they are running at the time, the harder they are pulled backward. And the harder they are pulled backward, the more their necks are wrenched and the greater the force with which they hit the ground. Some calves do not do encores. It's one performance and out. They either die in the dust or die soon thereafter.

So here we have today's brave cowboy, bending over and tying up a frightened, dazed, disoriented baby (the animals are all of four to five months old), with neck or back injuries, bruises, broken bones, and internal hemorrhages. Are those who are working to abolish rodeo in general, calf roping in particular, just overwrought, emotionally unbalanced calf huggers?

Before answering, consider the following excerpts from a letter by E. J. Finocchio, DVM, to the Rhode Island state legislature, in support of banning calf roping in Rhode Island. "As a large animal veterinarian for 20 years . . . I have witnessed firsthand the instant death of calves after their spinal cords were severed from the abrupt stop at the end of a rope when traveling up to 30 mph. I have also witnessed and tended calves who became paralyzed . . . and whose tracheas were totally or partially severed . . . Slamming to the ground has caused rupture of several internal organs leading to a slow, agonizing death for some of these calves." And they call this "sport."

Peggy Larson doesn't think so. "Based upon my extensive experience with large animals, I have come to the conclusion that rodeo events are inherently inhumane. The most cruel are the roping events."

Dr. Larson cites another authority, C. G. Haber, a veterinarian with thirty years' experience as a USDA meat inspector. "The rodeo folks send their animals to the packing houses where . . . I have seen cattle so extensively bruised that the only areas in which the skin was attached [to the body] was the head, neck, legs, and belly. I have seen animals with six to eight ribs broken from the spine and at times puncturing the lungs. I have seen as much as two and three gallons of free blood accumulated under the detached skin." So much for promoting animal welfare. In an effort to try to change reality by calling it by another name, PRCA's wordsmiths now call calf roping "tie down roping." Just like that, the victims—the calves—have disappeared.

Most of the national and many regional and local animal advocacy groups have antirodeo campaigns. SHARK (Showing Animals Respect and Kindness), under the leadership of Steve Hindi, is shining a spotlight on rodeo's hidden cruelty, using long-range cameras and even cameras that can film in the dark. Anyone who doubts that rodeos are guilty of the offenses described here can confirm the accuracy of the description by consulting SHARK's video archives.

Not Seeing Is Not Believing

People who know rodeo's hidden cruelty understand that what they see on television is not what actually takes place at rodeos. No electric prods and tail pulling on ESPN's telecasts. No discussion of what the flank strap is and why it is attached where it is. All this is predictable, given the corporate sponsors and the need to present rodeo as wholesome "family entertainment." What is worse goes deeper. It goes to the decision to edit out death and injury.

Writing in *Extra*, the magazine of Fairness and Accuracy in Reporting, Karen Chapman tells of how a horse died at the 2001 rodeo finals. "[A] 14-year-old bucking bronco named Great Plains broke its back and had to be carried out on an animal stretcher in front of the sold-out crowd of 17,000. Though the event was televised by the cable network ESPN, operating on a seven second tape delay, the TV audience had no clue about what happened. The camera cut just before the horse flipped over, and none of the announcers said one word about the incident. The horse was destroyed an hour later."

Then there is the matter of ESPN's noncoverage of calf roping. Without exception, television coverage of this event never lets viewers see what happens to the calf when the lasso pulls the animal back and to the ground. Without exception, those moments are edited out. If we ask why, the answer is not hard to find. When asked, PRCA commissioner Steve Hatchell had this to say: "We're really sensitive to people who might have a problem with calf-roping. We just want to showcase it in the best light. We want the show to be well presented to an audience broader than just rodeo people."

But how (one might ask) do PRCA's preferences translate into editorial policy? Isn't there a firm line between the event organizer and the professionals in the booth? "We [that is, PRCA] determine what goes on the air," Hatchell told the *Wyoming Tribune-Eagle*. "ESPN doesn't have anything to say about it."

It is hard not to become deeply cynical in the face of such power, not only the power that is exercised over other animals but also the power to control what people see. PRCA understands too well that viewers will not rise up against what they are not permitted to see. So what if viewers are denied the painful truth? The main thing is to have a show that is "well presented to an audience broader than just rodeo people."

GREYHOUND RACING

No one knows the origin of the name "greyhound." Some conjecture that in the past all greyhounds had gray coats; others, that the name is a corruption of "Greek hound," hearkening back to the breed's origins in Greece.

Whatever the true etymology, we know that greyhounds have had a special place in human history. In ancient Egypt, for example, greyhounds were associated with royalty; in keeping with the honorific practices of the times, their bodies were mummified along with their human caretakers. Homer celebrated the dog Argus because Argus was the only one who recognized Odysseus when he returned home after being away for years. Argus was a greyhound. And so revered was the breed when the Danish king Canute ruled England in the eleventh century, anyone convicted of killing a greyhound was put to death.

Among the oldest breeds of dogs, greyhounds are by far the fastest. Thin of body, long of leg, they are excellent sprinters. In their prime greyhounds can reach speeds in excess of forty-five miles an hour over short distances and average over thirty miles an hour when running up to a mile. Unfortunately for the dogs their great speed has been exploited by human beings who care more about making money than respecting rights.

Welfare Versus Rights

The National Greyhound Association, the official registry of racing greyhounds in North America, articulates the philosophy informing greyhound racing. It is a variation on a familiar theme.

> The animal welfare philosophy holds that it is both appropriate and necessary for humans to use animals for food, clothing, research, education, sport, recreation and companionship, as long as we do so responsibly and humanely.
>
> In contrast, the animal rights philosophy rejects all animal use, no matter how humane. . . .
>
> Animal welfare advocates accept responsibility for the humane treatment of the animals in their charge.

How far this is from the truth will be apparent in what follows.

And They Call This Humane?

Greyhounds race worldwide. Tracks operate in Australia, New Zealand, and throughout Asia, Europe, and North and South America. In the United States, there are forty-eight tracks in fifteen states, a third of them in Florida. According to the American Greyhound Track Owners Association, greyhound racing is the nation's sixth largest spectator sport, attracting more than thirty million paying enthusiasts annually.

Each year, some thirty-four thousand greyhounds are bred for the industry. The fastest and the fittest dogs begin racing at eighteen months. A few race until the mandatory retirement age of five years; the majority "retire" between three and four. Injuries (broken bones and heart attacks, for example) are an unfortunate economic cost that must be borne by humane trainers and owners.

Approximately a third of the dogs never race because they are lame, sick, or just not fast enough. Estimates place the number of greyhounds killed incidental to the racing industry at more than twenty thousand per year. Methods used include gunshot, bludgeoning, and electrocution.

Perhaps the cruelest insult to this noble breed occurs when dogs are sold or donated to research laboratories. These docile, trusting animals, with their pure bloodlines, make ideal "models" for a variety of experiments. The numbers are not inconsiderable. Between 1995 and 1998, researchers at Colorado State University used 2,650 greyhounds donated by local breeders. Figures for other universities for comparable years: Kansas State University, 111; the University of Alabama, 254; Iowa State University, 595.

Day-to-day life for racing greyhounds is characterized by chronic deprivation. Dogs are confined in small crates, some measuring three feet by three feet. On days when they are not racing, the animals can be crated for up to twenty-two hours, sometimes stacked in tiers. Except when eating, they are muzzled.

Asked why the dogs are crated so long, we are told (again, I am not making this up) by the Greyhound Lovers' League that "dogs are basically lounging animals. Once they reach maturity pet dogs spend the vast majority of their time lying around the house. A greyhound's crate is his bed." As for why they are muzzled, the explanation is an expression of the industry's commitment to humane treatment. After all, if their muzzles were removed, the dogs could injure their mouth, teeth, or gums when they gnaw on their wire cages. In other words, the industry's remedy for one kind of deprivation (keeping the dogs caged) is to impose another kind of deprivation (keeping them muzzled), the better to treat them more humanely. In the greyhound racing community, the Disconnect Dictum reigns supreme.

Special Cruelty

Accounts of special cruelty (dogs starving to death, abandoned, beaten) are plentiful and are not confined to the United States by any means. In the summer of 2000, ARAs throughout the world were horrified to learn of the atrocities committed in Medino del Campo, a small town located northwest of Madrid. Loles Silva, a writer for the magazine *Interviú*, reported that hundreds of greyhounds, no longer capable of competing successfully, were found hanging from trees in the neighboring pine groves. Evidently their owners believed the dogs had earned a "humane" death. Even worse, as hard as this is to believe, dogs who were too slow to compete in the first place were found hanging so that their rear feet barely touched the ground. No one knows how long these abandoned creatures struggled to remain alive before, exhausted by their efforts, they finally gave up and, gasping for one last breath, died.

Lest we think that nothing remotely like this could happen in America, the May 22, 2002, edition of the *New York Times* reported the discovery of the mass graves of thousands of greyhounds on ill-kept rural property outside Lillian, Alabama. Judged to be too slow for racing, they were sold to one Robert L. Rhodes, who killed them "humanely" with a single bullet to the head. "They didn't feel a thing," he told authorities investigating the carnage.

David Whetstone, the Baldwin County District Attorney overseeing the investigation, disputed Rhodes's assurance, saying that the dogs did not die instantly. Whetstone allowed as how he had gone to greyhound races in the past but was now having second thoughts after the discovery of what he described as "a Dachau for dogs."

"We've seen this before," Whetstone said. "A madman called Hitler was doing it, trying to create a super race. Well, they're over-breeding, because they're trying to get super dogs. These dogs were not unhealthy, they were just slow." How "clean," how "healthy" is greyhound racing? Who better to trust for an answer than the Baldwin County district attorney?

Thankfully, some ARAs are helping place "unwanted" greyhounds. Organizations specializing in greyhound adoptions can be found throughout the United States and in many other countries. (For more information, consult the web addresses in the online resources for this chapter.) As important and admirable as these efforts are, they come too late in the day for the dogs who have been subjected to the cruelty inherent in the industry. The real solution to the "greyhound problem" is to stop making greyhounds race. Animal rights advocates will not be satisfied with anything less.

CONCLUSION

As noted at the beginning of this chapter, the full story of the violation of animal rights in the name of sport cannot be told in these pages. Our conversation has covered only a few sentences from a few chapters of that much larger story. Even so, the sports discussed are representative and should help readers understand why ARAs are extremists when it comes to turning animals into "competitors," in one sport or another, in one way or another.

There is no "sport" in hunting, rodeo, greyhound racing, or in any other comparable activity, including horse racing, cockfighting, the bullfight, and the Iditerod, for example. What there is, is human domination, human exploitation, human avarice, human cruelty. A life in which respect for animal rights has a place can find no room for these barbarities.

It is only a matter of time, ARAs believe, before the civilized world evolves to the point where all such "sports" are banished. As Albert Schweitzer observes, "The time will come when public opinion will no longer tolerate amusements based on the mistreatment and killing of animals." Animal rights advocates believe this, to the very depth of our being. But we are also mindful of Schweitzer's final words: "The time will come. But when?"

TURNING ANIMALS
INTO TOOLS

When asked what we think about using animals in research, most of us will say something about the important medical benefits derived from using them. Life-saving surgeries (heart, kidney, and other transplants). Life-extending drugs (for cancer, diabetes, and hypertension). Where would we be if we did not use animals? Back in the dark ages, that's where.

Is this true? Are all or even most of the major advances in public health indebted to using "animal models"? And even if they are, what about the moral question: Would our benefits justify their harms?

I used to think the answers to both questions were easy and the same. Yes, to the first. Yes, to the second. Even after I started on my journey toward an expanded animal consciousness, I defended research using animals. If the researchers at General Motors said they had to use baboons in crash tests to make seat belts safer, who was I to argue with them? So long as animals were not caused any "unnecessary suffering," I was on board. Because no researcher ever denied this (none ever said, "I always make it a point to make sure my animals suffer unnecessarily"), it was hard for people who shared my views to be against much research.

Then I started to muddle along, first asking one question, then a second, then a third. In time I came to reject my earlier beliefs. Today, I no longer think that most of the major advances in public health are due to the use of the "animal model." Today, I think it is wrong to use animals as tools in research even if their suffering is "necessary." Today, I even think it is wrong to dissect dead animals or harm live ones for educational purposes or to use them to conduct product safety tests. In fact, as I hope to be able to explain, using animals for these purposes is not only archaic, there are superior ways to achieve the ends we seek without using them.

"HUMANE CARE"

The utilization of animals as tools in science usually is divided into three categories: education, testing, and research. It will come as no surprise to learn that those who favor using animals for these purposes embrace the philosophy of animal welfare. By way of illustration: the National Association for Biomedical Research (NABR) describes itself as "the only national, nonprofit organization dedicated solely to advocating sound public policy that recognizes the vital role of humane animal use in biomedical research, higher education and product safety testing." NABR members include "over 300 public and private universities, medical and veterinary schools, teaching hospitals, voluntary health agencies, professional societies, pharmaceutical companies and other animal research-related firms." NABR is, we are told, "the unified voice for the scientific community on legislative and regulatory matters affecting laboratory animal research." And what do NABR and its members support? They support "the responsible use and humane care and treatment of laboratory animals in research, education and product safety testing." In other words, NABR and the interests it represents are fertile ground for the application of the Disconnect Dictum.

USING ANIMALS AS TOOLS IN EDUCATION

Animals routinely are used in educational settings. For example, America's high school and university students annually dissect more than six million animals. Dissection was not standard practice until the 1920s. Perhaps partly in response to the antivivisection movement that was growing in strength at the time, the scientific establishment orchestrated changes that made it normal, even mandatory, for students to dissect dead animals as part of their courses in anatomy, physiology, and (as was true in my case) biology.

The animals dissected are either captured in the wild, purchased at animal shelters, stolen, bred at special facilities, or procured from slaughterhouses. Most of these animals pass through a biological supply company before ending up in the classroom. Providing animals for dissection is not on the margins of profitability; in America today, it is a multimillion dollar industry.

The care and treatment received by animals destined for dissection normally is hidden from public view. "Unauthorized personnel" are not admitted inside. Video footage obtained by an undercover investigator, working for People for the Ethical Treatment of Animals, offers a rare glimpse of that forbidden world.

The video shows cats arriving at a biological supply company crammed so tightly into crates that they cannot stand up. Some are visibly sick; others look as if they are dying. After their arrival, "[the] frightened cats come face to face with a worker," the investigator writes, "who jabs violently at them with a metal hook, forcing them from two or three already cramped crates into one. Then it's on to the gas chamber. Many of the cats are still moving when workers pump formaldehyde into their veins. They clench their paws as the chemicals surge through their bodies. They are then stored and packaged and eventually shipped to schools all around the country."

Is this standard operating procedure for suppliers? Are the millions of animals destined for dissection treated this harshly? Until the suppliers' walls are made of glass, who can say?

"Students Have to Dissect to Learn Anatomy."

Why are animals dissected in the classroom? "It's the only (or the best) way to learn anatomy." This is far and away the most common answer. It also happens to be untrue. Anyone who has kept abreast of how students actually learn anatomy will tell you the same thing.

Jonathan Balcombe, who has made a close study of the relevant literature, concludes that students who use alternatives, including high-tech computer demonstrations, score equally well or better than students who performed dissection. Balcombe cites more than thirty academic studies that all reach the same conclusion. Clearly, dissection is not a necessity, judged in terms of what students learn.

Perhaps it will be said that dissection's real purpose is to help students become skillful in using various scientific tools (scalpels, sutures, and the like). If this is the purpose, it is unclear why every student should be expected to participate since only a small percentage of them will go on to have careers that require the use of such tools. Moreover, even if it is desirable that all students try using these tools at least once, there are better ways for students to become tool users. Readily available interactive video programs permit students to repeat procedures over and over, without permanently injuring the "specimen" on which they are practicing. Programs of this same kind are increasingly used in human and veterinary medicine. Anyone who insists that high-tech alternatives might suffice for medical students but that only real, albeit dead, animals can serve the interests of elementary, high school, or college students risks ridicule, and deservedly so.

The Winds of Change

Today, a growing number of biology, anatomy, and physiology teachers are breaking with the past and turning to high-tech alternatives. Worldwide, the trend away from dissection is growing. Argentina, Israel, The Netherlands, The Slovak Republic, and Switzerland have eliminated dissection from their primary and secondary schools, and the practice has been all but eliminated in the United Kingdom, Germany, and Sweden. At the same time a growing number of students, asserting their personal integrity, are exercising their constitutional right to "Just say no!" to compulsory dissection and vivisection. How I admire their courage! How I wish I had had their sensibilities when I was handed the scalpel and sutures in my biology labs! These young people should serve as an inspiration to everyone. As ARAs they are willing to take a stand, even if this means questioning authority and risking punishment. Real terrorists, these young folks. They are so "out of touch with reality."

The "Dog Lab"

Pockets of resistance remain, even at the highest levels of education. The University of Colorado School of Medicine was a glaring example. CSMD administrators and faculty dug in their heels against the forces of progressive change. And what is it that they fought tooth and nail to preserve? The infamous "dog lab."

The dog lab has been a rite of passage for generations of American physicians, during which time neither the American Medical Association nor the American Veterinary Medical Association lifted a finger to try to stop it. Typically conducted during the first year of medical school, a dog is first anesthetized; then the dog's chest is cut open so that students can observe the beating of the heart and how the administration of various drugs affects the heart's behavior. The anesthesia used is not always adequate. CSMD's own logs indicated that some dogs (the animals sometimes were in use in the lab for up to seven hours) exhibit "pain response." At the end of the demonstration, the dog is killed. In such ways, defenders of the dog lab believe, students acquire important knowledge about physiology and pharmacology. Dozens of dogs were killed each year for this purpose, just at CSMD.

Whatever may have been said in defense of dog labs in the past (and it should be noted that British medical schools, including Cambridge and Oxford, have *never* made these labs part of their medical instruction), little can be said in their defense today. Superior alternatives (CD-ROMs, interactive computer programs, cadaver exercises, and firsthand observation of human surgery) are readily available and already widely used. Some of these software programs graphically represent human physiology and show how various pharmacological agents affect the heart, heart rate, and blood pressure.

All this said, sooner or later someone will say: "It is a *teacher's right* to decide how to teach! It is a question of *academic freedom*. So (this familiar protest concludes) don't you ARA extremists think you can tell us what we have to do!"

In the absence of laws prohibiting exercises like the dog lab, professors certainly are within their legal rights if they continue to make such exercises available to their students. But freedom of any kind, including academic freedom, is always associated with accountability. The real question is not whether professors can offer a dog lab this year, and the next, and the next. The real question is whether they should be doing this, not only because of the wasted death of the dogs but out of concern for their students' education. All the available evidence points to the same conclusion: dog labs are not the best way for students to learn what participation in the lab is supposed to teach. Three out of every four medical schools in America, including the best of the best (Columbia, Harvard, Johns Hopkins, Stanford, and Yale, for example) no longer use live animals in any way, for any purpose. Railing on behind the banner of academic freedom, recalcitrant medical professors may choose to keep an archaic tradition alive in their courses. However, students, administrators, trustees, and financial supporters should know that it is the personal obstinacy of a few, not a commitment to offering superior educational opportunities to the many, that is giving these medical schools a bad name.

For years, ARAs in Colorado waged an aggressive campaign to stop the dog lab (and all other harmful uses of animals) in the medical school. In January 2003 administrators surprised everyone when they announced that they would cancel the dog lab for students entering in the fall. Why? Not for "ethical considerations," God forbid. The reasons were financial; the decision was made "because of the cost" ($17,000 per year). And if the school should experience happier economic times in the future? "The decision is not permanent," we are informed. "University officials will revisit it at the end of the year." With medical school administrators who think this way, ARA extremists will need to exercise something approaching eternal vigilance. Fortunately, the larger Boulder community is getting into the act. A January 31, 2003, editorial in the *Boulder Daily Camera*, after characterizing the lab as "potentially cruel . . . and obsolete," called upon the university to "do the right thing and permanently end the dog labs"—which is what ARAs have been saying for years. Those who lack persistence never change anything.

CHAPTER 10

Your Animal Companion Could End Up in a Lab

It is important to realize this simple fact: Your animal companion could end up
in a lab. Despite assurances on the part of spokespersons for the animal research
industry that this never happens, make no mistake about it: it does.

Shelter is a word with a reassuring meaning. It means "a place of protection,"
"a refuge," "a haven." So "animal shelters" must be places where animals find
refuge, must be havens where they are protected. Given its natural meaning, the
last thing shelters would do is release animals to someone they knew would hurt
them. A shelter that did this would be a contradiction in terms. Unfortunately,
some shelters have no problem being contradictions.

"Pound seizure" is the name of an insidious practice that makes business
partners of animal shelters and the animal research industry. In jurisdictions
where it is legal, which is most places (only thirteen states prohibit the practice), pound seizure works like this. A Class B dealer (this is a government
designation) purchases animals from random sources. These sources include
people offering kittens or puppies "Free to good home" and shelters that are
willing or required by law to "surrender" them. The dealer, in turn, sells the
animals to biomedical research laboratories, pharmaceutical companies, or
universities, where they might be used for educational purposes (in the dog
lab, for example). It takes no special training or expertise to be a Class B
dealer. Even convicted felons qualify. All it takes is fifty dollars for a license
issued by the U.S. Department of Agriculture, and we're ready to start our
business.

Here is a thought experiment we can conduct. Let's imagine we are Class B
dealers. We ask ourselves, "Which dogs would we be looking for when we go to
shelters? Which ones will be the easiest for us (and the same considerations apply to our customers) to handle?" Not big, aggressive, strong animals. Not animals with an attitude. No, the ones we would prefer are small- to medium-sized
animals with good dispositions, animals who have been fully socialized, animals
who enjoy being around people. In other words, the animals we would purchase
are *the very animals who are most adoptable,* the ones who have the best chance
of making it out of a shelter alive.

One other thing about these animals should never be forgotten. They have
learned to trust human beings, something dealers and researchers can use to
their advantage. No fighting. No biting. Just calm, confident behavior, complete
with a friendly wag of the tail or, in the case of cats, a gentle arching of the back.
Forgive me if I seem overly cynical when I ask: Is there no limit to the depth of
betrayal to which we humans can sink?

What happens to these animals after they become the property of the biomedical industry? No one really knows because no one is paying very close attention. Undercover investigations and literature searches are two ways of trying to learn more. One such investigation, conducted by another PETA investigator, documented treatment received by pound-seized dogs used in scabies research at Wright State University, in Dayton, Ohio. Here is a summary of what was discovered:

> The dogs were infected with scabies, a skin disease caused by microscopic mites that spread over their entire bodies, causing intense, prolonged itching, open wounds, and, eventually, death. One dog named Genesee was infected so severely, she turned circles constantly, unable to rest because of the intense itching. She cried out when handled, wouldn't eat or drink, and lost her balance; her anguished howls could be heard through closed doors. She finally died, without veterinary treatment, because that would have "interfered" with the experiment.

People who love dogs will hope this research did not occur, it is so horrible. But believe it we must. On the basis of the investigation, in which APHIS played no role, Wright State University was fined twenty thousand dollars for violating the Animal Welfare Act.

The work of Robert Eckstein offers an example of what literature searches can reveal. Doing a random search of the relevant literature, Eckstein traced what happened to fifty-two dogs "surrendered" by shelters. Summarizing the findings, Dr. Neal Barnard, founder and president of the Physicians Committee for Responsible Medicine (PCRM), writes that "[t]he median length of experiments was about ten days. Thirty-two percent of the experiments lasted longer than one month. The longest in his study lasted five and one-half years. Sixty-six percent of the experiments involved significant pain. Thirteen percent involved severe pain on unanesthetized animals. One in ten dogs died accidentally in the course of experiments."

Knowing what happened to Genesee and the other dogs tracked by Eckstein's research is important. Although the knowledge is slight, it helps crack the laboratory door, even if only a little. It permits us to catch a glimpse inside that normally forbidden world. And it also gives us a basis on which to respond when someone defends pound seizure saying, "the animals were going to die soon anyway." Death for these animals is preferable to days or months or years of being confined to a cage, in many cases living with untreated pain.

Spokespersons for the animal research industry (Americans for Medical Progress (AMP), for example), glibly dismiss the problem I have just described as "another animal rights tall tale." ARAs, they say, "prey on the emotions of pet owners, by hoodwinking them into believing that pets are stolen and sold to research facilities. The fact is, there is no market for stolen pets in biomedical research." And the evidence that supports this finding? AMP cites a study showing that "there simply isn't the demand now to sustain a high-volume market for stolen pets in research," from which AMP concludes, "[n]o demand—no business."

With all due respect to AMP's spokespersons, one has to hope they understand medicine better than they understand logic. The absence of "a high-volume market for stolen pets" does not mean there is no market for stolen pets. It is utterly fallacious to infer that there is "no demand" and thus "no business" because no "high-volume market" exists, even assuming that this is true. Think of it this way. Suppose *your* dog was stolen, sold to a Class B dealer, and ended up being in the same scabies experiment as Genesee. And suppose some representative from AMP says, "All the evidence shows that there is not a high-volume market for stolen pets in research." Well, there does not have to be a "high-volume market" for this to happen to your dog. All there has to be is a market for one dog: yours. Anyone who doubts that this ever happens should contact Chris DeRose, at Last Chance for Animals, something AMP operatives have never taken the time to do. If they had, they would know there is a long list of people whose companion animals have ended up in one laboratory or another, not all of whom have been found in time to save them.

USING ANIMALS IN TOXICITY TESTS

Toxicity tests are one of the many ways animals are used in the name of science. These tests aim to establish a given substance's likely harmful effects on human beings by first administering the substance to animals. The substance varies, from potentially therapeutic (prescription) drugs to shampoos, deodorants, skin lotions, perfumes, drain cleaners, dishwasher detergents, pesticides, and industrial solvents. Prescription drugs will be discussed below, in the section on animal research. The present discussion of toxicity tests applies to cosmetics and household products.

Different toxicity tests use different methods. Sometimes animals are forced to ingest the test substance, sometimes they are made to inhale it, and in other cases the substance is applied to the skin or the eye. Though the exact figure is not known, there is no doubt that millions of animals are used in these tests or that their number will continue to increase. For example, current plans call for the chemical industry to conduct five types of animal-based toxicity tests on three thousand chemicals over the next six years. These tests alone, assuming they are carried out as they have been in the past, will require the utilization of hundreds of thousands of animals. And this is only one among the many ongoing and planned animal-based toxicity studies the future holds. In the general area of toxicity assessment, the number of animals used will run into the tens of millions.

Toxicity tests are carried out in the name of product safety, with a view to minimizing the known risk to consumers. Binding federal regulations are vague, at best. In the language of the Food and Drug Administration, manufacturers "must adequately substantiate for safety" before making their product available to consumers. *How* safety is "adequately substantiate[d]" is left for each manufacturer to decide. Despite widespread belief to the contrary, when it comes to cosmetics and household products, animal toxicity tests are not required in general and no one test is legally required in particular.

" LD_{50} "

Throughout the past sixty years, one common toxicity test conducted on animals is the LD_{50}. *LD* stands for *lethal dose, 50* for *50 percent*. As the words suggest, the LD_{50} seeks to establish at what dosage the test substance will prove lethal (that is, will kill) 50 percent of the test animals. There are both oral and dermal (skin) versions of the test. Only the oral is considered here.

The oral LD_{50} works this way. The test substance is orally administered to the test animals, some of whom are given the substance in more, others in less, concentrated forms. In theory, anything and everything has a lethal dose. As Paracelsus (1493–1541) observed centuries ago, "All substances are poisons; there is none that is not a poison. The right dose differentiates a poison and a remedy." Even water has been shown to be lethal to 50 percent of test animals, if enough is consumed in a short enough period of time. In order to control variables and because the animals themselves will not "volunteer" to swallow such things as paint thinner or Christmas tree spray, a measured amount is passed through a tube and down the animals' throats. Variables are also controlled by withholding anesthetic. Anywhere from ten to sixty animals are used. Observation of their condition may last up to two weeks, during which time the requisite 50 percent normally die, after which the remaining animals are killed and their dissected bodies are examined. Depending on the results, the test substance is labeled as more or less toxic if swallowed in full or diluted concentrations. Tests like the oral LD_{50} are the invisible history behind the "Harmful or fatal if swallowed" labels on cans of such items as brake fluids, household lubricants, and industrial solvents.

That manufacturers have a responsibility to inform consumers about the safety of their products is an idea no sensible person would dispute. As a nation America has progressed beyond the days of "Buyer beware!" Whether reliance on the oral LD_{50} test discharges this responsibility to consumers and whether using animals to discharge this responsibility is morally worth the cost to the animals are matters sensible people would do well to consider.

Scientific critics of both types of the LD_{50}, including many who are part of the regulatory toxicity industry, find the test to be badly flawed. Results have been shown to vary from one lab to the next and even within the same lab from one day to the next. The sex, age, and diet of the test animals have been shown to skew the outcome, as has their species. Even if the results were regularly reproducible in the case of the test animals, their usefulness for humans is negligible at best. Doctors and other hospital personnel who work in emergency rooms, where the majority of accidental poisonings are dealt with, do not consult LD_{50} results before treating their patients. To suggest otherwise reflects profound ignorance of the practice of emergency medicine.

Things only get worse when we learn that the results of toxicity tests in general, the LD_{50} in particular, don't protect consumers. Mindy Kursban, who serves as general counsel for Physicians for Responsible Medicine, notes that "[I]nstead of presuming chemicals dangerous until proven safe . . . [government policies] permit the use of known toxic chemicals in most household products, including soaps, shampoos, hair colors, perfumes, nail polish remover, detergents, bleach, paints, glues, motor oil, markers, crayons, gasoline, cosmetics, candles, carpeting, and furniture polish." In this case, the "protection" in "consumer protection" is more fiction than fact.

The consequences of utilizing animals in toxicity tests, when we consider the animals, are far from negligible. For them, life in a laboratory can be a living hell. In the case of LD_{50} tests, for example, animals frequently become quite ill before they die or are killed. Symptoms include diarrhea, convulsions, and bloody discharge from the mouth, eyes, and rectum. Richard Ryder, a former experimental psychologist who used animals in his research while at Cambridge and Columbia universities, characterizes the plight of animals used in LD_{50} tests of cosmetics as follows:

> Because most cosmetic products are not especially poisonous, it necessarily follows that if a rat or a dog has to be killed this way, then very great quantities of cosmetic must be forced into their stomachs, blocking or breaking internal organs, or killing the animal by some other physical action, rather than by any specific chemical effect. Of course the procedure of force-feeding—even with healthy food—is

itself a notoriously unpleasant procedure, as suffragettes and other prisoners on hunger-strike have testified. When the substance forced into the stomach is not food at all, but large quantities of face powder, makeup or liquid hair dye, then no doubt the suffering is very much greater indeed. If, for the bureaucratic correctness of the test, quantities great enough to kill are involved then clearly the process of dying itself must often be prolonged and agonizing.

And lest we think that, in the majority of cases, the animals used are "only rats" or "only mice," we should note that neither mice nor rats are able to vomit and so cannot find even the temporary relief this mechanism provides.

ARAs believe the LD_{50} test is wrong. We believe it is wrong because it violates the rights of animals. How could it be otherwise? Their bodies are grievously injured, their freedom denied, their very lives taken. And for what purpose? To conduct an unreliable, irrelevant test that gives manufacturers legal cover in case someone is injured or dies because of an accidental poisoning. After all, it says right on the label, "Harmful or fatal if swallowed."

Alternatives

In response to the growing chorus of criticism, some laboratories are moving away from the LD_{50} and using "limit" tests—the LD_{10}, for example, which uses only ten animals. However, the same scientific and moral objections apply, whatever the number of animals used. The test is both inaccurate and immoral.

If manufacturers were genuinely interested in protecting consumers, they would never use less reliable safety tests when more reliable tests are available. If they followed this simple rule, they would abandon the LD_{50} and other animal toxicity tests and in their place employ a battery of nonanimal (in vitro) methodologies. Swedish scientists have demonstrated that using four in vitro tests predicts a substance's toxicity for humans 80 percent of the time, compared with a 65 percent success rate when using the LD_{50}. A 15 percent difference is nothing to brush aside.

Where is our government when we need it? There is a simple win-win outcome here, a way to improve consumer protection and, at the same time, respect animal rights. Ban the LD_{50}. Don't permit it. ARAs lack the authority to do this. So does any other group of ordinary citizens. Only our elected and appointed representatives have the necessary power, and ARAs are resolute in our determination to see that they use that power properly, for everyone's good.

Elected representatives of the European Union are taking the lead in reforming product testing. In 2003 they voted to ban toxicity tests on cosmetics (no more LD$_{50}$, for example) manufactured in EU nations and to prohibit the sale of products from other countries in which these tests are done. This is not the end of all toxicity testing, not even within the EU. But it might well represent the beginning of the end.

Dirty Hair and Bad Breath

"It's bad enough," I can imagine someone saying, "that ARAs want us to stop eating meat and give up wearing wool. Now they want us to stop washing our hair and brushing our teeth!" Not true. Not true at all. There are wonderful cosmetics and toiletries on the market that have not been tested on animals, many of them found in our neighborhood drugstore or hairdresser's salon, or in various specialty stores in our local malls. You can't tell an ARA just by looking for dirty hair and sniffing for bad breath. In fact, ARAs can even keep our homes clean, from our floors to our toilet bowls, using quality products that are cruelty free. You'll find information about these products on the website mentioned in the prologue.

USING ANIMALS AS TOOLS IN RESEARCH

"Research" or "experimentation" (I will use the words interchangeably) can have one of two importantly different objectives. In therapeutic research the intention is to benefit the subjects on whom the experiments are conducted. For example, if I agree to undergo an experimental heart surgery, the surgeon and I both hope that I will benefit from the experiment. By contrast, in nontherapeutic research, subjects are harmed in the absence of any intended benefit for them; instead, the intention is to obtain information that might ultimately lead to benefits for others. The Tuskegee syphilis study illustrates research of this kind. Unless otherwise indicated, our discussion is limited to the use of animals in harmful, nontherapeutic medical research (which, for simplicity's sake, I will sometimes refer to simply as "research" or as "vivisection").

Kinds of Research

When asked what we think about using animals in research, most of us (I made this same observation earlier) will think about their use in medical research, the sort of research that leads to important advances in combating diseases like cancer and diabetes. However, research related to improvements of this sort is only part of the picture. Not to go unnoticed is research that hardly ever makes it to the media, as documented by Jeff Diner. Here is a summary of some of the examples he describes:

Eye research: Monkeys, rabbits, dogs, cats, and other animals are used. The animals' eyes are burned or injured in other ways; sometimes lids are sutured shut or eyes removed.

Burn research: Animals (guinea pigs, rats, mice, dogs, for example) are burned using chemicals or radiation, or they may experience "thermal burns," ranging in severity from mild to third degree. Thermal burns are caused by immersing all or part of the animals' bodies in boiling water, or pressing a hot plate against their skin, or by using steam.

Radiation research: All or part of an animal's body is subjected to radiation, or in some cases, the test animals are forced to inhale radioactive gases. Dogs, monkeys, rats, mice, and hamsters are among the animals used.

Brain research: Brain activity and behavior are studied in cats, dogs, monkeys, rabbits, and rats, for example. The animals suffer experimental trauma (usually produced by direct physical injury to the head), undergo surgical manipulation, or are stimulated electrically (for example, after undergoing surgical implantation).

Electric shock research: The physiological and psychological responses to electric shock are studied in various animals, principally rats. Electric shock of varying degrees, and at various intervals, is administered primarily through the feet or tail.

Aggression research: The effects of such factors as social isolation, induced brain dysfunction, and sleep deprivation on aggressive behavior are investigated.

Stress research: Test animals are exposed to extremes of cold or heat, deprived of REM sleep, immobilized, or malnourished, for example, to investigate physiology and behavior.

Military research: Funded by the U. S. Department of Defense, various animals, including nonhuman primates, are subjected to conventional, biological, and chemical weapons, nuclear radiation, lasers, and high-power microwaves.

That animals are harmed by such research, no reasonable person will deny. When (to cite some other outcomes) animals are drowned, suffocated, and starved to death; or when they have their limbs severed and their organs crushed; or when they are the recipients of heart attacks, ulcers, paralysis, and seizures; or when they are forced to inhale tobacco smoke, drink alcohol, and ingest various drugs, such as heroin and cocaine—when animals are on the receiving end of treatment of this kind, no reasonable person will say, "Yes, but are they ever harmed?"

It is important to realize that what I have just described is routine. From removal of eyes to thermal burns, suffocation to crushed organs, nothing I have described is the least bit unordinary. No law is broken, no codes are breached. Every experimental procedure listed is perfectly consistent with "the responsible use and humane care and treatment of laboratory animals in research." Those are NABR's words. It is a classic example of the Disconnect Dictum. People who drown, suffocate, or starve animals to death, and who say they believe in providing "humane care," are not to be believed.

"The (Some But Not All) Animal Welfare Act"

In the United States, various federal and state laws apply to the use of animals in research. At the federal level, the Animal Welfare Act (AWA) addresses only the care and treatment of animals outside the research itself; it explicitly removes the federal government from playing any role in the "design, outlines, guidelines, or performance of actual research or experimentation by a research facility as determined by such a research facility." Moreover, the AWA defines "animal" to mean "any live or dead dog, cat, monkey, [nonhuman] primate, guinea pig, hamster, rabbit, or other such warm-blooded animal as the Secretary [of the Department of Agriculture] may determine is being used, or is intended for use, for research, testing, experimentation or exhibition purposes." Conspicuously absent from the list are rats and mice, as well as all birds, farmed animals, and fish, which together account for at least 90 percent of the animals used in a research context.

In 2000 federal legislation was proposed to include rodents and birds within the meaning of "animal." The amendment was defeated (NABR was among its most vigorous opponents), to the great relief and delight of the animal research community. Never mind that the insincerity of the United States government's commitment to "animal welfare" and "humane and responsible use" was never more evident.

No one really knows how many animals are used for scientific purposes. Still, everyone agrees the number runs in the millions. So the dispute is over how many million. Fifteen? Fifty? Somewhere in between? Somewhere in between, somewhere between twenty-five and fifty million, may not be an unreasonable estimate.

Federal Enforcement

The Animal and Plant Health Inspection Service (APHIS, the same agency that has such a distinguished record of insuring that animals in circuses are treated "humanely") once again is called upon to enforce the AWA in America's laboratories. Facilities that do not use any of the regulated species are exempt from the Act, as are those facilities that do not receive federal funds and utilize animals they raise themselves. Despite these limitations, roughly nine thousand research facilities, animal dealers, animal shippers, and others are legally subject to inspection for compliance. It has been estimated that APHIS inspectors, whose primary responsibility is to prevent interstate shipments of diseased plants and livestock, devote a maximum of 6 percent of their time to enforcing the AWA.

As a result of steadily increasing budget cuts, the first half of the 1990s witnessed more than a 20 percent decline in the number of APHIS inspections performed. By 2001 (see our earlier discussion of animal acts in circuses), only one hundred APHIS inspectors remained on the job. Internal audits of APHIS, conducted in 1992 and 1995 by the Office of the Inspector General, found that "APHIS was still not able to make all the required inspection visits" to facilities *already* reported in violation of AWA. In response APHIS officials noted that "some of the follow-up visits were not made due to staffing limitations and budgetary cutbacks." Past violators were thus able to continue to treat animals in ways that [in APHIS's own words] could "jeopardize the health and safety of their animals without APHIS intervention."

All considered, then, the legally mandated and enforced protection afforded animals in labs is modest at best. Certainly it would be naive in the extreme to assume that "all is well" behind the locked doors blocking the day-to-day activities in America's laboratories from public view. Even APHIS officials, who hardly qualify as ARA extremists, would deny the credibility of such an assurance.

"Heads" the Researchers Win, "Tails" the Animals Lose

Most research facilities are required by law to have Institutional Animal Care and Use Committees. IACUCs are charged with the task of reviewing research protocols before they can go forward. Depending on the committee's assessment, the research may proceed as proposed, or it may have to be modified, or theoretically it can be disallowed. Among the criteria IACUCs use, some concern the invasiveness of the proposed research and the amount and intensity of the pain it will cause. The underlying principle is of the cost–benefit variety. Animals should not suffer "unnecessarily." Roughly speaking, invasive research that causes serious pain or death should only be permitted if the research promises important results.

The illusion of IACUC protection of animals was pierced by a study published in July 2001 in the prestigious journal *Science*. The study showed that, in the majority of cases, proposals that were approved by one IACUC were rejected by another. This does nothing to inspire confidence in "humane use" and "responsible care." As one of the authors of the study observed, "the reliability of [IACUC] reviews is at chance levels—literally, a coin toss." For the animals, it comes down to whether they happen to be in the wrong place at the wrong time. If they are, then "heads" the researchers win, and "tails" the animals lose.

The Benefits Argument

There is only one serious moral defense of vivisection. That defense proceeds as follows. Human beings are better off because of vivisection. Indeed, we are *much* better off because of it. If not all, at least most of the most important improvements in human health and longevity are indebted to vivisection. Included among the advances often cited are open heart surgery, vaccines (for polio and smallpox, for example), cataract and hip replacement surgery, and advances in rehabilitation techniques for victims of spinal cord injuries and strokes. Without these and the many other advances attributable to vivisection, proponents of the benefits argument maintain, the incidence of human disease, permanent disability, and premature death would be far, far greater than it is today.

Defenders of the benefits argument are not indifferent (at least they say they are not indifferent) to how animals are treated. They agree that animals used in vivisection sometimes suffer, both during the research itself and because of the restrictive conditions of their lives in the laboratory. These harms are regrettable, vivisection's defenders acknowledge, and everything that can be done should be done to minimize them. For example, to prevent overcrowding, animals should be housed in larger cages. But (so the argument goes) there is no other way to secure the important human health benefits that vivisection yields so abundantly, benefits that greatly justify any harms that animals endure.

Question Begging

One thing should be immediately obvious. The benefits argument has absolutely no logical bearing on the debate over animal rights. Clearly, all that the benefits argument *could* possibly show is that vivisection on nonhuman animals benefits human beings. What this argument *cannot* show is that vivisecting animals for this purpose is morally justified. Whether animals have rights is not a question that can be answered by saying how much vivisection benefits human beings.

In addition to begging the question, the benefits argument conveniently overlooks much and includes little. Until these omissions are addressed, the argument does not have a logical leg to stand on.

What the Benefits Argument Omits

Any argument that rests on comparing benefits and harms must not only state the benefits accurately; it must also do the same for the relevant harms. Advocates of the benefits argument fail on both counts. Independent of their lamentable tendency to minimize the harms done to animals and their fixed resolve to marginalize nonanimal alternatives, advocates overestimate the human benefits attributable to vivisection and all but ignore the massive human harms that are an essential part of vivisection's legacy. Even more fundamentally, they uniformly fail to provide an intelligible methodology for comparing benefits and harms across species. Let me address each of these three failures in turn.

Overestimation of Benefits

Proponents of the benefits argument would have us believe that most of the truly important improvements in human health could not have been achieved without vivisection. The facts tell a different story. Public health scholars have shown that animal experimentation has made at best only a modest contribution to public health. By contrast, the vast majority of the most important health advances have resulted from improvements in living conditions (in sanitation, for example) and changes in personal hygiene and lifestyle, none of which have anything to do with animal experimentation.

Underestimation of Harms

Advocates of the benefits argument conveniently ignore the hundreds of millions of deaths and the uncounted illnesses and disabilities that are attributable to reliance on the "animal model" in research. Sometimes the harms result from what reliance on vivisection makes available; sometimes they result from what reliance on vivisection prevents. The deleterious effects of prescription medicines are an example of the former.

Prescription drugs are first tested extensively on animals before being made available to consumers. As is well known, there are problems involved in extrapolating results obtained from studies on animal beings to human beings. In particular many medicines that are not toxic for test animals prove to be highly toxic for human beings. How toxic? This might surprise you, but it is estimated that one hundred thousand Americans die and some two million are hospitalized annually because of the harmful side effects of the prescription drugs they are taking. That makes prescription drugs *the fourth leading cause of death* in America, behind only heart disease, cancer, and stroke, a fact that, without exception, goes unmentioned by the benefits argument's advocates.

Worse, the Food and Drug Administration, the federal agency charged with regulating prescription drugs, estimates that physicians report only 1 percent of adverse drug reactions. In other words, for every adverse drug response reported, ninety-nine are not. Clearly, before vivisection's defenders can reasonably claim that human benefits greatly exceed human harms, they need honestly to acknowledge how often and how much reliance on the animal model leads to prescribed therapies that are anything but beneficial.

While vivisection's spokespersons in America continue to insist on business as usual, European Union researchers are developing drug tests using human blood cells. Not only are the tests less expensive and easier, they are proving to be more sensitive than tests done on rabbits, one of the vivisection industry's preferred "models."

Massive harm to humans also is attributable to what reliance on vivisection prevents. The role of cigarette smoking in the incidence of cancer is a case in point. As early as the 1950s, human epidemiological studies revealed a causal link between cigarette smoking and lung cancer. Nevertheless, repeated efforts, made over more than fifty years, rarely succeeded in inducing tobacco-related cancers in animals. Despite the alarm sounded by public health advocates, governments around the world for decades refused to mount an educational campaign to inform smokers about the grave risks they were running. Today, one in every five deaths in the United States is attributable to the effects of smoking, and fully 60 percent of direct health care costs in the United States go to treating tobacco-related illnesses.

How much of this massive human harm could have been prevented if the results of vivisection had not directed government health care policy? It is not clear that anyone knows the answer beyond saying, "A great deal. More than we will ever know." One thing we do know, however: Advocates of the benefits argument contravene the logic of their argument when they conveniently omit these harms in their defense of vivisection.

Research Ideology

Last, vivisection's defenders universally fail to explain how we are to weigh benefits and harms across species. Before we can judge that vivisection's benefits for humans greatly outweigh vivisection's harms to other animals, someone needs to explain how the relevant comparisons should be made. How much animal pain equals how much human relief from a drug that was tested on animals, for example? It does not suffice to say, to quote the American philosopher Carl Cohen (Cohen is the world's leading defender of the benefits argument), that "the suffering of our species does seem somehow to be more important than the suffering of other species." Not only does this fail to explain how much more important our suffering is supposed to be, it offers no reason why anyone should think that it is.

Plainly, unless or until those who support the benefits argument offer an intelligible methodology for comparing benefits and harms across species, the claim that human benefits derived from vivisection greatly outweigh the harms done to animals is more in the nature of unsupported ideology than demonstrated fact.

CONCLUSION

Human beings, not only nonhuman animals, have been used in harmful, nontherapeutic experimentation. Not surprisingly, most human "guinea pigs" have not come from the wealthy and educated, not from the dominant race, not from those with the power to assert and enforce their rights. No, most of human vivisection's victims have been coercively conscripted from the ranks of young children (especially orphans), the elderly, the insane, the poor, the illiterate, members of "inferior" races, homosexuals, military personnel, prisoners of war, convicted criminals, and humans with serious mental disabilities.

The scientific rationale behind human vivisection needs little explanation. Using human subjects in research overcomes the difficulty of extrapolating results from another species to our species. As such, human vivisection promises even greater benefits than any that might accrue from animal vivisection.

No serious advocate of human rights can support such research. This judgment is not capricious or arbitrary; it is a necessary consequence of the logic of our moral rights, including our summary right to be treated with respect. To use an analogy from a previous chapter, individual rights are the trump cards in the moral game. It is wrong to injure our bodies, take our freedom from us, or end our lives just because others will benefit by doing so.

ARAs hold the same position when other animals are vivisection's victims. The end does not justify the means. Even if it were true that humans reap great benefits and bear no harms from the practice, that would not justify violating the rights of the animals whose misfortune it is to find themselves in a cage in some laboratory somewhere. We are not to do evil that good may come. Vivisection is just the sort of evil we should not do.

MANY HANDS
ON MANY OARS

"YES . . . , BUT . . ."

Animal rights is a hard sell. ARAs can do our best to dispel myths about who we are. We can reason logically. We can make visible the many terrible things that are done to animals. We can unmask the deceptive rhetoric used by spokespersons for the major animal user industries. We can pierce the illusion that having laws on the books and inspectors in the field insure that "everything is just fine" on the farm and in the lab, at the circus and inside fur mills. We can do all the above, and what do we get (not all the time, just much of the time)? What we get is resistance. People with an expanding animal consciousness; people who genuinely care about animals; people who are open to change; people who are asking questions and finding answers—people who are Muddlers, as I call them: even after ARAs have talked the talk and walked the walk, many Muddlers just can't take that last step. Yes, what was invisible is now visible. Yes, they see the faces rather than the vase, or vice versa. But the image flickers; it comes and goes; it lacks constancy, permanence. Sometimes animals are seen as somebodies; more often, as old habits take hold, they are seen as somethings. Resistance. Resistance. Resistance.

Why? What is it that stands in the way of achieving a real change in perception, the settled conviction that, yes, animals have rights? There is no one answer. Different Muddlers have different reasons for staying right where they are. In fact, Muddlers have a long list of reasons for resisting the kind of fundamental change embracing animal rights entails, reasons commonly expressed in the form of "Yes, . . . but . . ." For example, "Yes, animal rights is backed by rational arguments, but," followed by one or another of the speaker's concerns.

On this score, I side with Muddlers, everywhere. Muddler resistance is entirely appropriate, given the magnitude of what is at stake (nothing less than how we should live our lives). I have been a Muddler. I know what it is like to stand on the precipice of indecision. Muddlers have every reason to hesitate before making animal rights part of their lives. In this final chapter, I want to explore some of the most common reasons (I call them "turn-offs") Muddlers have for looking *very* carefully at animal rights before they leap. First, though, a few preliminary remarks.

ARAs face many challenges. Paramount among them are (1) our small numbers and (2) our lack of credibility among the general public. How do we grow the animal rights movement? How do we go from where we are today, on the fringes of societal concern, to where we want to be, at the center of our culture's moral agenda? How do we undo several thousand years of history and habit? In other words, how do we turn around an iceberg in a bathtub?

ARAs are not naïve. We understand that the future of animal rights is bleak if too few people want to make the movement's goals a reality. Granted, hard work by some people might make some cages larger for some animals somewhere; but hard work by ARAs will never empty the cages if our numbers are too few, our influence, too feeble. Which is why I have dedicated this book to Muddlers, everywhere. Muddlers are the future of animal rights. The animal rights movement is not going anywhere (except maybe backward) if too few Muddlers join. So, yes, by all means, ARAs owe Muddlers honest responses whenever we hear them say, "Yes . . ., but . . ." Without making any claim to completeness, this is what I try to do in this chapter: offer honest responses.

The "Anti" Turn-Off

In an earlier chapter I mentioned how ARAs often are seen as a bunch of "anti" people: antimeat, antidairy, antifur, antileather, antihunting, antirodeo. This list goes on. This invites a familiar "Yes, but": "Yes, I would embrace animal rights, but who wants to be surrounded by such negative people?"

I make no apologies for ARAs. We really are against all these (in our view) abominations, and much else besides. But I hope no one will forget that there is another side to what we believe and value, the "pro" side. With rare exceptions, ARAs stand for love of family and country, for human rights and justice, for human freedom and equality, for compassion and mercy, for peace and tolerance, for special concern for those with special needs, for a clean, sustainable environment, for the rights of our children's children's children—our future generations.

To a Muddler who is thinking, "Yes, I would embrace animal rights, but who wants to be surrounded by such negative people?" I want to make a modest proposal: widen your circle of ARA acquaintances. You probably know too few rather than too many. We are more than happy to talk about the positive values we believe in. If the public doesn't hear this, if all they ever hear is the negative side of animal rights, there's a familiar explanation. The positive side doesn't "bleed" enough, isn't sexy or star-studded enough, to make it through the media's filters.

The "Merry Prankster" Turn-Off

Another turn-off for Muddlers is what they see as clownish or outlandish behavior. "Yes, animal rights is a noble idea," they say, "but I don't want to be associated with a movement that reduces serious social justice issues to a street carnival—like when people dress up as chickens or cows, to protest factory farming, or bounce around in gorilla suits, to protest vivisection."

Any helpful response to this concern begins with a reminder about the media mentality, which presents problems for ARAs, as it does for any other group vying to get its message heard. Question: How do we get the media's attention? Answer: Do something unlawful or outlandish. Either way, this kind of media exposure will turn off some Muddlers.

I will take up the topic of unlawful acts later. Concerning the outlandish: Major media want something to show besides talking heads. ARAs oblige by playing the role of merry pranksters. Must this be a bad idea? I don't think so. For example, having people running naked through the streets to protest fur *can* (note the italics) be a legitimate part of the educational process, *provided* that the noise generated by the event does not drown out the message, which should always be the same: Animals are in cages, and they should not be there. If (as could happen) some groups do too much by way of the outlandish, the appropriate response is to ask them to tone it down or to support some other groups, not to forgo animal rights completely.

Muddlers should note, moreover, that merry pranksterism is not unique to animal rights. Other social justice movements have engaged in the outlandish, the better to attract the media's attention. Any doubt about this, march in or attend a Gay Pride Parade in, say, San Francisco. The gays who dress up as grapes, oranges, and bananas ("fruits") are outlandish. There is no other word for it. Would the way they dress provide a sufficiently good reason for refusing to be supportive of gay rights? I don't think anyone really believes this. Well, the same thing should be no less true if a Muddler sees an ARA dressed up as a chicken outside the local Colonel Sanders. We should not make life-altering decisions depending on whether we hear someone going "Cluck. Cluck. Cluck."

The "Celebrity" Turn-Off

Some Muddlers are turned off to animal rights because ARAs court celebrity endorsements. Just take a look at the publications of the national ARA organizations. Sometimes they are so packed with pictures of celebrities you'd think you were reading *People, Ebony,* or *Hispanic* magazine. For any Muddler who thinks that part of the problem with today's world is the role played by the burgeoning celebrity culture, watching ARAs trip over one another as we race for endorsements from rock musicians and movie stars can be a real turn-off. "Yes, animal rights is an important idea," some Muddlers will say, "but I don't want to be involved in a movement that relies on celebrity endorsements."

When I started writing this book, I felt this way myself. It's not a good sign when *who* says something is viewed as more important than *what* is said. Now that I am almost finished, I have mellowed a bit. Celebrity endorsements of animal rights *can* (note the italics again) make an important contribution to the educational process. Face it. Celebrities open doors the rest of us can only bang on. That Kim Basinger and Paul McCartney don't eat meat will never be a good reason why anyone else should become a vegetarian. But some people (especially young Muddlers) might be moved to ask questions about their dietary ways once they learn what these celebrities do and don't eat. It's hard to be against that.

Besides, other social justice movements have played the celebrity card. The civil rights movement did not run away when the likes of Burt Lancaster, Quincy Jones, Carmen McRae, and Josephine Baker added their voice to the marchers singing "We Shall Overcome." And none of the activists who opposed the Vietnam War complained when Joan Baez, Country Joe McDonald, and Jane Fonda joined all the other antiwar activists, including Nancy and me, in speaking out against the war. Celebrity power always has been, is now, and will continue to be a fact of life. As such, it will always be used by all social justice movements, the animal rights movement among them. Sometimes we have to accept things as they are, not plant our feet in cement because the world is not the way we want it to be.

The "Tasteless" Turn-Off

ARAs can do some truly tasteless things. By way of illustration: An ARA organization creates advertisements that are supposed to help animals by capitalizing on hardships faced by people in the public limelight. A family is trying to cope with the death of their daughter at the hands of a serial murderer. The news is everywhere. The ARA organization uses these circumstances to promote animal rights in their ads. "If you think girls being killed by serial murderers is bad, think about the terrible things being done to animals in slaughterhouses." You get the picture. The media covers the ARA ad campaign like flies on week-old guacamole, and the organization thinks this makes the ads successful. They should think again.

Terrible things are being done to animals in slaughterhouses. You'll get no argument from me on this point. But here is a fact about the world that most people understand: Compassionate human beings extend their sympathy to other people in hard times. Compassionate people don't try to take advantage of the personal tragedies of others to advance their own cause. Evidently, the ARAs who create ads like this one live in some world other than the real one. Many people are turned off by such ads. *I* am turned off by these ads. *Everyone* should be turned off by these ads. All that such tasteless publicity achieves is bitterness, hostility, and resentment. Media coverage of this kind (coverage that confirms the stereotype of the misanthropic ARA) does not do the animal rights movement or the animals any good. You don't motivate people to become compassionate toward animals by showing a lack of compassion for humans in hard times.

When ARAs behave in this way, they don't speak for me. But neither do they speak for the vast majority of ARAs. We (the vast majority) duck and cover when this happens. The flack we take from friends and foes alike is unbelievable. So when Muddlers say, "Yes, I would join with ARAs, but they do such tasteless things," it needs to be remembered that "they" refers to only a small handful of ARAs. Their inconsiderate behavior is not a good reason for Muddler resistance.

The "Self-Righteous" Turn-Off

Some Muddlers are turned off by the self-righteousness they find in ARAs. "Yes, animal rights is a noble idea," they say, "but look at what it does to people; it makes them think they are *so* good, *so* pure. Who wants to be like that?" I can relate to this reaction. I know some ARAs who are so self-righteous that I'll go out of my way just so I don't have to deal with them. Here's one example.

ARAs have excellent reasons for not wearing fur, or leather, or wool. Just think about a fur mill, the treatment of cows in India, or mulesing as practiced by Australian sheep ranchers, and you can understand where we're coming from. We want none of this evil in our lives, thank you. We prefer cotton and fake leather.

Fair enough. Except I know some ARAs who *want you to know* how bad you are and how good they are, when it comes to the clothes on their backs and the shoes on your feet. I mean, I have known some ARAs who can *breathe fire* in the faces of people who don't dress right.

ARAs who behave this way do not live in the real world. Because the issues that surface here are important, I want to take a page or so to explore them.

Take cotton, for example. It is no free ride for animals. Cotton is one of the most chemically intensively raised crops in the world. Herbicides. Nematicides. Fungicides. All manner of chemical cides (*cide* means *death*) are administered to cotton. When the rains come (as they will) and the cides are washed into neighboring rivers and streams (as they are), fish and other animals are killed. Before that, many land animals are killed when mechanized tillers prepare the earth for planting. The result? Anytime an ARA buys something made from cotton, we take home clothes stained with the blood of animals.

As for shoes and belts made of fake leather: these are by-products of the petrochemical industry. This means oil spills, and that means countless numbers of injured and dead animals. Every time an ARA puts on a pair of fake leather shoes, we have the blood of animals on our feet.

Here is how I picture the ARA predicament. Imagine a large, intricate spider's web. The web has a center; it also has outer edges. Picture the web as representing the evil in the world. The worst things are at the center; the least bad things are at the edges.

Where do we find the evil visited upon animals by the major animal user industries? Let's think about it. The bodies of literally billions of animals are intentionally and deliberately injured every year. The freedom of hundreds of millions of animals is intentionally and deliberately denied every hour. The very life of tens of thousands of animals is intentionally and deliberately taken every minute. ARAs believe that what the major animal user industries do to animals is at or near the center of the web. What is done to them is this bad, in our view.

Where, then, do we find the evil visited upon animals by the cotton industry and the petrochemical industry? Not in the same neighborhood. The harm caused to animals by these industries is neither intentional nor deliberate. This makes a difference, given the way ARAs think. Our first duty is to remove our direct support from the major animal user industries by refusing to buy their products. We do not fail in this duty when we purchase products manufactured by other industries, though even here an expansive animal consciousness would counsel making do with less rather than making do with more. As is well and truly said, we should live simply so that others may simply live.

So, no, ARAs have no reason to be self-righteous, as if the world were divided into the Pures (that would be us) and the Impures (that would be the rest of humanity). Morally, we all are shades of gray. That said, Muddlers need to remember: that huffing-and-puffing ARA breathing fire about the clothes you're wearing is only one person, and no one person speaks for all ARAs. Self-righteousness is not a precondition of, nor a necessary consequence of, animal rights advocacy. Muddlers should not be deterred from moving forward on their journey because someone else doesn't understand where they are on theirs.

The "Outing" Turn-Off

An increasingly common educational tool used by ARAs is outing, understood as helping people learn what their neighbors do for a living. Here's how it works. Suppose the woman living next door spends her professional life blinding cats, while a guy down the street helps slaughter tens of thousands of hogs every year. "Outing" means taking steps to help people in the neighborhood know that these folks are not working at the local Wal-Mart or Jiffy-Lube.

There are different ways to do this. The classic outing goes like this. ARAs secure a permit to assemble beyond the proscribed distance from a given address (several states have laws defining what these limits are); then, using bull horns or other amplifying devices, they let the neighbors know who is living next door, so to speak. Other forms of education include in-your-face leafleting and intensive posting (on telephone poles, retail bulletin boards, and so on). The unifying object is to get the message out: When your neighbors go to work, here's what they do to animals.

Outings can target people who do not directly violate animal rights. Examples include people who write the insurance policies for major animal user industries, others who are large shareholders in these industries, public relations directors who put a happy face on what these industries do, and bankers who make loans to companies within these industries. On any given day or night, ARAs might pay a home visit to let others know that their neighbor's line of work contributes to the terrible things being done to animals.

This is not a pleasant time for the people being outed. They (and their families) can be embarrassed, frustrated, angry. Sometimes it is not blissville for the other good folk in the neighborhood. Picture the scene: Strangers on the streets. Noise disrupting the ordinary peace and quiet. Traffic snarled. A police presence. You have to wonder about the negative effects on real estate values.

So (perhaps some Muddlers will say), "Yes, I really do think animal rights has something important to say, but this 'outing' stuff is too much for me. I can't be involved in a movement that tolerates this kind of behavior." To which a relevant reply asks, "What kind of behavior?" At least until now, all Americans have rights protected by something called the First Amendment, a few words and a lot of history that guarantee our constitutional right to freedom of expression. So long as no law is broken (and no law need be broken), outing is just that: a constitutionally protected form of freedom of expression. People who are not ARAs might not like outings; personally, I don't *like* them. But everyone, including non-ARAs, should defend our precious right to freedom of speech. Anytime any of us loses some of our freedom, we all lose some of our freedom.

The "Vandalism and Violence" Turn-Off

Vandalism and violence are close cousins. Vandalism is the form violence sometimes takes when things, not people, are the direct object of damage or destruction. Vandals vandalize property, not people. Examples include breaking furniture or windows, painting houses or cars, uprooting plants or shrubs, and trashing offices or apartments. Vandalism involves violence on a small scale.

Without a doubt, some ARAs commit acts of vandalism. Without a doubt, many people are turned off when they read about ARAs breaking a furrier's windows or trashing a vivisector's office, or when an outing turns violent and houses or cars are painted. So let me say this as clearly as I can: the vast majority of ARAs are not into vandalism. Oh, we understand how it is that frustrated ARAs might find Ronald McDonald's windows or Ted Nugent's SUV mighty inviting targets for a little extracurricular animal rights activism. But frustration is not justification. Despite what some people say about us, most ARAs are not lawless fanatics.

Do ARAs ever go beyond vandalism? Is serious violence ever used? If we listen to the FBI, the answer is yes. The agency estimates that the Animal Liberation Front, along with the Earth Liberation Front, "have committed over 600 criminal acts in the United States since 1996, resulting in damages in excess of 43 million dollars." That adds up to a lot of violence in the minds of FBI agents. For their part, ALF spokespersons show that the Disconnect Dictum is not confined to the major animal user industries. They insist that ALF's record of property destruction is part of "a non-violent campaign, activists taking all precautions not to harm any animal (human or otherwise)."

Violence is not limited in the way the ALF or their supporters would have us believe. Someone who sets fire to an empty abortion clinic or torches a vacant synagogue causes no physical injury to any sentient being, but to suppose that these acts of arson are nonviolent distorts what violence means. When *The American Heritage College Dictionary* defines "violence" as "physical force exerted for the purpose of violating, damaging, or abusing," it does not say that the damage must involve a sentient being. We do not need to hurt someone in order to use violence against something. If the ALF uses an incendiary device to level a building, they engage in some serious violence. To speak of "the violent destruction of property" is not a contradiction in terms. Why persist in denying the obvious? In my opinion, unless or until ALF spokespersons acknowledge the violent nature of many ALF actions, everything else they say to the general public will fall on deaf ears. We never garner support for what we do if we are unwilling to admit what this is.

Many Muddlers are turned off by the violence attributed to ARAs. "Yes, I think animal rights is a wonderful idea, and I really would like to embrace it," they say, "but I can't abide all the violence." Of all ARA turn-offs, this may be the hardest to address. For this reason, we need to take our time in exploring it; even then what I have to say is far from complete.

We begin by reminding ourselves of something mentioned in chapter 1. Opponents of animal rights have crafted a strategy that requires reports of violent acts done in the name of animal rights. And not just a little; their strategy requires a lot of such violence. Personally, I do not doubt for a moment that some of the violence attributed to ARAs actually is done by somebody else, possibly even thugs employed by people who work in one of the major animal user industries. Remember Leon Hirsch? Remember "Animal Rights Terrorist Attempts to Murder Pillar of Community"? Enough said on this score.

Notice, too, how one-sided this discussion always plays out. On the one side we have all the wonderful law-abiding people who work for the major animal user industries. On the other side we have all (well, maybe not all) the law-breaking ARAs. Paragons of nonviolence on the one hand, beady-eyed flame throwers on the other. Not only is this absurdly unfair to ARAs, it is nothing less than a cover-up of the truth when it comes to what the major animal user industries do. Think about some of the things done to animals in the name of science, to take just one example.

Animals are drowned, suffocated, and starved to death; they have their limbs severed and their organs crushed; they are burned, exposed to radiation, and used in experimental surgeries; they are shocked, raised in isolation, exposed to weapons of mass destruction, and rendered blind or paralyzed; they are given heart attacks, ulcers, paralysis, and seizures; they are forced to inhale tobacco smoke, drink alcohol, and ingest various drugs, such as heroin and cocaine. And they say ARAs are violent? The violence done by ARAs (by which I mean the violent destruction of property, as explained below) is nothing compared to the violence done by the major animal user industries, a raindrop compared to an ocean. Just because a profession is legal, perhaps even (as in the case of vivisection) prestigious does not mean it is nonviolent. On a day to day basis, the greatest amount of violence in the "civilized" world occurs because of what humans do to other animals. That the violence is legally protected only serves to make matters worse.

I am not a Gandhian pacifist. I do not think it is always wrong to use violence. In particular, I do not think it is wrong to use violence to defend the innocent (for example, in order to rescue children from their estranged father who is threatening to kill them). Of course, we should not use more violence when less will suffice. And we should not use any violence at all until we have exhausted nonviolent alternatives, as time and circumstances permit. Nonpacifists like me (and this includes almost everybody) don't have to be trigger-happy anarchists. Morally, then, ARAs could attempt to satisfy these conditions by arguing as follows.

1. Animals are innocent.
2. Violence is used only when it is necessary to rescue them so that they are spared terrible harms.
3. Excessive violence is never used.
4. Violence is used only after nonviolent alternatives have been exhausted, as time and circumstances permit.
5. Therefore, in these cases, the use of violence is justified.

What should we say in response to this line of reasoning? If all the premises (1 through 4) are true, how can we avoid agreeing with the conclusion (5)? True, Gandhian pacifists can avoid the conclusion; they do not accept any violence, even in defense of the innocent. However, most of us are not Gandhian pacifists; for us, the plot thickens.

Personally, I don't think the second premise is true of all or even most of the violence done in the name of animal rights. Why not? Because the vast majority of this violence does not involve animal rescue. The vast majority (I estimate 98 percent) is property destruction, pure and simple. In cases like these, the defense we are considering contributes nothing by way of justification.

What of the remaining 2 percent of cases, cases where violence is used and animals are rescued? For example, suppose a multimillion-dollar lab is burnt to the ground *after* the animals in it have been liberated. Would this kind of violence be justified, given the argument sketched above?

Again, I don't think so. And the reason I don't think so is because I don't think the requirement set forth in premise 4 has been satisfied. Personally, I do not think that ARAs in general, members of the ALF in particular, have done nearly enough when it comes to exhausting nonviolent alternatives. Granted, to do this will take time and will require great patience coupled with hard, dedicated work. Granted, the results of these labors are uncertain. And granted, animals will be suffering and dying every hour of every day that ARAs struggle to free them using nonviolent means. Nevertheless, until ARAs have done the demanding nonviolent work that needs to be done, the use of violence, in my judgment, is not morally justified. (It is also a tactical disaster. Even when animals are rescued, the story the media tells is about the "terroristic" acts of ARAs, not the terrible things that were being done to animals. The one thing ARA violence never fails to produce is more grist for the mills run by spokespersons for the major animal user industries.)

Supporters of the ALF are certainly free to challenge my critique of ALF violence by arguing that violence is justified under different conditions than those I have given. For example, they could argue that violence is justified when the damage caused is so extensive that it puts an animal abuser out of business. In this case, no animals are rescued but (so it may be argued) some animals are spared the horrors of vivisection in a lab or a lifetime of deprivation in a fur mill, for example. However, to consider such an argument is premature. Before it merits consideration, ALF supporters will have to agree that the ALF sometimes uses violence, something that, as we have seen, ALF supporters are loath to admit.

The role of violence in social justice movements raises complicated questions that always have and always will divide activists on matters of substance—ethics and strategy in particular. It need not divide ARAs when it comes to assessments of character. I know ARAs who have spent years in jail because they have broken the law, having used violence as I understand this idea. To a person, these activists believe ARAs already have exhausted nonviolent alternatives. To a person, they believe the time for talking has passed. To a person, they believe the time for acting has arrived.

I have never doubted the sincerity and commitment—or the courage—these activists embody. I am reminded of an observation (I cannot find the source) Gandhi once made, to the effect that he had more admiration for people who have the courage to use violence than he had for people who embrace nonviolence out of cowardice. So, yes, members of the ALF are courageous in their acts and sincere in their commitment. And yes, perhaps some of us who reject the violence they employ do so out of cowardice. Nevertheless, violence done by ARAs, in my judgment, is wrong; it does not help, it hurts the animal rights movement.

Should Muddlers stay put in their journey because of the violence attributed to ARAs? This would not be a good reason to resist animal rights, any more than it would have been a good reason for Nancy and me to leave the antiwar movement because a small group of activists took it upon themselves to torch the ROTC building on the campus of Ohio State University. The vast majority of

ARAs (Norman Rockwell Americans, one and all) oppose violence. It is the propaganda machines of the major animal user industries that have made *violence* and *animal rights* synonymous in the minds of many people. It is these machines that have been doing (and are continuing to do) a special interest mind job on the American people. Why give these machines more power and influence than they deserve? People who think for themselves, Muddlers preeminent among them, just aren't built this way.

The "It's Hopeless!" Turn-Off

Animal rights is such a revolutionary idea that some Muddlers resist it because they think it is unrealistic. "Yes, the world would be wonderful if the rights of animals were respected," they say, "but it's never going to happen. It's hopeless!"

It's not hard to understand why some Muddlers might think this way. Let's take a simple inventory. First, we have several thousand years of Western civilization teaching that animals exist to satisfy human needs and satiate human desires. Next, we have the great masses of humanity buying into the wisdom of the ages. Then we have the major animal user industries, spending hundreds of millions of dollars in advertising money, protected by the laws of the land, telling the great masses that, yes, it is true, animals exist to satisfy our needs and satiate our desires. Finally, we have the social arrangements (the education system, religious institutions, legal traditions, restaurants, clothing stores, family-friendly forms of entertainment, the biomedical industrial complex, and what passes for sport among the adventurers in field and stream, for example). In the face of the sum of these powerful forces, a Muddler says, "Yes, animal rights is a wonderful idea, and I would like to help, but it's never going to happen. It's hopeless!"

I will say this. The animal rights movement does not create optimistic people. Rather, optimistic people must create the animal rights movement. ARAs need to bring a positive attitude to the movement. People who do not believe in the good of humanity, people who are barren of hope for a better future for the animals, people who are unable to take a long view of the struggle—these people do not last long. Like candles in a gale, they burn out quickly. The struggle for animal rights is not for the fainthearted, nor for those shopping around for the movement du jour. For committed ARAs, the struggle is a lifetime commitment. For committed ARAs, what we give of our time and talents and efforts is not hopeless. Those of us who stay the course do not see ourselves as counting the grains of sand of the Sahara.

Our faith in a better world is deeply rooted in history. There was a time when many thought it was utopian, unrealistic, and hopeless to achieve equal rights for

Native Americans, African Americans, women, the mentally disadvantaged, or the physically disabled, for example. If our forefathers and foremothers had accepted things as they were, if they had turned their backs to those calling for greater equality, many African Americans would still be enslaved and no woman would be entitled to vote. Granted, the struggle for equality among humans is far from complete. Granted, the challenges facing ARAs are huge, even when compared to those faced by human rights advocates in the past. Nevertheless, the verdicts of history teach that entrenched social practices not only *can* change, they *have* changed. But never without a struggle.

The "I Don't Have Anything to Contribute" Turn-Off

A proper humility teaches that none of us is the greatest thing since sliced bread. There are limits to what any of us can do. From this it is tempting sometimes to infer that we can't do anything. Animal rights advocacy can be one of these times. "Yes, I really think animal rights is a wonderful idea," some Muddler might say, "but I don't have anything to contribute." So, what? What is supposed to follow? What is supposed to follow (though unspoken) is: "Therefore, I'm not moving another inch toward embracing animal rights."

Clever, yes, but this way of avoiding the challenge animal rights presents is too convenient. *Every* ARA contributes something. For example, every ARA teaches by the power of example. Becoming an ARA never makes anyone "pure" by any means. But it does create the opportunity to witness for animal rights by how we strive to live. People who do not believe in animal rights cannot help but notice those who do. That alone is one form of activism. That alone gives other people (especially family and friends) something to chew on. That alone makes a contribution.

In addition to the testimony every ARA gives by how we strive to live, Muddlers who enter the movement can bring their special ways of contributing, whatever these might be. The animal rights movement moves forward because of the efforts of many hands, on many oars. The diversity of the contributions we can make, whether in art or debating, organizational skills or public relations, devising campaigns or writing letters, finding a home for rescued animals or answering the phone, contributing to a Web page or *just being there* to fold the newsletter, run the copying machine, or protest when Ringling Brothers comes to town—the diversity of our contributions is a cause for celebration. Every ARA has something to contribute to the animal rights movement. And not just any old something. What each person contributes is something special, something needed.

The "I Thought This Was Supposed to Be a Radical Movement" Turn-Off

Whereas some Muddlers are turned off because the animal rights movement is too extreme, others may be turned off because it looks too conservative. Muddlers who take the former view think ARAs are an unruly gaggle of no-goods whose idea of recreation is finding an animal facility to burn down. Muddlers who take the latter view think ARAs are a troop of do-gooders whose idea of pushing the envelope is to sell vegan cookies on Sundays. Muddlers who want to become part of a radical movement (because they believe, correctly, that radical changes are needed) are looking for something more than the usual animal rights drill: leafleting, tabling, holding vigils, writing letters (to politicians, newspapers, people in the major animal user industries), organizing boycotts, conducting demonstrations, and raising money at the annual dog wash. These are worthy endeavors, one and all. Still, they do little to identify the animal rights movement as a movement calling for fundamental change and even less to energize the movement or give it a sense of solidarity. The same is true when celebrities say bad things about meat or ARAs dress up as cows to protest the dairy industry. "Yes, I think animal rights is a revolutionary objective," some Muddlers will say, "but it doesn't accommodate revolutionary means. Something more is needed before I cross the line."

"Something more is needed?" I couldn't agree more. I'll discuss only two other kinds of advocacy, both of which invite the wise participation of the more daring among us.

My earlier discussion of the ALF might have created the impression that I think it is always wrong to break the law. This is not my view, anymore than it was Gandhi's or Martin Luther King's. I have broken the law in the same spirit in which they did: in the spirit of the civil disobedient. The watchword of the civil disobedient is openness, not secrecy; nonviolence, not violence. When acts of civil disobedience are performed, the agents do not run and hide. Those who break the law must face the law. To the extent that civil disobedients are successful, they cause no harm and instill no fear. Think Rosa Parks. When she refused to give up her seat and move to the back of the bus, she was the civil disobedient incarnate. A lawbreaker, yes. A violent lawbreaker, no. I believe that all ARAs should be willing to commit acts of civil disobedience even if this means going to jail. I believe, too, that until we are willing to do this, not capriciously but as part of well-conceived and well-executed campaigns, we will not have exhausted the nonviolent methods that must be exhausted before violent tactics can be contemplated.

A second way to push the envelope is to follow the example of Compassion over Killing. Their special brand of lawbreaking is called open rescue. In open rescue, unlike classic civil disobedience, participants break the law by stealing someone's "property"; however, unlike some ALF actions, open rescue does not involve violence of any kind.

One of COK's stories goes like this. In April 2001, they learned about deplorable conditions at a large battery hen operation. They wrote the company, requested a tour, and received no reply. Under cover of darkness, four COK members paid an unauthorized visit and found that things were even worse than they imagined: dead hens were in the same cages as live ones, others had their feet or wings entangled in the wire caging, many were injured in a variety of ways. All this COK documented, with video and photographs, during several visits.

Armed with this damning information, they requested an investigation. "Sorry," they were told, "the state's attorney only carries out investigations when requests are made by law enforcement agencies." So COK contacted the local sheriff and made the same request. That was more than two years ago. The sheriff still has not called back.

COK decided to take matters into their own hands. When they returned from their final visit, they brought eight hens with them, all of whom were in desperate need of medical attention. And then COK did the right thing. They said, so all the world could hear, "We just broke the law by stealing these hens. Arrest us if you will." And do you know what happened? They never were arrested, and the hens they rescued were adopted and allowed to be real chickens for the first time in their lives.

And here's another noteworthy fact: major newspapers and television programs gave COK's open rescue extensive, positive coverage. Hundreds of thousands of Americans learned that hens are in cages and they should not be there. Moreover, from beginning to end, *the story was about the hens*, without any competition from what a celebrity or some ARAs dressed in chicken outfits had to say about eating eggs. Oh, and without anyone having to call a fire truck, either.

Can this sort of nonviolent lawbreaking be replicated? COK already has shown that it can, having exposed the same kind of barbaric conditions (eleven birds wedged into a space the size of a file cabinet drawer) in another battery hen factory. This time COK rescued ten hens and again dared the world to arrest them. Again, there were no takers. However, Ken Klippen, vice president of government relations for United Egg Producers, was not the least bit bashful in defending business as usual in the egg industry. He assured reporters (this will come as no surprise by now) that "having chickens in cages is the humane way of producing eggs." For anyone still looking for a good reason not to eat eggs, Mr. Klippen has provided one.

Muddlers who want to do something more radical than sell vegan cookies on Sundays should not succumb to the "I thought this was supposed to be a radical movement" turn-off. Without having to take the path favored by the ALF, the animal rights movement offers plenty of opportunities for creative, nonviolent lawbreaking. Even Gandhi and King would approve.

MOVING FORWARD

Here is another picture. In front of us stands a large brick wall. It symbolizes the oppression of animals. ARAs have one overriding objective: to make this wall history, to make it a thing of the past. There's just this small problem: there is no way we are going to do this all at once or any time soon. What, then, can we do? In my picture, I watch as we take the wall down, one brick at a time. Although we cannot abolish every form of animal exploitation today, we can abolish some tomorrow. Instead of merely changing the conditions in which animals are exploited, sometimes we can end their exploitation.

Here are some specific examples of the kind of change I mean. Each assumes that there is strong collaboration between the major national groups together with active, honored collaboration with individual ARAs in the grassroots. Legislation will be necessary in some cases, which means ARAs must be willing to work vigorously in the political arena, mindful of its many challenges and shortcomings. And ARAs may be called upon to engage in direct action, whether in the form of civil disobedience or open rescue. Sometimes some of us may have to do something illegal. Some cages that can be opened are:

- The elimination of elephants and other performing animals from circuses
- The liberation of dolphins currently imprisoned by the captive dolphin industry
- The total cessation of canned hunts
- The total demise of the greyhound racing industry
- No more fur mills
- An end to seal slaughter
- A ban on compulsory dissection
- No more dog labs
- A ban on the use of animals in toxicity tests, beginning with the LD_{50}
- An end to pound seizure
- The total elimination of Class B dealers

I was once described by another philosopher as "a starry-eyed optimist," and I suspect some Muddlers will be thinking the same thing. "Do you really believe this is possible?" they will ask. To which I will reply, "I really do. It's just a matter of taking the energy that is out there, in the person of every ARA, including the many new ones who are needed, and giving that energy the focus that only a unified movement, working collaboratively, can provide. If we do this, everything I've listed—and much, much more, more than we have ever imagined—is possible." Surrounded by a sea of uncertainty, one thing is clear: we'll never know if we never try.

Is it hopelessly unrealistic to imagine a day when fur coats will follow whalebone corsets into fashion oblivion, when slaughterhouses will exist only in history books, and when all the scientific laboratories of the world will have a sign over their entrances proclaiming No Animals Allowed? Those who are pessimistic about the moral possibilities of humanity will answer yes. But those who believe in the human capacity for good, as I do, will answer *no*. Not in my lifetime, perhaps, but someday surely, ARAs will be on hand to witness the triumph of animal rights, the happy day when, after years of struggle, all the cages will be empty.

CONCLUSION

Even after ARAs have made the case for our position and even after we have unmasked the untruths that are the stock in trade of the major animal user industries, there is Muddler resistance. The plain fact is, ARAs sometimes do some things that turn people off. Self-righteous preening. Tasteless ads. Violence. I cast my vote with Muddlers on those three. That said, Muddlers should not be turned off from growing into a more expansive animal consciousness because they don't agree with everything every ARA believes or does. That would be impossible, in any case. Nor should they be turned off because they are "only one" person with "nothing to contribute." As I noted earlier, the animal rights movement goes forward because of the efforts of many hands, on many oars. For every Muddler who stays on the shore, an oar lies limp in the water.

I have dedicated this book to Muddlers, everywhere, for two reasons. My first reason was stated earlier. Muddlers are the future of animal rights. The plain truth is simple: the animal rights movement is not going anywhere (except maybe backward) if too few Muddlers join. Muddlers really are this important.

My second reason is personal. Having been a Muddler myself, I feel a real kinship with others who are muddling along, asking questions, finding answers; experiencing one thing, then another; moving forward, sometimes quickly, sometimes slowly, toward a more expansive animal consciousness; seeing other animals, however fleetingly, as unique somebodies, meriting respect. What has motivated me to write this book is the possibility that I might say something that would help some Muddler, somewhere, somehow, to keep moving forward, to keep growing against the grain of our cultural paradigm concerning animals.

Maybe you are that Muddler. And maybe a day will come when, to your surprise, you look in the mirror and (as happened to me) you see an Animal Rights Advocate looking back. My hope is that some of the words I have written may have been of some help to you on your journey.

EPILOGUE: THE CAT

Recall that fluffy white cat we met in the prologue. Innocent of any wrongdoing. Powerless in the face of human disrespect. Even as I write these words, I want to shout, "Stop it! What are you doing? Stop it!"

As badly as this poor cat was treated, the major animal user industries treat animals just as badly, if not worse. Industry spokespersons *say* their industries treat animals humanely; they *say* they always show due regard for their welfare. But what they say is not what they do. We have confirmed this, many times over. Dare we say, as I said in the prologue, that compared to how animals are treated in these industries, the fluffy white cat was one of the lucky ones?

Think about it. Although she lived in a small cage and the last minutes of her life were full of terror and excruciating pain, she may have had a reasonably decent life before this. This is never true of greyhounds exploited by the racing industry. This is never true of sows confined to stalls. This is never true of elephants, or tigers, or lions who are born to the circus industry and spend years being "trained" to perform tricks. This is never true of mink and other animals who are confined their entire lives in a wire mesh world. This is never true of chimpanzees used in research for twenty, or thirty, or forty years. This is never true of hens in battery cages or veal calves raised in crates. This is never true of *billions* of animals, just in America. Was the cat one of the lucky ones? As hard as it is to say or believe, I think she was.

The cat episode invites two further observations. First, there was no pretense on the part of the cook in the video that he was treating the cat humanely or that he cared about her welfare. He treated her ruthlessly, heartlessly, without remorse. Of him, however, it can be said: at least he was an honest man. Second, there was no pretense that government officials were ensuring that the cat was indeed being treated "humanely" in accordance with the Chinese equivalent of America's Animal Welfare Act. No counterparts of APHIS inspectors were anywhere in sight. Of how things were done in this Chinese village, however, we may say the same thing: at least they were honest.

Can the same be said about the major animal user industries? Can we say: at least they are honest? Many ARAs give a negative answer. They believe that major animal user spokespersons are lying through their teeth. I have not made this accusation. I accuse these spokespersons only of saying what is false. As for the question of honesty: I am prepared to let the record of these industries speak for itself and to invite every fair-minded person to judge accordingly.

How that fluffy white cat has haunted me all these years! I think it is because her plight has come to symbolize for me the plight of all animals caught in the grip of human exploitation. All innocent of any wrongdoing. All powerless in the face of human disrespect. Which might explain why I have always felt the need for another variation to the story, this one ending the way it should.

Final variation: The HBO video team has spent a full day getting ready to film the episode at the restaurant. When they arrive the next morning, the cook is beside himself, the patrons, perplexed. "What's the problem?" they are asked. The crew is led to where the animals have always been kept. All the cages are empty. All the dogs are gone. All the cats (first among them, the fluffy white one) are gone too. In their place stand the two of us, you and I, waiting, ready to explain, ready to face whatever the future holds.

ACKNOWLEDGMENTS

Many people have given generously of their time when I asked for their help. I am particularly indebted to Jeffrey Masson for his more than generous foreword. I only hope my book is half as good as he says it is.

Sue Coe, a dear friend of many years, knows how grateful I am without my having to say so. But let me say so anyhow. I have no doubt that Sue's art (and the same is true of Jeffrey Masson's writings) is of historic importance. A hundred years from now and more, assuming our species has managed to survive, Sue Coe's work will hang in all the great museums of the world. Imagine what a rush it is for me to have a sample of it on the cover.

Laura Moretti, one of the few DaVincians I have ever known, created the website www.tomregan-animalrights.com that supplements these pages. *Supplements* may be the wrong word. What Laura has created is a work of great merit in its own right. What a piece of good fortune it is to have a person of such remarkable talents devote her life to using them in the struggle for animal rights. What a privilege to have those talents used to help this work reach a larger audience. *Thank you* says too little for so large a gift.

Eve DeVaro, the philosophy editor at Rowman and Littlefield, was tireless in representing the merits of the book to the publisher. It might not have seen the light of day but for her good efforts. Much thanks to you, Eve. I am also pleased to thank Leslie Evans for the many improvements she made to the text.

I was not the least bit bashful in asking experts questions I did not know how to answer. They were indefatigable even when I took more of their time than my good upbringing should have allowed me to ask for. My thanks to Jonathan Balcomb, Teri Barnato, Kim Bartlett, Gene Bauston, Marion Bolz, Andy Breslin, Ned

Buyukmihci, Merritt Clifton, Christine Dorchak, Catherine Doyle, Mylan Engel, Lisa Franzetta, Jennifer Lanier, Debbie Leahy, Donna Litowitz, Mike Markarian, Eric Mills, Alisa Mullins, Ric O'Barry, Wayne Pacelle, Kim Stallwood, and Paul Watson.

Gary Comstock, Sid Gendin, James LaVeck, and Dietrich von Haugwitz read all or large parts of the manuscript at various stages and offered many helpful comments.

Bruce Friedrich, in addition to reading and commenting on several drafts, called my attention to pertinent information and put me in touch with quite a few of the experts listed above. I cannot remember anyone helping me so much, in so many different ways, over so long a period of time. Such large debts I hope somehow to repay.

In addition, I want to thank all the anonymous ARAs who have spent hours updating the many useful websites I have consulted and from which I have learned so much. My special thanks to those brave souls who have conducted undercover investigations that permit the trusting public to catch a glimpse inside the major animal user industries. But for your risk taking, we would know far less than what we do. It remains for the rest of us to do something good and lasting for the animals, to eliminate the hidden horrors you have revealed to us.

Above all others, I give my thanks to my dear wife, Nancy, my constant companion during the many years we have shared our lives with one another. No words adequately express what she means to me or what she has done to enrich my life. It is no exaggeration to say that I would not *be* me but for the role she has played in shaping both my character and my outlook. Emerson contrasts friends and lovers by saying that lovers look at one another, face to face, whereas friends look ahead, their eyes on the same values. As is true of lovers, I look at Nancy, face to face. With her, however, I also look ahead. How blessed I am to find in her, in one, the person I most love and my best friend.

NOTES

Quotations are arranged by subsections within each chapter. When material is quoted from websites, the web address is given.

PROLOGUE: THE CAT

To Love or Kill: Man vs. Animals, directed by Anthony Thomas, HBO Original Programming/America Undercover Series, 1996.

CHAPTER 1: WHO ARE YOU ANIMAL RIGHTS ADVOCATES ANYWAY?

Untruth in Labeling

The Animal Liberation Front (ALF) is described as being involved in "a non-violent campaign, activists taking all precautions not to harm any animal (human or otherwise)." See www.hedweb.com/alffaq.htm. I examine ALF actions in chapter 11. A small handful of people who say they are ARAs sometimes beat their breasts about their willingness to hurt animal exploiters, but these malcontents have no place in the animal rights movement and no standing in it.

The Media

Paul Watson's quotation appears in a February 12, 2003, story by Brook Griffin, "Paul Watson Uses His Boat As a Method of Stopping Illegal Poachers," *The Collegian* (Fresno: California State University), 2.

Special Interest Politics

An American Medical Association white paper, "Use of Animals in Biomedical Research: The Challenge and the Response," 1992 (revised).

The Foundation for Biomedical Research www.fbresearch.org/

All Aboard!

The Fur Information Council of America www.fur.org/

They Would Never Do That, Would They?

For more information about the Fran Trutt case, see my essay "Misplaced Trust," *The Animals' Voice Magazine* 3, no. 1: 22–26.

John C. Stauber and Sheldon Rampton, *Toxic Sludge Is Good for You* (Monroe, Maine: Common Courage Press, 1995), 62–63.

It Only Gets Worse

See Merritt Clifton's account of the circumstances of the publication and the identity of the publishers of *A Declaration of War: Killing Animals to Save Animals and the Environment*, in "A Late April Fool? Or Something Worse?" *The Animals' Agenda* (June 1991): 34–35.

For a more complete account of the *Screaming Wolf* book, see my review, "Reader Beware: When It Comes to a Declaration, What Is Meant May Not Be What Is Said," *The Animals' Agenda* (October 1991): 24–26.

CHAPTER 2: HOW DID YOU GET THAT WAY?

Animal Consciousness: The DaVincians

Quotations concerning Leonardo appear in David Hurwitz, "Leonardo DaVinci's Ethical Vegetarianism," available at www.ivu.org/history/davinci/hurwitz.html; and *The Extended Circle: A Commonplace Book of Animal Rights*, compiled by Jon Wynne-Tyson (New York: Paragon Books, 1989), 65.

Martin Buber, *I and Thou*, trans. Walter Kaufman (New York: Scribner, 1970).

A Change in Perception

James LaVeck and Jenny Stein, *The Witness*, 2000. Information at www.tribeofheart.org/.

Animal Consciousness: The Muddlers

Kim Bartlett's observations about the animal consciousness of her and her son, Wolf, were included in correspondence with Australian ARA, Christine Townsend. I am grateful to Kim for sharing this with me.

First Steps

Mohandas Karamchand Gandhi, *An Autobiography: The Story of My Experiments with Truth* (Boston: Beacon Press, 1957).

An Expanding Animal Consciousness

My early position on using animals in research is "Animal Experimentation: First Thoughts," in Tom Regan, *All That Dwell Therein: Essays on Animal Rights and Environmental Ethics* (Berkeley: University of California Press, 1982), 65–74.

CHAPTER 3: HUMAN RIGHTS

My argument in this chapter can be supplemented by two of my other efforts, *The Case for Animal Rights* (Berkeley: University of California Press, 1983), and *Animal Rights, Human Wrongs: An Introduction to Moral Philosophy* (New York: Rowman and Littlefield, 2004). See, in addition, my contribution to *The Animal Rights Debate*, with Carl Cohen (New York: Rowman and Littlefield, 2001), and the following essays in *Defending Animal Rights* (Urbana: University of Illinois Press, 2000): "Mapping Human Rights" (66–84) and "Putting People in Their Place" (85–105).

The Tuskegee Syphilis Study

Useful information about the study will be found at www.kn.pacbell.com/wired/BHM/tuskegee_quest.html.

Moral Protection: No Trespassing

I owe the No Trespassing analogy to Robert Nozick, *Anarchy, State, and Utopia* (New York: Basic Books, 1974).

Moral Weight: Trump

I owe the trump analogy to Ronald Dworkin, *Taking Rights Seriously* (London: Duckworth, 1977).

Unsatisfactory Answers

1. "Humans Have Rights Because Humans Are Human."

Carl Cohen seems to hold this position, among others. See his contribution to Carl Cohen and Tom Regan, *The Animal Rights Debate.*

2. "Humans Have Rights Because Humans Are Persons."

This widely held view is taken by Michael Tooley, for example, in *Abortion and Infanticide* (Oxford: Oxford University Press, 1983).

3. "Humans Have Rights Because Humans Are Self-Aware."

Again, Tooley is among many philosophers who take this view. See his *Abortion and Infanticide.*

4. "Humans Have Rights Because Humans Use Language."

R. G. Frey is representative of the philosophers who believe that possession of rights presupposes the ability to use language. See his *Interests and Rights: The Case against Animals* (Oxford: Clarendon Press, 1983).

5. "Humans Have Rights Because Humans Live in a Moral Community."

Cohen adopts this position in *The Animal Rights Debate.*

6. "Humans Have Rights Because Humans Have Souls."

The "soul argument" is very common among people of faith.

7. "Humans Have Rights Because God Gave Them to Us."

A classic work that addresses these issues is Andrew Linzey, *Christianity and the Rights of Animals* (New York: Crossroad, 1987).

CHAPTER 4: ANIMAL RIGHTS

Common Origins

Charles Darwin, "The Descent of Man," in Tom Regan and Peter Singer, eds., *Animal Rights and Human Obligations* (Englewood Cliffs, N.J.: Prentice Hall, 1976), 72.

James Rachels, *Created from Animals: The Moral Implications of Darwinism* (Oxford: Oxford University Press, 1990), 133, 166.

Line Drawing

Thelma Lee Gross, DVM, DACVP, "Scientific and Moral Consideration for Live Animal Practice," *Journal of the American Veterinary Medical Association* 222, no. 3 (February 1, 2003): 285–88.

The summary of fish cognition is taken from Redouan Bishary, Wolfgang Wickler, and Hans Fricke, "Fish Cognition: A Primate's Eye View," *Animal Cognition* 5 (2002), 1–13. The authors present their findings as "purely functional."

Objections to Animal Rights

2. "Animals Are Not Human."

For a fuller critical discussion of speciesism, see chapter 8 of *Animal Rights, Human Wrongs*.

8. "Animals Are Not Aware of Anything."

Descartes's views about animals may be found in selections from his work in Regan and Singer, eds., *Animal Rights and Human Obligations*, 13–19.

10. "Well, at Least God Gave Us Dominion!"

For a more expanded discussion, see my essay "Christians Are What Christians Eat," in *The Thee Generation: Reflections on the Coming Revolution* (Philadelphia: Temple University Press, 1991), 143–57.

CHAPTER 5: WHAT WE LEARN FROM ALICE

Humpty Dumpty's Arrogance

Peter Heath, *The Philosopher's Alice* (New York: St. Martin's Press, 1974), 193.

"Sadistic Nazi Liar Scum"

The Congressional statement of policy www.aphis.usda.gov/ac/awa.html#2131.

American Veterinarian Medical Association's Policy on Animal Welfare and Animal Rights www.avma.org/care4pets/morewelf.htm#rights.

The Association of Veterinarians for Animal Rights (AVAR) embraces the philosophy of animal rights. For information see avar.org/avar.

CHAPTER 6: TURNING ANIMALS INTO FOOD

Rebekah Harp, "The Sounds of the Knives," in *Voices from the Garden: Stories of Becoming a Vegetarian*, ed. Daniel and Sharon Towns (New York: Lantern Books, 2001), 35–36.

The Veal Industry

The estimate of eight hundred thousand veal slaughtered annually is given by the American Meat Institute www.meatami.com/. Other numerical estimates in this chapter are those of the USDA www.usda.gov/nass/pubs/histdata.htm.

Quotations from *The Stall Street Journal* are from Peter Singer, "Down on the Factory Farm," chap. 3 in *Animal Liberation*, 2nd ed. (New York: *New York Review of Books*, 1990).

Scientific studies showing the physical and psychological illness of veal calves and other farmed animals raised in close confinement, including repetitive motion and other behavioral signs of maladjustment, were first documented in Britain by an independent government-appointed committee, headed by zoologist Professor F. W. Rogers Brambell. See *Report of the Technical Committee to Enquire into the Welfare of Animals Kept under Intensive Livestock Husbandry Systems* (London: Her Majesty's Stationary Office, 1965). A second study, *Animal Welfare in Poultry, Pig and Veal Calf Production* (London: Her Majesty's Stationary Office, 1981), submitted by the House of Commons' Agriculture Committee, was highly critical of the intensive rearing methods that continue to dominate contemporary American animal agribusiness. A brief overview of scientific studies of animal welfare is Joy A. Mench, "Thirty Years after Brambell: Whither Animal Welfare Science," *Journal of Applied Animal Welfare Science* 1, no. 2: 91–102. A more detailed account covering the same period is Richard Ryder, *The Political Animal: The Conquest of Speciesism* (Jefferson, N.C.: McFarland and Company, 1998); see, in particular, chapter 3, "The Science of Animal Welfare." Ryder coined the word *speciesism*.

Factory Farming

General surveys of factory farming include Michael W. Fox, *Farm Animals: Husbandry, Behavior, and Veterinary Practice* (Baltimore: University Park Press, 1984), and Jim Mason and Peter Singer, *Animal Factories* (New York: Crown, 1980). See, as well, Matthew Scully, *Dominion: The Power of Man, the Suffering of Animals, and the Call to Mercy* (New York: St. Martin's Press, 2002).

The American Veal Industry www.vealfarm.com/education/pdfs/special-product.pdf.

The Hog Industry

Dutch animal behaviorist G. Cronin is quoted in Singer, *Animal Factories*, p. 25.

Matthew Scully, *Dominion*, 258, 267–68, 274.

Bernard Rollin, *Farm Animal Welfare: Social, Bioethical, and Research Issues* (Ames: Iowa State University Press, 1995), 74–75.

National Pork Producers Council www.nppc.org.

The quotation of the manager of Wall's Meat Company appears in *National Hog Farmer* (March 1978): 27.

The Poultry Industry

The U. S. Poultry and Egg Association www.poultryegg.org.

The Cattle Industry

The National Cattlemen's Beef Association www.beef.org.

"Humane" Slaughter

Gail Eisnitz, *Slaughterhouse: The Shocking Greed, Neglect, and Inhumane Treatment inside the U.S. Meat Industry* (Amherst: Prometheus Books, 1997), 71, 105, 181, 206, 228–29.

Results of the Zogby poll were reported by Reuters on March 30, 2002, available at nodowners.org/poll.htm.

The dairy industry's opposition to downer legislation was reported by Frederic J. Frommer, for the Associated Press, on June 9, 2002, under the headline, "Dairy Groups Spent Generously on Lobbying, Contributions in Winning Farm Bill Battles." Available at www.farmedanimal.net.

The American Meat Institute www.meatami.com.

Fish Slaughter

Estimates of the total number of fish killed in commerce and "sport" are taken from private correspondence by Bruce Friedrich, "Annual Aquatic Animal Mortality Caused by Fishing Practices in the United States." The figures are for 1997. No doubt the total is higher today.

Joan Dunayer, *Animal Equality: Language and Liberation* (Derwood, Md.: Ryce Publishing, 2001), 137–38.

The Humane Slaughter Association www.hsa.org.uk/recent%20event.html#link7.

The descriptions of "humane" ways "sportsmen" can kill fish will be found at "How to Humanely Kill Fish," www.geocities.com/tony2kuk/fishkill.html.

Farmed-Animal Sanctuaries

United Poultry Concerns www.upc-online.org/.

Farm Sanctuary www.farmsanctuary.org/

Animal Place www.animalplace.org/

The Suwanna Ranch www.hfa.org/refuge/suwanna.html.

The study showing that pigs are as intelligent as nonhuman primates in some respects was reported by Reuters on September 11, 2002, under the headline, "Pigs and Chickens Are Smarter Than You Think." Available at www.enn.com/news/wire-stories/ 2002/09/09122002/reu_48402asp.

The study showing that sheep have remarkable memories was reported by Margaret Munro, in the *National Post* (Canada) on November 9, 2001, under the headline "'We Should Accord Them More Respect': Signs of Intelligence."

Information about the film *Peaceable Kingdom* can be found at www.tribeofheart.org.

The study showing that chickens are capable of learning and teaching was reported in a news release from the University of Bristol (U.K.) dated September 12, 2002, under the headline "Q. Why Did the Chicken Cross the Road? A. To Take a Lesson in Diet and Social Behavior." Available at publicrelations@bristol.ac.uk.

Conclusion

The quotation of Gandhi appears in Jon Wynne-Tyson, ed., *The Extended Circle: A Commonplace Book of Animal Rights* (New York: Paragon House, 1988), 91.

CHAPTER 7: TURNING ANIMALS INTO CLOTHES

The American Fur Industry

Fur Mill Fur

Statistics concerning the number of fur mills comes from the Fur Commission USA www.furcommission.com/who/index.html.

Information about the Chinchilla Industry Council can be found at www.chinchilla. com/ranch.html.

Trapped Fur

Friends of Animals www.friendsofanimals.org.

The quotation of Desmond Morris appears in Mark Glover, "Eye of the Beholder," *The Animals' Voice Magazine* 5, no. 4 (1992): 33. Morris also addresses trapping in *The Animal Contract: An Impassioned and Rational Guide to Sharing the Planet and Saving Our Common World* (New York: Warner, 1990), 116–18.

Marshall Cohen's quotation appears in a December 3, 2002, *New York Times* story by Ginia Ballfante entitled "Staying Warm and Fuzzy during Hard Times."

Robert Verdi's quotation appears in a January 8, 2003, *New York Daily News* story by Alev Aktar, "Adventures in the Skin Trade. Used to Be Fur Coats Were for Ladies or Joe Namath. Today, Men Love Their Minks."

Keith Kaplan's quotation appears in a February 8, 2003, *Atlanta Journal-Constitution* story by Shelley Emling, entitled "Fashion Trumps Compassion As Fur Makes a Comeback. Bright, Hip Styles and Chilly Temps Fuel Its Return to Favor, But Animal Activists Cry Foul."

The International Fur Market: Three Examples

The Northwest Atlantic Seal Hunts

General information about both hunts is from Pagophilus http://pagophilus.org/hunt/ index.htm.

The quotation of Newfoundland's Minister of Fisheries and Agriculture, John Efford, appeared in St. John's *Evening Telegram*, March 31, 1999.

Canadian Fisheries Minister Robert Thibault quotations appear in a February 3, 2003, *Toronto Globe and Mail* "Update" by Jeff Gray.

The quotation of Dr. Roberts is included in the International Federation for Animal Welfare's publication *Canada's Commercial Seal Hunt, 1998 Investigation*. His words are quoted in "Seal Song: Canada's Shame," by Rebecca Aldworth, www. animalsvoice.com/PAGES/features/seal.html.

Information about the veterinarians' study of the 2001 Canadian seal hunt will be found at the website for Fur Free Alliance www.infurmation.com/infurdesk/press/pres0206.htm.

Michael J. Dwyer, *Over the Side, Mickey: A Sealer's First-Hand Account of the Newfoundland Seal Hunt* (Halifax: Nimbus, 1998), 140.

"A Cruel Slaughter on Ice," Rebecca Aldworth, *The Toronto Star*, May 9, 2003. Available at www.thestar.com.

The finding that the Canadian sealing industry is exceeding "a truly 'precautionary' management model" is set forth in "Harp Seal Population Likely Declining," www.imma.org/PBR/.

The quotation of Wilfred Grenfell appears in Paul Watson, *Seal Wars: Twenty-Five Years on the Front Lines with the Harp Seals* (Toronto: Key Porter, 2002), 29. Watson's book is a "must read" for anyone interested in an informed account of this annual tragedy.

Persian Lambs

Information about the HSUS video on Persian lambs will be found at www .hsus.org/ace/a2046.

Bont voor Dieren's website concerning karakul lambs www.bontvoordieren.nl/eglisg /index.php?action=karakul.

Cat and Dog Fur

Information from HSUS will be found at www.hsus.org/ace/12014.

Leather

Elliot Gang, "The Skin off Their Backs," *The Animals Agenda*, October 31, 1999 at www.animalsagenda.org.

Information about PETA-India's video of leather production will be found at www.petaindia.org/cleath.html.

Wool

The description of the behavior of lambs after mulesing will be found at the Vegan Society's website www.vegansociety.com/html/info/info21.html.

The quotation of M. D. Kirby appears in "Horrors on the Sheep Farm," *Agscene*, July 1986.

Jennifer Greenbaum, "What's Wrong with Wool?" at www.animalsvoice.com/PAGES/invest/wool.html.

CHAPTER 8: TURNING ANIMALS INTO PERFORMERS

Limitations of Space

Information about the home range and social structure of lions, tigers, and elephants can be found at (for example) www.oaklandzoo.org/atoz/atoz.html.

Both quotations are of Ernest Albrecht, *The New American Circus* (Gainesville: University of Florida, 1995), 207, 218.

Loss of Social Structure

Earl Chapin May, *The Circus from Rome to Ringling* (New York: Dover Publications, 1932), 109.

No Pain, No Train

Clyde Beatty is quoted in Wilton Eckley, *The American Circus* (Boston: Twayne Publishers, 1984), 75.

"Don't Touch 'Em! Hurt 'Em!"

Carson and Barnes www.carsonbarnescircus.com/.

People for the Ethical Treatment of Animals (PETA) www.peta.org/.

A summary of Barbara Byrd's interview with the Associated Press can be found at www.impactpress.com/articles/junjul02/circus6702.html.

Information about the trial of David A. Creech can be found in the October 19, 2002, issue of *The Virginian-Pilot*. "Circus Trainer Convicted, Fined for Cruelty to Elephant," by Matthew Roy.

Legal Illusions

Peggy Larson's testimony was presented to the Board of Supervisors, County of Riverside, Riverside, California on May 1, 2000. Available at www.api4animals.org/doc.asp? ID+806.

The figure of 100 APHIS inspectors is given by Michael Satchell in "Cruel and Unusual," *US News*, August 5, 2002, 31.

"Radical Views"

Ringling Brothers and Barnum and Bailey Circus www.ringling.com/.

"No 'Boutique Circuses' for Me."

Alan Slifka is quoted in *The New American Circus*, 206.

The Boston Herald, July 26, 2002. Quoted in People for the Ethical Treatment of Animals, "State of the Circus," www.circuses.com.

Melissa Draper wrote the story about the Cirque du Soleil appearance in Raleigh, in *The News and Observer*, January 17, 2003.

Marine Mammal Display

Sea World-San Diego www.buschgardens.com/seaworld/ca/.

Dave Barry, "Theme Park Fever: You'll Know When You Go," *The News and Observer*, Raleigh, N.C., April 4, 2003.

General information about dolphins will be found at the Dolphin Project www. dolphinproject.org/.

The quotation of Giorgio Pilleri will be found in William Johnson, *The Rose Tinted Menagerie* (London: Heretic Books, 1990), 168.

The quotation of Jean-Michael Cousteau will be found at the Dolphin Project's website.

CHAPTER 9: TURNING ANIMALS INTO COMPETITORS

Hunting

Hunting statistics available at http://www.fund.org/library/documentViewer.asp? ID=85&table=documents.

"Humane" Hunting

Ann S. Causey, "On the Morality of Hunting," *Environmental Ethics* 11 (Winter 1989): 334–35.

List Hunters

C. J. Chivers, "A Big Game," *New York Times*, August 25, 2002.

Canned Hunts

Humane Society of the United States www.hsus.org/ace/12017.

"The Animals Come from Where?"

The role played by America's leading zoos in supplying animals for canned hunts is documented by Michael Satchell in "Cruel and Unusual," *US News* (August 5, 2002): 29–32.

The number of "surplus" animals sold by accredited zoos appears in Linda Goldstein, "Animals Once Admired at Country's Major Zoos Are Sold or Given Away to Dealers," *San Jose Mercury News*, February 11, 1999.

"Real" hunters

1. *"My Genes Made Me Do It."*

Aldo Leopold, *A Sand County Almanac* (New York: Baltimore Books, 1970), 227.
Jose Ortega y Gasset, *Meditations of Hunting*, trans. Howard B. Wescott, with a foreword by Paul Shepherd (New York: Scribner, 1985), 29.

2. *"Love Made Me Do It."*

Jose Ortega y Gasset, *Meditations on Hunting*, 92.
Randall L. Eaton, "The Hunter as Alert Man: An Overview of the Origin of the Human/Animal Connection," in *The Human/Animal Connection*, ed. Randall L. Eaton (Incline Village, Nev.: *Carnivore Journal* and Sierra Nevada College Press, 1985), 9.

3. *"It's a Spiritual Thing."*

David Petersen, *A Hunter's Heart: Honest Essays on Bloodsport* (New York: Henry Holt, 1996), 161.
James A. Swan, *In Defense of Hunting* (New York: HarperCollins, 1995), 35.
Jim Motavalli dismissed "this spiritual mumbo-jumbo" favored by hunters like Petersen

and Swan in a talk he gave at The Seventeenth Annual Compassionate Living Festival, sponsored by the Culture and Animals Foundation, October 4–6, 2002.

5. "It's Fun!"

Information about increased heart rate among hunters at rest will be found in *Energy Times: Special Heart Issue* (February 2003): 48.

"Send in the Vandals!"

National Rifle Association www.nrahq.org/hunting/ hunterimage.asp.

Rodeo

Professional Rodeo Cowboys Association www.prorodeo.com/.

"Why Do Those Horses Buck?"

This and the later Peggy Larson quotation is from Merritt Clifton, "Anti-rodeo Vet Was Performer," *Animal People* 3, no. 6 (July–August 1994), available at www.animalpeople. org/94/6/antirodeo_vet.html.

Roping Babies

Dr. Finocchio's quotation is available at the Animal Protection Institute website, www.api4animals.org/doc.asp?ID=1276.
   Dr. Larson's quotation appears in Merritt Clifton, "Anti-rodeo Vet Was Performer."
   C. G. Haber, DVM, from a 1979 interview by the Humane Society of the United States. Showing Animals Respect and Kindness, www.sharkonline.org/.

Not Seeing Is Not Believing

Karen Chapman, "Riding, Roping—and Editing," *Extra!* (May/June 2002): 25.
   Steve Hatchell quotation ("We're really sensitive . . .") from Thomas Mitchell, "Giving Credence to the Rodeo Banner," *Las Vegas Review-Journal* (December 16, 2001).
   Steve Hatchell quotation from the *Wyoming Tribune-Eagle* edition of December 24, 2000, cited by Karen Chapman, 25.

Greyhound Racing

General information about greyhounds presented here is based on material available at the Grey2K USA website: www.grey2kusa.org.

Welfare versus Rights

The National Greyhound Association www.ngagreyhounds.com/.

And They Call This Humane?

Greyhound Lovers League www.geocities.com/greyluvrsleague/myths.htm.

Special Cruelty

The story about the mass graves of greyhounds in Lillian, Alabama ("Dismal End for Race Dogs, Alabama Authorities Say") was written by David M. Halbfinger.

Conclusion

The quotation of Albert Schweitzer appears in William Johnson, *The Rose-Tinted Menagerie* (London: Heretic Books, 1990), 150.

CHAPTER 10: TURNING ANIMALS INTO TOOLS

"Humane Care"

National Association for Biomedical Research www.nabr.org/.

Using Animals As Tools in Education

People for the Ethical Treatment of Animals petacatalog.com/peta/product.asp?dept%5 Fid=12&pf%5Fid=VP511&mscssid=.

"Students Have to Dissect to Learn Anatomy."

Jonathan Balcombe, "Dissection: The Scientific Case for Alternatives," *Journal of Applied Animal Science* 4, no. 2 (2001): 117–26.

The Winds of Change

Jonathan Balcombe, "Student/Teacher Conflict regarding Animal Dissection," *The American Biology Teacher* 59, no. 1 (2000): 22–25.

The "Dog Lab"

Colorado dog lab website www.stopcudoglabs.org/.
  "CU Halts Last Dog Vivisections. Decision Made for Fiscal Reasons, Official Says," *The Boulder Daily Camera*, by Katy Human, January 30, 2003.

Editorial, *Boulder Daily Camera*, "Saving Dogs and Money. CU Should Make Dog-Lab Ban Permanent," January 31, 2003.

Your Animal Companion Could End Up in a Lab

PETA peta.org/mc/facts/fsc15.html.
    PCRM www.pcrm.org/issues/Animal_Experimentation_Issues/pound_seizure.html.
    Americans for Medical Progress www.amprogress.org/.
    Last Chance for Animals www.lcanimal.org/.

Using Animals in Toxicity Tests

"LD_{50}"

For a classic scientific critique of the variability in LD_{50} results because of environmental and other factors, see R. Loosli, "Duplicate Testing and Reproducibility," in Regamay, Hennessen, Ikic, and Ungar, International Symposium on Laboratory Medicine (Basel: Karger, 1967).
    Mindy Kursban, Esq., "PCRM Brings EPA to Court over Cruel and Useless Tests," *Good Medicine* (Winter 2003): 11.
    Richard Ryder, *Victims of Science: The Use of Animals in Research* (London: Davis-Poyter, 1975), 36.

Alternatives

For detailed information about the in vitro alternatives to the LD_{50}, see www.pcrm. org/issues/Animal_Experimentation_Issues/ in_vitr_test.html.
    The results of the research conducted by Swedish scientists are summarized in "In Vitro Acute Toxicity Tests More Predictive Than Animal Tests," available at www.pcrm.org/issues/Animal_Experimentation_Issues/in_vitro_tests_html.

Using Animals As Tools in Research

The Federal Food, Drug, and Cosmetic Act can be found at www.fda.gov/cvm/index/ffdc_act/ffdcatoc.html.
    Information about the European Union's changing policy concerning product testing can be found at the British Union for the Abolition of Vivisection's website: www.buav.org/fcampaign.html.

Kinds of Research

A classic description of the kinds of research to which animals are subjected is Jeff Diner, *Beyond the Laboratory Door* (Washington, D.C.: Animal Welfare Institute, 1985).

"The (Some But Not All) Animal Welfare Act"

For information about the number of reportable animals used in research, see Animal and Plant Health Inspection Service www.aphis.usda.gov.

Federal Enforcement

Data about the number of facilities subject to APHIS inspection and the shortcomings of these inspections are quoted from Office of the Inspector General's Animal and Plant Inspection Service Enforcement of the Animal Welfare Act, Audit Report No. 33600-1-Ch (Washington, D.C.: U. S. Government Printing Office, January 1995). An informed overview of APHIS practices will be found in Michael Budke, "Are Laboratory Animals Protected in the U.S.?" *The Animals' Voice Magazine* (Spring 1996): 6–9. Gary Francione offers a sustained critique of the Animal Welfare Act and APHIS's enforcement of its provisions in *Animals, Property, and the Law* (Philadelphia: Temple University Press, 1995).

"Heads" the Researchers Win, "Tails" the Animals Lose.

Scott Plous and Harold Herzog, "Reliability of Protocol Reviews for Animal Research," *Science* 27 (July 2001): 608–9. The quotation is of Herzog and is contained in an undated press release from Wesleyan University News.

Overestimation of Benefits

For an overview of how much the benefits of animal research are exaggerated, see Hugh LaFollette and Niall Shanks, *Brute Science: Dilemmas of Animal Experimentation* (New York: Rowman and Littlefield, 1996). In addition, see C. Ray Greek, MD and Jean Swingle Greek, DVM, *Sacred Cows and Golden Geese: The Human Costs of Experiments on Animals* (New York: Continuum, 2000), and *Specious Science: How Genetics and Evolution Reveal Why Medical Research on Animals Harms Humans* (New York: Continuum, 2002).

Underestimation of Harms

The statistics concerning the toxicity of FDA-approved drugs will be found in U. S. General Accounting Office, *Report to the Chairman, Subcommittee on Human Resources and Intergovernmental Relations, Committee on Government Operations, House of Representatives, FDA Drug Review, Postapproval Risk, 1976–1985* (Washington, D.C.: U. S. Government Printing Office, 1990).

The estimate of 1 percent of adverse drug reactions that are reported is given in D. A. Kessler, "Introducing MedWatch: A New Approach to Reporting Medication and Adverse Effects and Product Problems," *Journal of the American Medical Association* 269 (1993): 2765–68.

The estimate of 60 percent of total health costs that are attributable to smoking is included in a comprehensive economic analysis prepared by Robert Shubinski, M.D. Available at unr.edu/homepage/shubink/smokost1.html#cost2.

Information about using human blood cells to replace rabbits in drug tests will be found at www.euobserver.com/index.phtml?sid=9&aid=11188.

Research Ideology

Carl Cohen, *The Animal Rights Debate*, 291.

CHAPTER 11: YES . . . , BUT . . .

The "Vandalism and Violence" Turn-Off

The FBI estimate of combined ALF/ELF damages will be found at www.fbi.gov/congress/congress02/jarboe021202.htm.

ALF arson and other actions are described as part of a "nonviolent campaign" by the North American ALF's Supporters Group www.hedweb.com/alffaq.htm.

The "I Thought This Was Supposed to Be a Radical Movement" Turn-Off

Compassion over Killing www.cok.net/.

Ken Klippen is quoted in a December 4, 2002, Associated Press story entitled "Group Alleges Egg Farms Are Cruel," www.cok.net/camp/inv/rb/article_ap.php.

INDEX

African Atto, 17
Aldworth, Rebecca, 116
Alice (from *Alice in Wonderland*), 77, 78, 80
American Greyhound Track Owners Association, 155
American Medical Association, 14, 15, 133, 162; opposes animal rights, 12; supports humane treatment and responsible care, 12
American Veal Industry: supports humane production, 92
American Veterinary Medical Association, 82, 92, 105, 111, 162; opposes animal rights, 82; supports humane treatment and care, 82
American Zoological and Aquarium Association, 145
Americans for Medical Progress, 165, 166
animal consciousness. *See* Damascans, DaVincians, Muddlers
Animal Liberation Front, 10, 11, 80, 189, 190, 191, 194, 195, 196
Animal Meat Institute: supports humane handling, 101

Animal People, 27
Animal Place, 103
Animal and Plant Health Inspections Service, 131, 165, 172, 173, 200
animal rights: argument for, 53-62; consequences of, 61-62; contrasted with animal welfare, 12, 13, 14, 15, 77; contrasted with anti-cruelty to animals, 9-10; contrasted with kindness to animals, 9-10; objections to, 62-71; simple, profound idea, 9-10
Animal Rights Advocates (ARAs): forthrightness of, 78; as Norman Rockwell Americans, 19; portrayed as extremists, 10-11, 12, 13, 14, 77; as portrayed by the media, 11, 14, 18; portrayed as misanthropic, 17, 18, 77; as portrayed by spokespersons for major animal user industries, 10, 12-15, 16, 18; portrayed as terrorists, 12, 14, 15, 16, 18; positive values of, 19, 182; public's perception of, 11, 18; stereotype of, 3, 17, 18, 77; terminology explained, 34; types of. *See* Damascans, DaVincians, Muddlers.

Animal Rights Advocates' positions: on turning animals into clothes, 123-24; on turning animals into competitors, 157; on turning animals into food, 106; on turning animals into performers, 139; on turning animals into tools, 162, 169, 177

Animal Rights, Human Wrongs: An Introduction to Moral Philosophy, 3, 62

Animal Rights Movement, 15, 16, 18, 19

animal welfare: contrasted with animal rights, 12, 13, 14, 77

Animal Welfare Act, 81, 82, 101, 131, 132, 172, 173, 200; some animals excluded from, 171

Anthony, Susan B., 32

Association of Veterinarians for Animal Rights: supports animal rights, 82

baboons: used in crash tests, 33

Balcombe, Jonathan, 161

Barnard, Neal, 165

Barry, Dave, 135

Bartlett, Kim, 27

Bauston, Gene and Lorri, 104, 105

Beatty, Clyde, 130

beaver. *See* turning animal into clothes

Big Apple Circus, 127, 133

Binder, Paul, 127

"blink" test, 155, 116

birds: intelligence of, 59-60

Bont voor Dieren, 117

Bronte, Charlotte, 32

Buber, Martin, 22, 29

Byrd, Barbara, 131

captive dolphin industry, 135-39. *See* marine mammal display

Carroll, Lewis, 78

Carson and Barnes Circus, 130-31

The Case for Animal Rights, 72

cats: eating of, 1, 2, 118; fur (*See* turning animal into clothes); used in brain and eye research, 171; used in dissection, 161

cattle industry, 98-99; beef, 98-99; dairy, 98

Causey, Ann S., 143

change in perception, 23, 24, 25, 87, 88, 118, 119, 137, 139, 181. *See* Damascan moment

Chapman, Karen, 153

chickens: intelligence of, 105. *See* poultry industry; turning animals into food

chinchilla. *See* turning animal into clothes

Chinchilla Industry Council: supports humane treatment, 110

Chivers, C. J., 144, 150

Christianity: and animal rights, 69-70; and human rights, 48-49

Cirque du Soleil, 126, 134

civil disobedience, 194

Class B dealers, 164, 166, 196

Clifton, Merritt, 27

Clifton, Wolf, 27

Clinton, President, 42

Clyde Beatty-Cole Brothers Circus, 125

Coe, Sue, 103, 201

Cohen, Carl, 177

Cohen, Marshall, 112

Compassion over Killing, 195

Comstock, Gary, 202

Cousteau, Jean-Michael, 139

cows: cognitive abilities of, 104-5. *See* cattle industry; turning animals into food

Coyote. *See* turning animals into clothes

Creech, David A., 131

cruelty to animals, 9-10

cultural paradigm: how animals are viewed in, 17, 18, 23, 25, 28, 29, 198

Cutick, Gary and Gillian, 87, 88

dairy industry. *See* cattle industry; turning animals into food

Damascan moment, 87, 129, 137. *See* change in perception

Damascans, 23-24, 28, 32, 34, 62, 87

Darwin, Charles, 57-58

DaVinci, Leonardo, 22-23

DaVincians, 21-25, 26, 27, 28, 32, 34, 62, 87, 88

Davis, Karen, 103, 105

Day, Dorothy, vi

Declaration of War: Killing People to Save Animals and the Environment, 17

DeRose, Chris, 166

Descartes, Rene, 67

Disconnect Dictum, 79, 81, 92, 98, 101, 102, 111, 123, 133, 160, 171. *See* Humpty Dumpty

dogs: eating of, 1, 2, 118; fur (*See* turning animals into clothes); used in "dog lab," 162-63; used in eye, burn, radiation, and brain research, 171; used in practice surgery, 162-63

Dolphin Project, 138

dolphins: deprivation in captivity, 136-39; in Greek thought, 135; method of capture, 136; in nature, 136

dominion, given by God: meaning of, 69-70

"downers," 100-101; dairy industry's attitude toward, 101; public's attitude toward, 101

Dunayer, Joan, 101

Dwyer, Mickey J., 115, 116

Earth Liberation Front, 188

Eaton, Randall, 146, 147

Eckstein, Robert, 165

Education, animal use in, 160-63; dissection, 161-62, 196; "dog lab," 162-63, 196

Efford, John, 113, 114

egg industry. *See* poultry industry; turning animals into food

Eisnitz, Gail, 100

elephants. *See* turning animals into performers; traditional circus

empty cages, 10, 34, 61, 70, 78, 105, 139, 182, 197. *See* animal rights, consequences of

European Union, 111, 114, 119, 169, 176

evolution: theory of, 57-58

extremism: two senses of, 10-11

factory farming, 93-94

Farm Sanctuary, 103, 105

farmed animal sanctuaries, 103-5

FBI, 188

Finocchio, E. J., DVM, 152

First Amendment, 187

fish: cognitive abilities of, 60-61

fish industry: "humane" methods of, 102; slaughter, 101-2

fox. *See* turning animal into clothes

Food and Drug Administration, 107, 176

Foundation for Biomedical Research: opposes animal rights, 13; supports humane treatment, 12

founding fathers: and human rights, 48, 49

Friedrich, Bruce, 202

Friends of Animals, 16, 110, 112

Frisco, Tim, 130-31

Fund for Animals, 142

Fur Commission USA: supports humane treatment, 110

fur industry. *See* turning animals into clothes

Fur Information Council: opposes animal rights, 14, 15; supports humane treatment and responsible care, 14, 15, 112

Gandhi, Mahatma, 30, 31, 32, 49, 72, 88, 105, 106, 120, 194, 196
Gandhian pacifism, 30, 190
Gang, Elliot, 119, 120
Garden of Eden, 70
Gates, Bill, 40, 41
Gendin, Sid, 202
Genesee, 165, 166
Gleco, 28, 31, 54
God: and human dominion, 69-70; and moral rights, 48-49; and origin of human life, 56-58, 70
Greenbaum, Jennifer, 122
Grenfell, Wilfred, 117
Greyhound Lover's League, 156
greyhounds. *See* turning animals into competitors
Gross, Thelma Lee, DVM, 60
guinea pigs: used in burn research, 171

Haber, C. G., DVM, 153
hamsters: used in radiation research, 171
Harp, Rebekah, 87
Hatchell, Steve, 154
Hindi, Steve, 152
Hirsch, Leon, 16, 18, 189
hog industry, 94-100; slaughter, 99-100
hogs: intelligence of, 104, 105
human rights, 37, 39, 40; nature and importance of, 43-52; and subject-of-a-life, 50-52; unsatisfactory explanations of, 44-49. *See* moral rights
humane: discussed, 77-83; meaning of, 78-79
Humane Farming Association, 103
"humane" hunting, 144
"humane" slaughter, 99-101
"humane" traps, 116
Humane Slaughter Act, 99, 100
Humane Slaughter Association, 102
Humane Society of the United States, 117, 118, 145

humaneness, 4
Humpty Dumpty, 78, 79, 80, 113, 127, 142. *See* Disconnect Dictum
Hunting. *See* turning animals into competitors

International Fund for Animal Welfare, 115, 116
Institutional Animal Care and Use Committees: inadequacy of, 173-174

Jesus: speaks to Saul, 25
Johnson, President Lyndon, 62

Kaplan, Keith, 112
kindness: to animals, 9-10
King, Martin Luther, 194, 196
Kirby, M. D., 122
Klippen, Ken, 195
Kursban, Mindy, 168

Lama, Eddie, 23-25
Larson, Peggy, DVM, 131, 151, 153
Last Chance for Animals, 166
LaVeck, James, 23, 104, 105
leather. *See* turning animals into clothes
Leopold, Aldo, 146, 147
lions. *See* traditional circus; turning animals into performers

Macias, Roberto, 100
major animal user industries, 4, 5, 11, 13, 14, 15, 16, 17, 18, 19, 61, 70, 73, 82, 133, 176, 186, 189, 192, 199, 200; spokespersons for, 4, 14, 18, 73, 74, 77, 79, 80, 81, 101, 130, 181, 191, 199, 200. *See* Disconnect Dictum, Humpty Dumpty
marine mammal display, 134-139, 196
Masson, Jeffrey Moussaieff, ix, 201
May, Earl Chapin, 128
McCurdy, Edward, 22

Mendel, Mike, 105

Merejkowski, Dimitri, 23

mice: used in burn and radiation research, 171; used in toxicity tests, 167-169

mink. *See* turning animal into clothes

monkeys: used in eye, radiation and brain research, 171

Montavalli, Jim, 148

moral rights, 38-52; and assistance, 41-42; to bodily integrity, freedom, life, 37, 42, 43, 46, 48, 49, 50; and equality, 39; and justice, 40-41; and No Trespass, 38-39; and respect, 42; summary of, 43; and trump, 40. *See* animal rights; human rights

Moretti, Laura, 201

Morris, Desmond, 111

Muddlers, 19, 26, 28, 34, 62, 74, 88; "anti" turn-off, 182-83; "celebrity" turn-off, 184; "I don't have anything to contribute" turn-off, 193; "I thought this was supposed to be a radical movement" turn-off, 194-96; "It's hopeless!" turn-off, 192; "merry prankster" turn-off, 183; "outing" turn-off, 187-88; resistance to animal rights, 181-98; "self-righteous" turn-off, 185-87; "tasteless" turn-off, 184-85; "vandalism and violence" turn-off, 188-92

Mules, J. H. W., 121

mulesing, 121, 122

National Association for Biomedical Research: supports humane treatment, 160, 172

National Cattlemen's Beef Association: supports humane treatment, 99

National Greyhound Association: opposes animal rights, 155; supports humane treatment, 155

National Pork Producers Council: supports humane treatment, 96

National Rifle Association: defense of "hunting heritage," 149, 150

Nugent, Ted, 146, 188

O'Barry, Helene, 135, 138; open rescue, 195

O'Barry, Ric, 135, 137-38

Over the Side Mickey: A Sealers First-Hand Account of the Newfoundland Seal Hunt, 115

Ovid, 32

Paracelsus, 167

Parks, Rosa, 194

Paul, the apostle, 25

The Peaceable Kingdom, 104

People for the Ethical Treatment of Animals, 130, 160, 165

People for the Ethical Treatment of Animals–India, 120

Persian lambs. *See* turning animal into clothes, fur industry

Peterson, David, 147

Pilleri, Giorgio, 137

Physicians Committee for Responsible Medicine, 165, 168

Plutarch, 32

poultry industry, 96-98; broilers, 96-97; layers, 97-98

pound seizure, 164-66, 196

Professional Rodeo Cowboys Association, 151, 152, 153, 154; supports humane treatment, 150

rabbits: used in eye and brain research, 171

Rachels, James, 57

Rampton, Sheldon, 16

rats: used in burn, radiation, brain, and electric shock research, 171; used in toxicity tests, 167-69 research (vivisection), animal use in, 170-77; Benefits Argument, 174; critique of Benefits Argument, 175-76; kinds of research, 170-71

Rhodes, Robert L., 156

Ringling Brothers and Barnum & Bailey Circus, 125, 127, 128, 134; opposes animal rights, 133; supports humane treatment, 133

Roberts, Mary, DVM, 115

Rodeo. *See* turning animals into competitors

Rollin, Bernard, 95

The Romance of Leonardo DaVinci, 23

Ryder, Richard, 168

Sea World-San Diego, 134, 135, 138

seals (harp). *See* turning animal into clothes, fur industry

Schweitzer, Albert, 157

Screaming Wolf, 17

Scully, Mathew, vi, 95, 96

sheep: cognitive abilities of, 104. *See* turning animals into clothes

Showing Animals Respect and Kindness (SHARK), 152

Silva, Loles, 156

Slifka, Alan, 133, 134

Snickers, 104

souls: and animal rights, 68-69; and human rights, 47-48

speciesism, 64

Stall Street Journal, 91, 93

Stauber, John C., 16

Stein, Jenny, 23, 104, 105

Sterling and Reid Brothers Circus, 131

Studwell, Peter, 144

subject-of-a-life, ix, 50-52, 53, 54; and animals, 54-59; and animal rights, 59-62; and birds, 59-60; and evolution, 56-58; and fish, 60-61, 101-2; and human rights, 50-52; and line

drawing, 59-61; and mammals, 59; and religious teachings, 58

Suwanna Ranch, 103

Swan, James A., 147

Thibault, Robert, 116

Through the Looking Glass, 78

tigers. *See* traditional circus

"To Love or Kill: Man vs. Animals," 1, 2

toxicity tests, 166-70, 196; alternatives to using animals in, 169; European Union ban on, 169, 170; LD$_{50}$, 167-69; types of tests, 166-67

traditional circus, 125-34, 196; deprivation of elephants in, 127, 128-29; deprivation of lions in, 127, 128; deprivation of tigers in, 127, 128; inadequacy of legal protection, 131-32; methods of training, 130

Trutt, Fran, 16

turning animals into clothes, 107-24; American fur industry, 108-12; cat and dog fur, 118-19; and "downers," 120; fur mill fur, 108-10, 196; in India, 120; International fur industry, 112-19; leather, 119-20; live transport of manufacture of, 119; merino sheep, 122-23; merino wool, 120; mulesing, 121; Northwest Atlantic seal hunts, 112-17, 196; Persian lambs, 117; tooth grinding, 121, 122; trapped fur, 110-12; wool, 120-23

turning animals into competitors, 141-57; calf-roping, 152-53, 154; canned hunts, 144-146, 196; cruelty inherent in, 153; ESPN coverage of rodeos, 153, 154; greyhound racing, 154-57, 196; greyhounds bred by racing industry, 155; greyhounds crated by racing industry, 156; greyhounds in history, 154-55; greyhounds sold by racing industry for biomedical

research, 155-56; "humane" hunting, 144; hunting, 142-50; list hunters, 144; NRA defense of, 149-50; "real" hunters, 146-50; rodeo, 150-54; role of circuses and zoos in, 146; saddle bronc riding, 151-52; special cruelty to greyhounds, 156, 157; spurious defenses of, 146-49
turning animals into food, 87-106
turning animals into performers, 125-140
turning animals into tools, 159-177
Tuskegee Syphilis Study, 38-43, 170

United Egg Producers: supports humane treatment, 195
United Poultry Concerns, 103
United Poultry and Eggs Association, 97-98; supports humane treatment, 98
United States Department of Agriculture, 131, 132, 164
University of Colorado School of Medicine, 162-163
U.S. Surgical Corporation, 16

vandalism, 188
veal industry, 90-93

vegan diet, 106, 107; and Garden of Eden, 70
vegetarian diet, 107
Verdi, Robert, 112
Vietnam War, 29, 30, 37, 184
violence: how to defend use of, 190; meaning of, 188-89
vivisection: using animals (See turning animals into tools); using humans, 177
Voltaire, 60
von Haugwitz, Dietrich, 202

Watson, Paul, 11
welfare: discussed, 77-83; meaning of, 79
Wesley, John, 68
Whetstone, David, 157
Wiesel, Elie, vi
The Witness, 23, 24
wool. See turning animals into clothes
Wright State University, 165
Wynne-Tyson, John, 23

y Gasset, Ortega, 146, 147
Yankovic, Weird Al, 32
Yourofsky, Gary, 129

zoos: role in canned hunts, 146

ABOUT THE AUTHOR

Tom Regan (Emeritus Professor of Philosophy, North Carolina State University) is universally recognized as the intellectual leader of the animal rights movement. During his more than thirty years on the faculty, he received numerous awards for excellence in undergraduate and graduate teaching; was named University Alumni Distinguished Professor; published hundreds of professional papers and more than twenty books; won major international awards for film writing and direction; and presented hundreds of lectures throughout the United States and abroad. Upon his retirement in 2001, he received the William Quarles Holliday Medal, the highest honor North Carolina State University can bestow on one of its faculty.

In that same year, using his donated papers and extensive personal library, the North Carolina State University Library established the Tom Regan Animal Rights Archive, the world's leading archival resource for animal rights scholarship. Information about Tom Regan's career and the archive named in his honor is available at http://www.lib.ncsu.edu/arights/

With his wife, Nancy, he cofounded The Culture & Animals Foundation (www.cultureandanimals.org).